Top Level Talks:
The Christian Summit Meeting

T. D. MEADLEY

Top Level Talks: The Christian Summit Meeting

Studies in Scriptural Holiness or the Doctrine of Entire Sanctification

LONDON
EPWORTH PRESS

© T. D. MEADLEY 1969
FIRST PUBLISHED IN 1969 BY
EPWORTH PRESS
Printed in Great Britain
at the St Ann's Press, Park Road,
Altrincham

SBN 7162 0056 2

To Joan and Margaret,
John, Robert, and Paul,
with love

'Peter, an apostle of Jesus Christ,
To the exiles of the Dispersion . . .
chosen and destined by God the Father
and sanctified by the Spirit
for obedience to Jesus Christ
and for sprinkling with his blood:
   May grace and peace be multiplied to you . . .
in the things which have now been announced to you
by those who preached the good news to you
through the Holy Spirit
sent from heaven,
things into which angels long to look . . . .
as he who called you is holy,
be holy yourselves in all your conduct;
since it is written,
"You shall be holy,
for I am holy". . .
That word is the good news
which was preached to you.'

(I Peter 1: 1–2; 12; 15f.; 25; RSV.)

Foreword

BY HAROLD K. MOULTON

I ONCE had a student who confided in me just before an examination that he was going to aim at forty per cent, the bare pass mark. How he thought he could achieve this precise result I do not know, but the true student can never aim at less than a hundred per cent, however far short he actually falls, as he inevitably will.

That is the parable of the biblical teaching on Perfection. Its standard is nothing less, frighteningly absolute. Its realistic appraisal of the candidate is minimal. But the Bible introduces a dimension not provided for in the percentage system: the almighty love of God in Christ. Nothing but that could bridge the gap.

In a century that was content to make forty per cent the maximum, the Wesleys took men back to the Bible with the alarming doctrine of Entire Sanctification or, to give it the terms they perhaps preferred, Perfect Love.

No teaching was—or is—more essential. None has more pitfalls in its path. It is not necessary to go into detail here. Mr Meadley has done that in the book. He has wrestled with the doctrine carefully and joyously, brilliantly in places, plainly and practically in others, but always whole-heartedly, convinced of the need to keep this Christian possibility centrally and sanely before men's eyes.

During his time as Principal of Cliff College this was his chief aim, an aim that concerns me very nearly because of the long tutorial connexion with the College of my uncle, Fiddian Moulton. My sister and I lived with him and that wonderful woman our aunt for many years, and saw how they realized this as the heart of the work there. They longed for it to be presented and lived, persuasively and lovingly. This is Mr Meadley's longing too.

I would underline one sentence on p. 135: 'Entire sanctification means that the given Christian message is treated with supreme reverence, subjected to the ablest and most sincere examination, and demonstrated as capable of exerting itself in relation to whatever changing circumstances may arise.' That is not one of the most striking sentences in the book, but it is one of the deepest—and it describes exactly what Mr Meadley has done. Yet he would not claim that he is therefore entirely sanctified. Nor would any true Christian. And that is just it!

Acknowledgements

FOR PERMISSION to quote from copyright material the author and publishers are indebted to: Geoffrey Bles, *The Great Divorce* by C. S. Lewis; Jonathan Cape Ltd, 'A Relativist' from *The Room* by Cecil Day Lewis; the Congregational Church in England and Wales, *Congregationalism and Reunion* and *The Soul of Prayer* by P. T. Forsyth; Miss Phyllis Hartnoll, 'The Carpenter'; and The Nonesuch Press, 'Christ in the Universe' from *Selected Poems of Alice Meynell*.

Contents

Foreword   vii

Acknowledgements   viii

Preface   1

1   Setting the scene   5

2   Learning the language   19

3   Compiling the agenda   37

4   Outlining the programme   59

5   Watching the snags   90

6   Generating the energy   117

7   Conducting the operation   144

8   Concluding the process   191

Bibliography   234

Subject Index   237

Index of Scriptural Passages   239

'I must make it plain that, in spite of all the uncertainties and confusion in which world affairs are plunged, I believe that a conference on the highest level should take place between the leading powers without long delay. This conference should not be overhung by a ponderous or rigid agenda, or led into mazes and jungles of technical details, zealously contested by hordes of experts and officials drawn up in vast, cumbrous array. The conference should be confined to the smallest number of powers and persons possible. It should meet with a measure of informality and a still greater measure of privacy and seclusion. It might well be no hard-faced agreements would be reached, but there might be a general feeling among those gathered together that they might do something better than tear the human race, including themselves, into bits.

'For instance, they might be attracted by the idea of letting the weary, toiling masses of mankind enter upon the best spell of good fortune, fair play, wellbeing, leisure, and harmless happiness that has ever been within their reach or even within their dreams. I only say that this might happen, and I do not see why anyone should be frightened at having a try for it.'

(Sir Winston Churchill, House of Commons, 11 May, 1953.)

'The message I send you today is this word of God: "Be ye holy as I am holy." To become occupied with the holiness of God is the surest sign of entering on Christian moral manhood. We leave behind the ideas even of pity, peace, and love and we find them all again made solemn, eternal, and almighty in the holiness of God. It was for this Christ came. It was this that sustained Him in His work even more than the love of men. You are not really fit to preach the fullness of His gospel till you realize that. How are you to realize the holiness of God? Not by introspection, not by painful soul exercises, or pieties forced and fanciful, not by holiness movements, conventions and the like. But by dwelling on Christ where you have God's holiness in no human mirror, but in itself. By poring upon the love of Christ. By leaving behind the hobbledehoyisms both of the natural man and the religious man, and entering into the nature of Christ's atonement as a standard of Christian faith. This will be the work of years. It is just what you have come here to do. God help and bless you in the doing of it, and defend you from all the dangers that beset you—of which the worst are the dangers and debasements of the religious world. Your souls have more to fear from the religious world than from the wicked world. Betake yourselves to your Bible, your Christ, and to a serious dealing at first hand with both.'

(A letter from Dr P. T. Forsyth, sent on request, when illness prevented his weekly personal meeting with the students of Hackney Congregational College. The senior student, the Revd J. Allardyce, kept the letter, later quoted in the *Christian World*, 7 November, 1935.)

Preface

ONE of the greatest needs of the world, the Church, and the individual is evidence that Christianity really works out in practice in this world. Our Lord's model prayer places high on the list of requisites the passionate longing for our Heavenly Father's will to be done, and His Kingdom come on earth as in heaven. Jesus envisages a genuine out-working of his intention. In any walk of life incompetent, half-hearted workmanship is always demoralizing and everywhere despised. Is the Master Craftsman likely to be less competent or enthusiastic than the man He has created?

The terms used in the Bible and among Christians to describe the end-product and its processes are apparently not so familiar and appealing as they sometimes have been in the past—holiness, perfection, sanctification. A shudder of dismay disturbs a congregation when accused of sanctity. Holy Joes are treated like lepers. A young film-star who achieved enormous success as Saint Joan expressed the hope that she would not be type-cast as a saint for ever. Most of us sympathize with the shoe-shop assistant who had to cope with a finnicky customer. A microscopic examination exposed a tiny scratch in the first pair, and also in the second. Sizing up the customer, the girl brought eight pairs in the next journey. After similar scrutiny in each case detected a flaw the customer discarded the last pair with the comment, 'They're all imperfect': whereat the sales-girl wearily replied, 'Madam, I'm not perfect; you're not perfect; how do you expect a poor benighted snake to be perfect?'

Nevertheless, these words are integral to Christianity, whether it is thought of as a programme or a way of life. The Bible is all about holiness, sin, salvation, sanctification. The Pharisees, or Separatists, sought to give detailed guidance,

1

and pushed the process to its logical conclusion in their more than six hundred extra rules. God appeared as a fussy house-proud housewife with a perpetual turpentine rag in His hand rubbing out tiny spots, or a sergeant-major fiercely inspecting his troops with a pernickety and barrack-like precision. Nevertheless the caricature witnesses to the original, and no one can competently study the Scriptures without finding holiness at the heart of it all.

Methodism in particular has focused this theme with special clarity in John Wesley's phrases about Scriptural Holiness and Entire Sanctification. While the Methodist Church as a whole has not of recent years laid much stress in fact upon this doctrine, it has been much in evidence at Cliff College, a Methodist training-college for lay workers, especially in evangelism. The claim would be made that only if a person had been through some decisive experience of the reality enshrined in this doctrine could such a one be an effective evangelist. It will readily appear that such claims need very careful examination, whether they are right, wrong, or somewhere in between.

A whole set of associations has gathered round the subject and rendered it for many either taboo or touchy. Once the challenge is raised anyone's spiritual integrity and foundation is involved one way or another, for or against, so that calm investigation and impartial discussion are hard to achieve. Feelings run deep; mutual criticism comes all too easily; and consequently unnecessary controversy dogs the subject and obscures the genuine benefits. The result, in Kai Lung's phrase, is 'a great depth of no enthusiasm'.

If we are to extract the truth we need sympathetic, detailed, and constructive investigation, seeking to return to first principles. This book endeavours to sort out the material freshly and vividly, with the Bible as the prime source, and practical outworking very much in mind. There is no pretence at an exhaustive survey, but only an elementary introduction, uninhibited by too much or too reverential reference to past formulations. It is an interim assessment after eight years of living inescapably in the midst of a community consciously asserting this teaching and offering experimental appropriation.

Wesley himself, it is generally agreed by those best qualified through extensive study to express an opinion, never quite achieved consistency in this doctrine. He was naturally a lucid thinker, trained in logic, who did not normally commit himself in print till he had made up his mind on a subject. Once he had stated his thought in authorized documentary form he could henceforth refer to it as the final expression of his mind on the subject. There is, however, one notable exception in his writing on this very theme. To meet outside criticism and also the progress of his own thinking he revised from time to time *A Plain Account of Christian Perfection,* his attempt at a definitive statement. Even after the final revision in 1777 he returned to the subject in correspondence.

In spite of any criticism which may be made of Wesley's statement of his teaching we may well be reminded of the famous comment on the two climbers Mallory and Irvine making the final assault on Mount Everest in 1922: they were last seen 'going hard for the top'. Nobody knows how near to the summit they reached, but on that side nobody climbed higher. Wesley possibly managed to get nearer the peak in thought than anybody else, and it is better to risk the perils of the heights than play safe on the foothills. George Croft Cell ventured the view that Wesley's doctrine combines the Protestant ethic of grace with the Catholic ethic of holiness. Quite apart from the truth of such a statement, the fact that it could be made is itself indicative of the possible truth in our claim.

At the same time have we anything to learn from the fact that Sir Edmund Hillary actually reached the summit of Everest from the other side, previously inaccessible? Perhaps a fresh approach from another angle may help both comprehension and achievement. The mind can become too accustomed to a well-worn path. The history of controversies, while necessary to know, can clog the mental machinery and unnecessarily complicate the problems to be solved. A great deal depends not only on the basic facts in a situation but also on their arrangement.

I should like to thank Mrs Margaret Parish and Mrs Ruth Hughes for help in preparing the typescript, and my wife and family both for their forbearance during the period of writing and for not stressing unbearably the noticeable contrast between theory and practice both in the writer and the College. I am grateful also to the Revd Harold K. Moulton, M.A., Bible Society Assistant Translations Editor, for his friendship and encouraging Foreword.

1   Setting the scene

> '. . . good news to you through the Holy Spirit
> sent to you from heaven, things into which
> angels long to look.' (1 Peter 1:12.)

ONE of the greatest figures of the twentieth century is Sir
Winston Churchill. When the cause of freedom and the dignity
of man seemed on the verge of collapse he stood calm and
immovable as the servant of destiny, uttered the challenging
and invigorating word, waved high the victory sign and vindicated the power of faith. After victory, although advanced in
years, he spoke with vision and realism about the situation still
confronting the human race. His words to the British House
of Commons on May 11, 1953, provided a dramatic picture
within and through which we may begin to see a prior and
profounder realistic vision of the One who stood calm and
immovable as the Servant of destiny, uttered the challenging
and invigorating word, lifted high the victory sign, and vindicated the power of faith in the supreme battle of time and
eternity for the freedom and dignity of the human race at a
place called Calvary.

The gist of the matter

The gist of the speech was that a Conference on the highest
level should take place between the leading Powers at the
earliest possible moment. An agenda is obviously required
but let it be pruned to the minimum, unencumbered at this
stage with detail, however necessary later, confined to the
really powerful people, with as little formality and as much
seclusion as possible. The aim is not bargained agreements but
a mutual concern that instead of the human race tearing itself
to bits it should be afforded an undreamed of opportunity for

well-being, fair play and happiness. 'I only say this might happen, and I do not see why anyone should be frightened at having a try at it.' Since that day indeed the world has become familiar with the sight of massive power-blocs holding summit meetings and momentous top level talks, where the supreme wielders of earthly power survey the world-scene, and seek mutually satisfactory policies in relation to large-scale problems of world-order and peace.

A profounder set of talks

Behind this necessary and attractive appeal lies a profounder question and a more realistic vision. The question is whether the human conferences sufficiently estimate the depths of the problems they face, and whether they can ever move from the dimension of expectation disappointed and hope deferred until they take into account the fundamental diagnosis of the human situation offered by the Christian Gospel. The Bible offers a glimpse of the world family and supreme discussions in celestial government circles, divine top level talks, the Christian summit meeting. Everything else in the Christian life is determined by such consultation. Human summit meetings are inevitably composed of fallible participants and need a wider context than their own wisdom, a built-in structure of universal support for perspective and persistence. Moses, one of the few humans recorded to have held top level talks with God, was instructed to make all things after the vision shown him in the mountain (Hebrews 8:5).

Where to begin

Here is an angle of approach to the very proper and devastating question, What is Christianity all about? Obviously it centres round the historical personage Jesus Christ, but why is He so significant? To answer the question we need to see Him in His proper setting, which is unfolded in the Bible. The theme of the Bible is the nature and purpose of God, so we must begin at the top if we are to understand the proceedings. 'In the beginning God . . .' (Genesis 1:1) is the first phrase of the Bible, and it is the proper starting-point for our studies. The landscape painter Corot, famous for his talent in conveying the impression of light, was once asked about his secret, and replied, 'I paint the sky first.' It is the source of light which determines the effect of light as it illumines landscape and people. Thus for correct perspective in all matters to do with our religion we begin on the heights in the light. 'God is light . . .' (1 John 1:5). 'And God said, Let there be light, and there was light' (Genesis 1:3). Before John saw a new earth he saw a new heaven (Revelation 19:6), i.e. a new view of God and the world of the spirit.

Who is in charge?

Since in our story God is the controller of the universe, God Almighty (Genesis 17:1), the omnipotent ruler of all (Revelation 19:6), King of kings and Lord of lords (Revelation 17:14; 1 Timothy 6:15), it is not unfitting to picture Him in terms of government, kingdom, power, and glory (Matthew 6:13). The supremely important factor in any situation is authority. Who is in charge? Whose hand is on the buzzer to say in or out, up or down, hit or miss? Mao Tse Tung once doodled a verse, when bored with a business meeting, which asked precisely this question and which comes with all the more force from one who exercises vast power in a confessedly atheistic movement.

> *Alone in the desolate vastness*
> *I ask of this ageless earth:*
> *Who is the ruler of the universe?*

Central to our thought of holiness will be the other idea of the kingdom of God, just as it was central to the teaching of our Lord Jesus Christ. The model prayer links holiness and the kingdom with the fatherhood and will of God inextricably at the outset; 'Our Father which art in heaven, Hallowed (recognized as holy) be thy name (or nature). Thy kingdom come. Thy will be done on earth as it is in heaven' (Matthew 6:9-10). Again, everything begins at top level with God, and relates to purpose, order, control, and divine government.

Preliminary preparations

Now we are in a position to consider the development of

the illustration of top level talks, or the Christian summit meeting. A number of preliminary matters must be attended to before the talks take place, or at least until we are allowed to ascend the Christian summit and listen in. The limits of invitation need to be fixed. Sufficiently important business must warrant the occasion, and an agenda be drafted. A good deal of homework has to be done, relevant material gathered and formulated sufficiently for handling without waste of time, documents must be prepared and summarized, and arrangements made for translation. The remainder of this first session deals with the end-product envisaged, a survey of the authorities engaged in the discussions, and a rough glance at the kind of subject likely to be on the agenda. The other sessions go in greater detail into the agenda and its proper order, explanation of the terms used, the proposed line of action, a consideration of the possible snags, and the actual procedures to be followed. Even so, nothing like the whole ground can be covered; we can only hope that an adequate shape will have been drawn and the central matters opened up.

The aim

First we look at the aim of the operation. When we examine the Bible carefully we see that one overall theme holds it together, despite many criss-crossing tie-rods. It is about the effecting of the will and rule of God, imparting His nature to man. God is understood to be Spirit, which is impalpable energy, from whom the whole creation is projected. His message determines the patterns of energy which constitute the universe. Therefore man is in the hands of supreme power, and must humbly trust and obey. He rightly trembles before the One who has the power of life and death. This final power is what is meant by holiness. We adjust or perish. Such power when manifested in a huge fire at once terrifies and fascinates us. 'Our God is a consuming fire' (Hebrews 12:29). 'The fear of the Lord is the beginning of wisdom' (Proverbs 1:7). Reverence, worship, adoration, trust, obedience, are the proper response to this almightiness. The totality of this supreme power, and the appropriate response are sometimes summarized in the technical word *numinous*.

A risky experiment

According to the authorized story, this holy Being has made a man with a likeness to Himself, with sufficient freedom to enter into relationship with Himself. If this freedom is to be genuine, however restricted, the possibility of rebellion or indifference remains. Where such defiance, evasion, or apathy takes place the purpose of God is to that extent thwarted, and a disastrous state of impaired confidence results. The story of the Garden of Eden illustrates vividly the process whereby man, to ensure his own independence and security, seeks to lift himself beyond the limits set by God, only to overbalance and fall. He then builds up alibis, defences, hide-outs from the truth, but is inevitably exposed and punished. The moment of truth always comes. He is out of Paradise, away from home, with every man's hand against his brother's. Blood flows, violence abounds, relationships deteriorate, and the inner world of imagination, where motives originate, is corrupted. This disordered state of affairs achieves a kind of cancerous life of its own, providing an environmental pressure on its members, and developing an entail of degenerating influences which affects social behaviour and reaction, both within and outside the human personality, individual and corporate.

If it comes to the worst

The exerciser of governmental control must recognize and make provision for the possibility of this catastrophic situation, both to subdue rebellion and disorder, to make his authority manifest, and if possible to restore and develop the original intention. All relevant authority must consult, decide, and act. The will of the sovereign must prevail. Law must be enacted, penalty exacted, and, if possible, reconstruction inaugurated.

Framework of understanding

It is within the framework of some such picture as this that our theme can be understood. Our total confidence in the government of the universe is at stake, so no trivial or superficial treatment will suffice. All relevant factors in the situation must be brought to light and sorted out. Total treatment must be applied if there is to be any justifiable hope, and we must

9

have a clear view of the complete work to be done. The final purpose must be envisaged, and all thought and action related thereto. If there is such a purpose it must be present from the beginning in the mind of the organizer. Hence we keep reading in the Bible of plans hatched from the foundation of the world, and this Jesus Christ, who is obviously the central clue, is described as the embodiment of the mind, the will, the heart, and the message through whom the creation came to be. He is built in to the structure of the universe (John 1:1ff.). Such claims are staggering, incredible, but strangely convincing once we raise the question of ultimate meaning or purpose, and contrast it with the actual state of mankind.

Command, exhortation, promise

To cut a long story short at this point, before entering upon more detailed discussion, the Bible is about shaping human beings, human society, and the total structure of reality itself, into the pattern and will of God. The Bible is essentially about action, ultimate and intimate, to this end. Both command, exhortation, and promise agree: 'Be ye holy, for I am holy' (Leviticus 19:2); 'Be ye perfect as your heavenly Father is perfect' (Matthew 5:48); 'Ye shall be partakers of the divine nature' (2 Peter 1:4); 'For it became him, for whom are all things, and by whom are all things, in bringing many sons into glory to make the Captain of their salvation perfect through sufferings. For both he that sanctifieth and they who are sanctified are of one: for which cause he is not ashamed to call them brethren' (Hebrews 2:10–11). The purpose is 'to present every man perfect in Christ Jesus' (Colossians 1:28), 'perfect in every good work' (Hebrews 13:21). 'Beloved, now are we the children of God, but it doth not yet appear what we shall be, but we know that when we see him, we shall be like him, for we shall see him as he is' (1 John 3:2–3).

Picture language

We must now remind ourselves that we are using pictorial language, but after all there is little else to use. Abstract language has its use for sorting out, tidying up, and labelling ideas for quick accessibility, but what matters most in life is the living situation. We ought to be grateful, not apologetic, that the Bible is a book full of stories, which begins with the tale of a garden and ends with a city of gold. The scenery helps us to see the meaning more clearly. Thus we shall be talking about heaven and God as He is revealed in the Bible, which includes references to the Father, the Son, and the Holy Spirit, who are the persons engaged in the top level talks. It is important to remember that the three persons of the Holy Trinity are not three individual beings in the separated sense of human individuals. The point is that there are distinctions within the Godhead, and while in the nature of the case there must be identity of nature, will, and purpose, there is an element of social relationship which belongs to the Creator, Judge, and Ruler of the universe. We can therefore without impropriety for the purpose of our subject visualize a cabinet meeting in the heavenly courts, rather as for another purpose the Bible play *Green Pastures* frankly portrays God like a Negro grandad Sunday School Superintendent consulting with the Angel Gabriel.

Summary to date

We can now summarize the position to date. The Creator of the world is responsible for its maintenance, and in so far as other responsible beings are brought into existence He is their Controller and Accountant. Their responsibility must include an element of free choice, otherwise they cannot be called to account and either blamed or praised. If they have failed in their responsibilities they have hindered the Lord's will, and are to be judged guilty. If the divine purpose is to be achieved at all, the guilty status must be altered, the accompanying sinful state must be eradicated, and a new condition must be created, including both decontamination and rehabilitation, and a constructive dynamism for the future. The divine will of the Ruler of the universe has to be established upon the earth, both negatively in judgement and penalty, and positively in renewed obedience, trust, and cooperation.

Some inevitable terms

In such a setting certain concepts and technical terms become inevitable—will, purpose, covenant, law, penalty, pardon, and the like. In a human sense this is true, but more than human possibilities must be envisaged if there is to be any positive progress. In so far as the original purpose has been damaged repairs are required. In so far as there has been wreckage and waste a salvage operation is called for, unless the whole project is to be a write-off. The term salvation summarizes all the elements needed in such a situation. Since the heart of the scheme has to do with obedience and trust in terms of personal and social relationships, terms like justification, atonement, and reconciliation enter our vocabulary. Since the project operates in the setting of organic concepts like life and death, there is a clamant call for new life and power, so that terms like regeneration and resurrection are included. Last of all there is the perfecting of the work against a background of imperfection and failure. It is at this point that we introduce the distinctive word of our discussion, sanctification, which includes a thorough clean-up and actual impartation of the purified life as essential elements in any setting apart for total service of the sacred.

God's initiative

The situation we face, then, is the sad and sordid result of a breakdown on man's part of an originally happy and effective relationship of God and man, Creator and creature, King and subject. God is not prepared to accept the situation lying down. He therefore takes the initiative and intervenes by a series of moves. He calls to man, questions him, exposes him, punishes him, but also continuously seeks to restore him to his proper state. Man has no right, merit, or claim, but God is prepared to do everything necessary for this purpose, at whatever cost. Plainly the price will be immense, and the energy to be expended beyond human calculation.

The inner debate

We have therefore to imagine the inner debate in heaven prior to creation and during the process. In a sense the essential elements are present before the beginning, though they are only manifest as the creative process unfolds. It is not that God has a series of *ad hoc* emergency measures, endless improvization to meet unforeseen circumstances, with the Holy Spirit continually panting up breathlessly at the last minute to overtake a chaos engendered by lack of previous forethought. Even though there is an element of the indeterminate at any given juncture, this does not inevitably mean that the contingency was unforeseen or unprovided for. However, this must be dealt with more intensively when the agenda is formulated. Our immediate concern is to observe the personnel, if one might put it so without irreverence.

Architect of destruction

The official consultants are the Father, the Son, and the Holy Spirit. There is an element of secrecy about such confidential talks (Ephesians 3:9–11). Whatever other celestial beings may exist, such as angels, they are incapable of full understanding, even though they may be curious (1 Peter 1:12). It would appear that one angelic being was rebellious and nosy, narked by his exclusion. He appears variously as the Devil, Satan, the Dragon, Beelzebub, Lucifer, and the serpent. Each term has its contribution to our understanding of his nature, and certainly he appears as the leading architect of destruction. His jealous aim is to foil whatever God plans. He cannot bear undiluted human happiness, and therefore gate-crashes to spoil the party. He is the father of lies, a misleading angel of light which dazzles rather than illuminates. Satan was originally the eyes of the king, mixing with the people to keep the king informed of the state of public opinion, otherwise concealed behind the elaborate arras of court flattery. It is a simple step to provoke disaffection in order to report it. Hence he becomes an *agent provocateur,* a tempter, a sneak. The serpent is the symbol of power misused. Its silent, wriggling evasiveness, below eye-level, allows easy access to entangle the feet, and extend its sinuous folds to an embrace of doom. The Bible carries echoes and glimpses of a dimension of the spirit where there is wickedness in celestial places (Ephesians 6:10–20; cf. Job, chapter 1). His activities, however, are essentially parasitic.

Distinctions in unity

The participants in the meeting by right are the members of the Trinity, but the unity of the Godhead is basic to our thinking. There is one heart, mind, will in control of the universe. Science, art, theology, and common sense agree about the necessity for a foundation of unity in the structure of life and thought. Yet by analysis we can recognize distinctions of function in the one final personality. Without unduly pressing the point we note how the official and socially representative plural first personal pronoun appears in the creation story, like the editorial or regal 'we': 'let *us* make man in *our* own image' (Genesis 1:26).

The divine dynamism

This one God is essentially living, creative, purposeful. His dynamism accounts for the creation of the cosmos over against chaos. He creates the world in ascending order of significance with man as the climax for cooperative oversight and direction. This God is the Father in the sense of creator, controller, provider, the source of personal relationships and standing. He must be reliable and fair (Genesis 17:7), and able to accomplish His will in His own way, which is the real meaning of the word righteous. The indestructable intertwining of holiness and righteousness is one of the distinctively Biblical contributions to man's understanding of the ultimate meaning of life.

Potent idea, shape, communication

However, such ideas and forces can hardly be comprehended fully in personal terms unless they are capable of taking shape in specific individual form. If the idea and power originally generated spontaneously are to be communicated they must take shape, and if they are personal they must be capable of taking shape in individual life, accepting the limitations of the material chosen for incarnation. The shape is inherent in the structure of the Godhead, and yet in terms of thought and projection in space and time the shape is an extension of the idea, and to that extent subordinate to it, though of equal weight and status with identity of will. In so far as these two are perfectly in accord there becomes possible the imparting of the original personal idea, energy, relationship through the Incarnation to the mind of the human race, which already bears traces of its creative origin in itself, though limited and distorted. The original Spirit, through the Son, leaps like a spark across a gap and establishes itself within the personality of human beings, and thus the nature and purpose of God are recreated within the human race. There is communication, communion, and community because there is unity in reconciliation. The Holy Spirit proceeds from the Father and the Son.

Reading backwards

The rich harmony, at once complex and simple, of this view is not fully seen until events call it forth. Thus the doctrine of the Trinity does not emerge till after the work of Christ and the Day of Pentecost, but God was always like this. Whatever came to light eventually was but the unfolding of what was present from the beginning. This is the meaning of such phrases as 'in the beginning was the Word, and the Word was with God, and the Word was God . . . and without him was not anything made that was made' (John 1:1, 3). John the Baptist says of Jesus, '. . . he was before me' (John 1:30), while Jesus says of Himself, 'before Abraham was I am' (John 8:58). So also the same Spirit which brooded over the chaos, and entered into Bezaleel, Samson, David and many others, to enhance their natural powers, is the Spirit which drove Jesus into the wilderness to be tempted of the Devil, inspired the fellowship at Pentecost, and enables believers to say 'Jesus is Lord'. We are in fact reading backwards and upwards into the heavenly scene what has since been revealed, rather like running a film backwards and seeing the ball bounce higher and higher back into the hand which originally propelled it downwards, or even the shattered fragments of a cup or plate reassembling at the original point of unity before any division took place.

The summit scene

The scene includes therefore the original, eternal, infinite dimension of the Spirit commonly called heaven (in temporal and spatial terms) and God (in personal and metaphysical terms). God is seen in His fulness as finally revealed in Christ and realized in the Spirit. The top level talks are about the purpose and plan of this Triune God in Creation. We have therefore set the scene so far as the personal elements are concerned, and also the dimension of existence within which the talks take place. Heaven is the Christian summit. Holiness and heaven and the reign of God are at this point almost interchangeable terms, with love as the inextricable intertwining bond and interfusing essence at every point.

Willing and able

We now turn to the general purpose of the meeting, and begin to consider the type of subject which will eventually appear on the official agenda of business. The first point to be discussed is the willingness and ability of the Godhead to cope with the potential problems inherent in the experiment of creating free beings. Creation in itself is a proper and natural, not to say almost inevitable, outcome of power and love united. In itself it is a good thing, but in so far as purposiveness is inherent in the character of God the creation itself must be purposive, and to the best of our knowledge purpose is a personal characteristic at its highest, and is therefore directed to personal ends. Mankind is to share by delegation and loan the nature of God, and take charge of the subhuman creation to direct it to social ends and human use (Genesis 1:26–30; 2:15). The possibility of the misuse of such freedom and power is obvious, but an inescapable part of the experiment.

Necessary elements

Whatever happens the general oversight of the creation must continue; the Father must remain the Father. If there is breakdown on the human side a precise work is called for, which includes pardon, power, and price. The final limits will be stretched as much as in the creative act itself; it is a kind of new creation, a life and death issue. A variety of measures of increasing weight could be brought into play, but there is always the possibility that the extremest measures might be called for, and thus provision to the utmost must be reckoned for. Sacrifice, pain, patience, creative love in some final, decisive, and universal act may be required. There must be an entrance into the conflict, a bearing of the consequence in terms of physical, moral, emotional expenditure and endurance, as part of a clear and wholeheartedly accepted plan, with preparatory stages, a ripe time, a prepared follow-up, a concluding climax, of which the turning-point will be at once the core and clue of the whole business. 'The Lamb was slain from the foundation of the world' (Revelation 13:8; cf. 22:1–3). The Incarnation is part of the Cross, and both reflect the nature and purpose of the Creator of the universe, which was so constructed that God was free to enter the limits of His own world without being finally conquered by them. The ground plan of the universe is cruciform. The roots of the Cross are fast within our fairest fields, as Francis Thompson put it.

Present from the beginning

The whole potential process of incarnation, atonement, resurrection, and the gift of the Spirit are present from the beginning and written in to the constitution of things. The breaking involved removes the separating factors, the middle-walls or partitions, the veils and curtains, the fences and barriers, thereby opening up the way to meet and share, and releasing energy to shatter the tomb and allow the atmosphere of the Spirit to circulate freely. It will readily be seen that this theme represents the end-product of the whole Christian message. All the different terms used, the plans and processes outlined, the powers employed are part of a consistent whole. If we remember this we need not get bogged down in superfluous detail, even though the large general picture may seem almost too grandiose and remote, while impressive.

Recapitulation

To recapitulate, the original summit meeting is between God the Father, God the Son, and God the Holy Ghost. The basic concept is of a world of free persons in fellowship, both intimately as a family, and publicly as a kingdom. The norm of this concept is to be found in the teaching and life of the Son become human, with such preparation as we read of in the Old Testament, the log-book of the student-teacher race, the Jews. The function of the Spirit is to impart special energies, skills and spontaneous guidance over and above the legal requirements which can be codified. In case the experiment misfires at any point the same creative love which initiates the whole proceeding is able, willing, and ready to uncover its total resources in sharing the situation, bearing the consequences, absorbing the shock, and reversing the process. Such involvement and identification inevitably includes total sacrifice, the possibility of violent death, a freely offered recovery at infinite cost and expenditure of recuperative energy. In fact, the Triune Godhead is prepared for what we see faintly foreshadowed in the Jewish sacrificial system and starkly outlined and completely effected in the crucifixion. The Cross is not an afterthought. Since the eternal God was operating the project, the death, while actual, was not the final fact. The pure spirit of love broke through the dungeon of the tomb, and Christ was raised from the dead, 'according to the spirit of holiness' (Romans 1:4). By this means the Holy Spirit, always operative, possessed a new fulness of meaning and a more extensive field of application. These dramatis personae and themes will inevitably appear and reappear as the talks and their outcome develop. The most extended glimpse of this intimate discussion is in John 17, called by Father John O'Connor (the original of G. K. Chesterton's Father Brown), 'the inmost shrine of revealed religion'.

Summing up

In summing up we may say that the God of the Bible is distinctively a saving God, who imparts His nature, understood as holiness identified with righteousness, moving out as a free gift of graciously restored and reconciled relationships, at infinite cost to Himself. This attitude is His perfect love, and represents His nature and His purpose. To be holy is to be like Him in approach to all situations, i.e. a saving person, or part of a saving community. Our sanctification is to this end, and expresses itself in this way. We become minor mediators, supplementary saviours, extensions of the atonement, crucified with Christ, risen with Him, filled with the Spirit, agents of the Kingdom of God, colonizers of heaven.

2 Learning the language

*'. . . we do hear them speak in our tongues the
wonderful works of God.'* (Acts 2:11.)

ALL trades and professions have their own technical terms.
The purpose is to provide a handy and commonly recognized
label to store, with easy availability for use, the materials,
equipment, facts, processes, ideas involved. There is a natural
tendency for those in the know to be mysterious and impressive
about their special expertise, and exploit the ignorance of the
outsider. Theology is no exception, and preachers can be as
guilty as the next of the vulgar error. Equally, of course, the
outsider, the amateur, the layman, can just as easily belittle the
necessity for such technical languages, and be impatient of its
use. The answer is that the layman, if he finds it necessary to
know the subject, must learn the language, and the professional
must be willing to teach and explain it.

Using the dictionary

The subject of holiness has its own technical terms, and it
is important to know them, understand their meaning, and
not confuse one with another. Although nobody becomes
completely the man God wants him to be because of knowing
these words and using them correctly, it helps to clear the mind,
makes for sound thinking and mutually comprehensible communication. If mankind is to benefit by the top level talks
and reach the Christian summit he must be able to grasp
what the discussion is all about, so a language lesson is called
for which includes a session on vocabulary with a dictionary.
There are two main sections to cover; first, words describing
the general structure of the work of salvation; and second,
words about sanctification specifically. Although holiness is the

19

final element in God's series of moves to deal with the human situation, in surveying the total work involved it will be necessary to use the terms describing the earlier stages. The best form of explanation is to visualize the human scenes from which the terms were themselves drawn.

Salvation

The most comprehensive term is *salvation,* which means to rescue from any kind of harmful restriction, and bring forth into a large place, as from slavery, prison, defeat, disease, into freedom, victory, health. Weakness and death are transformed into strength and life. It is a vast salvage operation. Someone outside the situation must get in with power to get out again with his prize.

Redemption

The actual work of deliverance requires vast expenditure of energy. The cost is enormous. In so far as the cause is sacred, *sacrifice,* or holy action and making is inescapable. If debt is involved then payment is required. There is a ransom-price. *Redemption* is the precisest word for this works-costing. Someone in a sufficiently favourable position must assume the responsibility. Expenditure will be involved to the limit at every stage of the job in hand, with probably a different application or minting, though the currency and bullion remain the same throughout.

Covenant

In any binding relationship involving people there will be some form of *covenant,* which has a legal core because it is of public significance. The heart of it will be a freely entered association, yet with permanent elements which require more than the initial impetus to guarantee perpetuity. The covenant is most successful when the legal skeleton is covered with a living body of loyal love. Someone in a stronger position must make the first effective move, and the burden will fall most heavily on such a one. Such a relationship develops responsibility because conditions must be kept, not only literally but also in intention and spirit.

Law

To face up to the realities of human weakness and perversity despite good intentions the legal aspect must be codified in reasonably precise form. The Jewish *Law*, or *Torah*, included such specific enactment, but was always based on the prior benefits received from the providential activity of God. It included first principles, energetic manifestations, statutes and case-law. When a covenant is broken the law, meant to be a friendly guide and support, becomes a menace and destroyer. Its aim was to safeguard freedom in community; its result is bondage, both in isolation and community. It is a tutorial overseer at its best, at its worst a tyrannical bully; and, in between, a standard of accusation, revealing the status of guilt and a state of sin.

Guilt

Guilt is our greatest, as *death* is our last, enemy. It is our proclaimed standing as outlaws to be punished. Whether we feel it in our conscience or not, God's judgement stands. Equally, if we have a morbid sense of guilt over trifles not in God's law, it does not follow that we are guilty.

Sin

Sin is a condition of wrong relationship with God, distrustful and disobedient. The sinner has stepped over the boundary-line or tripped up in the penalty area. He is offside, which disables his effectiveness. Again, he may or not feel pangs of conscience, but his state is as it is, apart from his personal views on the subject. The Bible sees all mankind as a sinful race with a guilty status, the bandit caught with the offensive weapon in one hand and the other hand in the cash-box.

Justification

Such a wrong relationship with God involves a wrong standing at every level. Guilt at one point affects the whole man (James 2:10). The law-court is the obvious picture. Somehow guilt must be dealt with, and the unjust *justified*, with the consequent standing of innocence. Without indicating how at this point, we assume its actuality and press on to the next picture.

Regeneration, conversion, adoption

Suppose the status has been put right, what about the state? New energy and drive is required, therefore the generating plant has to go into production. Life begets life, and so here. The people need to start afresh with a new life from above. This is *regeneration*, sometimes linked with *conversion* or turning round on the turntable and shooting off in a new direction. The maternity-ward is the simplest picture. The link between the law-court and the maternity ward is the *Adoption Society*.

Sanctification

Once this new life has begun to grow, resistance is encountered. Old habits and patterns have to be broken, and new ones found. Accumulated, ingrained dirt has to be soaked and swooshed away. The stain and smell of the foetid life remain. We need to be made whiter than white. To force the grey out we must force the white in, to quote the detergent advertisements. Here we reach the area of *sanctification*, decontamination, cleansing, setting apart for training, rehabilitation, and toughening up to achieve the maximum fitness for the use of God. This is the cleansing department.

Reconciliation and atonement

The aim of the operation is the restoration of relationships, so it will include *reconciliation, reparation, atonement*, or the removal of the radical cause of the separation in the first place, with all its complicated tangles. The Hebrew word for atonement, *kippur*, means covering.

Propitiation and expiation

In terms of authority *propitiation* and *expiation* are required. The workshop is a useful setting to consider these words. A bad piece of work has been produced, or a mess has been made. The inspector in charge must examine, expose, blame, and in general make clear that an offence has been committed. While in any relationship involving people a personal element must enter, the inspector is not primarily expressing a sense of personal offence or pique, but officially passing an adverse verdict. The botched job is offensive and must be removed, either by covering over or by clearing up, and in fact by both. Someone has to intervene and perform both the distasteful task of undoing and cleaning, which is expiation, and also of redoing the work and re-presenting it, a sacrifice of obedient and perfect workmanship. The offence is removed and a proper work substituted. The authority concerned and the inspector can then be satisfied and propitiated. But nothing can alter the fact that there has once been an offence. The gracious, freely offered act which put matters right was performed by the authority in charge, and so the offender is eternally in a debtor's relationship. Thoughout life it remains true that we are daily constrained to acknowledge a great debt. The recipients of the grace are bound for life.

Sacrifice, altar, priest

The mention of *sacrifice* inevitably conjures up the picture of an *altar* and a *priest* whose function it is to be the linkman between the holy, living God and mortal, sinful men, and to preside at the sacrificial meal of communion. The priest can be thought of as the liaison-officer interpreting each to the other with the altar as the counter where the two-way traffic of sharing and communication takes place, or the priest may be the master of ceremonies and the altar the table for the feast of fellowship.

Assurance

Since all these varied terms describe inevitable elements on the agenda and the programme all who would profit thereby must both know the terminology and the inner meaning. The latter can only be achieved by some kind of experiment and first-hand testing. The appropriate pressures must be applied, and thereafter there exists an assured body of knowledge, practical as well as theoretical. In other words there is *assurance*. The whole process has been through the experimental station.

Faith

The remaining words have mainly to do with appropriation. The apprehending link-word is *faith*. In general this means, in

C

terms of a mathematical formula, evidence plus reason plus imagination plus fascination plus courage plus persistent experimentation. Faith is not contrasted with evidence and reason but incorporates and transcends both. In relation to persons it is summed up as trust issuing in confidence. It seeks the reliable and the genuine, which in an unfinished world demands a careful estimate of the probable balance of power at the ultimate conclusion of all things.

Prayer

Prayer is the final, and possibly most familiar, word. It really means a mutually trustful conversation, focusing the total relationship in verbally framed form, and including all the potential items of any personal relationship, especially help and gratitude. It operates in the elusive world of personal response, which by its very nature cannot be predicted or mechanically determined.

Specific holiness words

Now we turn to the specific words about our main theme. There are at least three ways in which this section can be approached, and all three have their uses. *First,* the original Bible words in Hebrew and Greek, together with their English equivalents, can be listed and expounded. Nobody need be alarmed at this prospect. Some will be helped by seeing the original words, in which the precious truths were first conveyed, put into English letters, while those who feel out of their depth can tread water for a moment until we all enjoy examining the English meaning. *Second,* the terms which have grown up in English among those specially interested in the subject can be explained and arranged in ideal relationship to each other. *Third,* the various English words involved can be subjected to careful analysis to discover their essential meaning and relationship.

Some Hebrew words

First we turn to the main Hebrew word for *holy, qadesh* or *qodesh.* The whole subject relates to mankind's original and elemental reactions to the surroundings of mystery and energy.

It would appear that the root meaning of the word concerns something cut or pierced, and therefore separated, set aside for special use. The holy is the divine power which draws things and people into its own orbit. The basic idea as it affects the world is setting apart for the service of sacred, supernatural power, which suffuses the thing or person with its own nature. Thoughtless or forbidden infringement of the sacred protection has fatal consequences as when Achan ransacked Ai (Joshua 7:18–26), Uzzah touched the Ark (2 Samuel 6:3), Uzziah handled the shewbread (2 Kings 15:13), and Annas and Sapphira lied about their share in the apostolic commonwealth (Acts 5:1). Three words which are related in idea are *cherem*, which means a *ban*, destroying the accursed object because of its offensive state; *chol* which includes *commonness* and *profaneness*, and therefore unsuitable by nature or in condition to be considered in the context of God; *ellu* with the emphasis on *clarity* and *brightness*, *free from any defect*, like a tempered, sharp and shining sword. In actual use the precise distinctions are not invariably kept. There are a good number of physical objects which could be separated for God's use, such as receptacles (1 Kings 7:51; Exodus 22:31). Ritual washing is a feature of the process (Leviticus 15:3; 22:4–6; Isaiah 65:8; Ezekiel 44:9). Dr Norman Snaith teases out five strands in the concept in his book *The Distinctive Ideas of the Old Testament*. *Separateness* to the divine nature is primary; second, there is the *aboveness* of the great ceiling of the sky which gives the impression of *loftiness*, as with the Holy One of Israel, high and lifted up (Isaiah 6:1 ff; Psalm 99:24), requiring the upward look. *Brightness* reflects the glory of God in the incandescent bush and on Mount Sinai, inducing reverent, humble obedience. *Power* is present by definition. Abraham takes upon him to address the Lord, though he is but dust and ashes, with fear and trembling. The psalm of the seven thunders (Psalm 29) reminds us of the overwhelming impact of God. *Righteousness* is linked with holiness, and represents the vindication of the norm, immovably straight and dependable (cf. Amos's plumb-line and everflowing stream). Another word is *tamin*, which symbolizes the *completeness* as against a part, and therefore without deficiency or blemish: RSV often translates as *blame-*

25

less. Shalom is also relevant, emphasizing *wholeness* as *peace* and *harmony,* trained absence of fuss, efficient control, as with the rippling muscles of the police horse, and usually applied to the heart (1 Chronicles 28:9; 29:9, 19; Isaiah 38:3).

Holiness: divine and human

Holiness has two aspects which need to be both distinguished and related. Only God is holy in the absolute sense. Man becomes holy in so far as he is brought into the area of God's service and use. The first holiness is objective and exists apart from man, which is probably why contemporary translations are reluctant to use holiness and perfection about human beings. The second aspect is derived, given, imparted. The aim of the operation for man is to fulfil the conditions of receiving without infringement of God's holiness or damage to man's nature, and thereafter to adjust as rapidly and completely as possible to the standard required. Such adjustment is partly man's effort to sanctify himself, but mainly glad submission to the powerful influences of God.

Relation of Hebrew and Greek words

Before we turn to the New Testament words it is important to note one fact. In 270 B.C. the Hebrew Old Testament was translated into a Greek version known as the *Septuagint* (so called because of the seventy who supposedly translated it). It was this Greek Septuagint that was the early Christians' Scriptures. In English versions, however, including the Authorized Version, the Old Testament is translated direct from the Hebrew while the New Testament, of course, is translated from the original Greek. This explains why in our English versions there is sometimes a difference between two passages that should be identical—for example when the New Testament quotes the Old Testament or when Isaiah is called Esaias. However, the Greek words are reasonably accurate indications of the Hebrew meaning; the two languages and the two parts of the Bible are adequately linked.

New Testament Greek words

The most important New Testament words in Greek are *teleios, hagios, katartisis,* and *naos. Teleios* is the adjective

formed from the very important word *telos,* the *end* or *purpose.*
If we pick up a novel in the library it is very hard not to glance
at the last page to see how the story concludes. The end is
the finish, but also the climax where the meaning of it all is
made plain. An unfinished story is very teasing, like Dickens's
The Mystery of Edwin Drood. It is the end that makes sense
of things, and everything else in a book is significant in proportion to the completeness of its relation to the end. All behaviour
is related to some purpose. Everything depends on what proves
triumphant at the final test. This word *teleios* therefore teaches
one of the most vital truths about *holiness, perfection, sanctification.* They are all related to the final power in control, from
beginning to end. It is not an accident that some of the clearest
teaching on this subject comes in the letters to the Thessalonians,
dominated by the thought of the final winding-up of all things
at the return of our Lord. A number of Paul's prayers are
scattered through these two earliest pieces of writing in the
Christian Church, and each is a prayer for the complete perfecting of this little back-street group of believers. The basic
thought, then, is of perfection as fulfilling the purpose for whatever the thing or person was intended. It will readily be seen
that the combination of finality in time and space and completion in purpose, can only be at the climax of all things,
but at any stage of time there can be the proper and complete response which fully contributes to the whole process.
In its fullest sense the word deals with the completed operation.
The student, for instance, has passed the elementary stages
and his final examinations; the rose-bud is transformed into
full bloom; the athlete has reached the tape; the child has
reached full stature. The word can relate to physical, moral,
intellectual, and spiritual states. Anything lacking has been
supplied. The man is mature, adult; the game is finished and
won; the promise is kept; the fruit is ripe; the pregnancy has
issued in birth; the process is complete, and the errand
performed.

Perfection as movement to climax

In order to achieve this overall aim we need to know what
we are aiming at, what is available to receive, and the resources

provided. At the beginning, in the middle, and at the end we must faithfully aim, study, work, and appropriate. Each stage has its own responsibilities and opportunities. We note therefore for all future occasions that complete concentration, trust, and obedience is called for, whatever we are doing, and this is an essential element in *sanctification, perfection, holiness.* Each point in the process may be utterly related to the final purpose and totally further its consummation. The difference in this sense between the perfect and the imperfect is not between completion and incompletion absolutely, but between the perfect and the imperfect adjustment at the stage in question. Our thought must take account of space and time. Most of our difficulties of thought on this subject arise from a static picture of frozen immobility, as of some waterfall arrested in mid-flight in all the majesty of its mass and pattern. All perfection in this world is perfection of movement, even if it includes stillness. Perhaps the ideal would be to confine the word to its adverbial form, where it modifies a verb describing some specific action, e.g. 'perfectly joined together' (1 Corinthians 1:10). Perfection relates to fitness for the job in hand viewed as part of a total operation; it furthers the end in view. All the powers of mind, conscience, affection, and body are bent to one and the same object, the will of God.

Drawn into divine orbit

The next word is *hagios*, which means *holy, sanctified, partaking of the nature of God, arousing and imparting reverence and worship.* It includes the total reality of the characteristics of God which produce awe, including especially power, purity, and purpose. God is flawless, genuine through and through, and in perfect control. His nature is of this kind from beginning to end. All the fulness of meaning in such words as *consecration, dedication, sanctification* here apply. This complex yet coherent personality we call God justifiably fascinates mankind, and arouses a mingled sense of attraction and repulsion. To be drawn into the purposes of such a being is devastating. 'Who may abide the day of his coming, and who shall stand when he appeareth? For he is like a refiner's fire . . .' (Malachi 3:2). Such an experience must leave a mark, like a searing flash. In so far as men remain within the radius of influence there is a permanently radioactive effect, transforming the nature. The direction of life changes; a new atmosphere is breathed; new food is eaten; 'behold, old things are passed away . . .' (2 Corinthians 5:17). Incidentally the verb *hagiadzo* is used twenty-seven times in the New Testament.

Completely fit

Katartidzo means to *make fit*, put in *sound condition*, which includes *mending*, like Peter and Andrew, James and John, with their respective fathers, keeping the fishing nets in repair. Whatever equipping, arranging, adjusting is necessary must be done. The property must be in a perfect state, furnished from top to bottom. The battalion must be up to strength, a full complement; the athlete must be in the pink of condition; the competitor must be thoroughly disciplined and prepared. The emphasis is on *fitness for purpose,* and the activities engaged in the process of achievement.

The holy place

Naos refers to the central and distinctive parts of the Jewish *Temple* in Jerusalem, the sanctuary where the priests alone entered, *the holy place* and the *Holy of Holies*. It applied also to the Temple in the New Jerusalem above, and to any true temple or place of worship where God is realized as spirit and truth. It also refers to the body of believers which is the Body of Christ, and to the Christian's own personality, which is a holy place by the work of the Holy Spirit.

Fullness

A group of words so far not mentioned is developed from *pleres,* which means *filled up,* as with a container of any kind, or a surface entirely covered, as with a fitted carpet, or a material soaked and permeated, a culvert flooded. It is used of a grain of corn packed to capacity, The related words strike the note of abundance, fullness, confidence, the overflowing cup full to the brim in unrationed, uninhibited abandon, intoxicated like the Spirit-filled believers on the first Christian Pentecost.

Such accomplishments cannot be kept quiet; they bubble out, up and over. There is therefore complete communication. We are to 'be filled with all the fullness of God' (Ephesians 3:19). Here is the consummation of God and man in creative encounter.

Entire sanctification

The general drift and precise meaning of the words in use is now evident. In various ways they stress the overmastering power and perfection of God, and the call to men to cooperate with Him and be set apart for trained fitness for His use. The whole of this process is readily understood as *sanctification*. Wesley adds a distinctive word to underline the point. The first half of two Greek words used in the same passage (1 Thessalonians 5:23) is identical: *Holo–* means *complete*, entire through and through, but with two different endings. *Holoteles* means completely related to its *purpose*, and at the end everything gained. *Holokleres* means *completely responsive to a calling* in the first place, with nothing lost on the way. Thus Wesley describes his doctrine as *Entire* Sanctification. The verse in question needs writing down for intensive study. 'The God of harmoniously controlled order sets you apart wholly for the purpose in hand, and may your spirit, soul and body be preserved in entire retention of your original calling without blame.' We recall our Lord's love of the word *all;* He warmed to whole-heartedness.

Specialized English terms

We have examined the Hebrew and Greek words in use, and their English meaning. As time proceeds, however, the various English words gain accretions of their own, and get used interchangeably. While it is hardly likely that such a process can be overtaken, reversed, and sorted out so far as the mass of those interested in the subject is concerned, it still remains possible to suggest to all who will listen the advisability of such a process. Indeed, there are a few other words which have become associated with the subject. In addition to *holiness, sanctification, perfection, fullness,* there are terms or phrases like *perfect love, maturity, wholeness, saints, fullness of the Spirit, purity of heart, blessing,* and *Second Blessing.*

Keep terms distinct

Each of the terms may well have validity in its own sphere, and nothing is to be gained by mixing them up, substituting one for another, or reacting violently against or for any because of ignorance or impatient revulsion against inexpert use. *Holiness* is the primary *Scriptural* and *religious* term. *Sanctification* is the *theological* term, *perfect love* the *ethical* and *relational* term, *maturity* the *psychological* term, *sanctity* or *sainthood* the *personal* term, always understood socially. *Completeness* is practically a *numerical* term, stressing the sum of the parts, and *wholeness* verges on the *metaphysical* and *teleological*, stressing the concept of *coherence, harmony, unity,* and *fulfilment. Fullness* includes completeness and wholeness but adds the distinctive note of *largesse*, superabundance, pulsing, irrepressible, unquenchable, *eternal life*, 'like a fountain rich and free', the original creative energy, measurable and immeasurable, having free play, pressed down and running over. It is *sui generis*, incorporating all other analysable factors, but transcending all. Powerful religion must be *pleromatic*. Whatever emptying takes place is not for its own sake but for unrationed filling. Obviously all the terms are describing the same dynamic condition and observe the identical subject from a variety of angles, each of which adds its shaft of illumination. It is supremely important, however, to keep the Godward side predominant, otherwise the result becomes either stunted and rigid, feverish and fungoid, or anaemic and spineless. Holiness and Sanctification are the primary terms, with perfect love the integral outworking, just as our Lord bound together inseparably with an unalterable order of priority, the double commandment to love God with the totality of powers, and our neighbour similarly.

Purity of heart

While the pressure comes down from the clouds via the reservoir in the hills, the immediate access is from the artesian well within the heart, which must be thoroughly free from sediment or impediment. The heart is the inner citadel of the personality, the headquarters where policies are decided, plans are made, and the spring of motive and action released. 'The pure in heart shall see God' (Matthew 5:8). *Purity* is undistorted concentration, vision, aim, and dynamic fully in accord, correctly directed with unimpeded efficiency of operation.

Reaching the essential

Each of these terms has a history, and books have been written about each of them. It is important to remember that they are in simple essence descriptive of the way things work and people behave. Life is full of deviations, complications, twists and turns, but it is impossible to cope with the abnormal unless there exists a relatively simple norm, which is first realized and then accepted as the basis of judgement. The great aim of this series is to list all the essentials, sort out and assemble them in the most logical and coherent manner, and then condense into a vividly viable proposition.

Second blessing

Once the subject has been raised among English-speaking people, a whole vocabulary of its own develops. Naturally those who do not know the original language discuss such matters in their own language, and thus a secondary series of semi-technical terms arises. Some of these we have already glanced at, but there remains the phrase *Second Blessing*, which has developed from an apparently casual remark by John Wesley. It is perhaps unfortunate that the phrase has become almost a technical term with an aura of sanctity around it, so that to ask straightforward and unprejudiced questions about its accuracy, its meaning, its practical implications or its Scriptural base tends to arouse more feeling than reason, both for proponents and opponents.

Blessedness

First we must examine the term *blessing*, which so easily becomes a religious commonplace, yet has a definite and infinitely rich meaning in Scripture. *Berhakha* is the Hebrew word for blessing. *Makarios* is the Greek adjective describing those who enjoy the divine favour, approval, and total benefits. In secular Greek the idea can be applied to the upper classes, and hence religiously to the spiritual aristocracy, who, as the

Beatitudes reveal, by no means necessarily coincide with the ruling powers of this world. While it is impossible to be the recipients of bounty and approval from supreme power without some degree of joyful feeling-tone, the central meaning is the objective fact of God's attitude. Since He approves of His own nature, and has imparted it to man through the unique Son Jesus Christ, He approves of those who are united to Christ, or incorporated into Him. Since His nature is holy by definition, and since His *holiness* manifests itself in *judgement, righteousness, pardon,* and *grace,* it follows that those who respond to the call to receive and cooperatively manifest this nature are in fact blessed. They have received everything summed up in the word *Blessing,* which is really *the summary of all God has to give.* Since those who are in any way separated from such joyous, unclouded confidence are to that extent cursed, which is the opposite of being blessed, the means by which they can be restored are obviously blessings. Therefore *salvation in all its aspects,* general and particular, *is the blessing.* Since the supreme end, humanly speaking, of salvation is *entire sanctification,* this latter state must be the supreme blessing. In terms of the Trinity this means that the *gift of the Holy Spirit,* with the full content explicit in the person and work of Christ, is the blessing. Since, however, human capacity for reception is usually extremely limited it may well be that the cup of blessing cannot contain all that God offers at once, and the believer indeed may not realize for some time just how much more is available. A second conflict, issuing in a second crisis may well ensue, and what is meant by the *Second Blessing* appears to be the realization of this deeper need and higher offer, and the willing acceptance thereof with all the conditions and consequences involved.

Beware the mechanical

It is extremely important not to harden this teaching into an almost mechanical, doctrinaire scheme whereby God always operates a two-stage impartation of blessing, pulling first lever one and then lever two. Thus it has been known for a young person to undergo the experience of conversion or the new birth in the afternoon, and a few hours later profess to have entered the Second Blessing or experience of *full salvation*. While such experiences are not impossible it would hardly seem a responsible method for normal use. Such teaching needs to be surrounded with the most careful instruction in the significance, conditions, and consequences of the offer, otherwise a later experience of disappointment may result in disheartenment or disillusionment, and the last state be worse than the first.

Valuation of the second blessing

Just as the automatic scheme is inadequate to the known nature of God, so we must note that God can act in this way if He sees fit, and that such an experience is unique in comparison with other crises of blessing still to come, because it is the first time that the person concerned has realized the necessity of a complete work, with some understanding of the radical nature of the operation. There is therefore force in the reply, to those who claim many blessings without the Second, that these are no substitute. The whole point of the teaching is that every Christian must face up to the challenge to complete surrender of self-will to the Divine Will, and the offer of supreme Divine assistance to this end. John Wesley himself stressed the immediacy of the experience and had the impressive evidence of his preachers, every one of whom recorded in the *Lives of the Early Methodist Preachers* became effective as he received the blessing. As a historic phenomenon the recorded amount of unflagging pioneer work achieved by these ordinary men appears to be without parallel. However cautious we may naturally be about teaching of this kind the phraseology cannot lightly be cast aside without serious and respectful consideration.

Use of verbs

Before turning to the last section of our word-study a note may be inserted about the use of verbs, which are the distinctive word-form of the Bible, with its emphasis on dynamic action, so congenial to our own day and the various mass media of communication. There is one Greek tense which is peculiar to that language, and which it is not easy to translate succinctly

34

into English, the aorist, which describes an action at a point in time as if the action were complete, or at any rate 'frozen' at that moment, even though in fact it may be continuous. It is rather like the deliberate, almost arbitrary, selection of one moment to freeze for inspection, a kind of cross-section of a temporal process, with the opportunity to investigate at depth to discern the inner consistency of an action still in progress.

Validity of religious language

The final assignment we set ourselves was to study various English words related to the concept of holiness in order to discern any common elements which would help to render this elusive word holiness more communicable in terms able to stand the test of contemporary linguistic philosophy. The assumption is that words are tools for human communication which must be within the scope of the world of experience potentially knowable to men as men. The complaint against religious vocabulary is that in its distinctive words it does not measure up to this test. Apart from the term *God, holiness* (which is almost identical) is at once the most typical and the most elusive. Words like *creation, love, providence,* and the like have more obvious relations with everyday speech, but there is no accepted method of testing *holiness* scientifically. The nearest kind of perceptive method which has any chance of coping with such ideas is used in apprehending relationships between things or persons. If related words cover some of the same area within the measurable world, to that extent a *prima facie* case is made out for further investigation of the claim that an immeasurable element is also present.

Linguistic analysis of holiness

A thorough examination of the subject from this point of view has been recently undertaken (O. R. Jones, *The Concept of Holiness*, 1961) which surveys the allied terms *fearfulness, powerfulness, wholeness, separatedness,* and *goodness.* In each case an element of personality and purpose was discovered, and was the dimension of thought which most successfully illuminated the words in isolation and together. The impersonal measurable element was clearly present, so that the words had

35

significance, but at the same time the significance was increased, and not decreased, by the personal factor, even though it was impossible to pin down completely. Since holiness includes all these terms it implies a personal and purposive nature and yet is operating partially in the recognizable world of human experience. *Holiness* is therefore seen as the comprehensive term which unites the fragmented glimpses of the allied words into one complete vision, which emerges from the logical order of thought in the parts, and in turn illuminates each and all. The ultimate personality, with purpose and power combined in moral integrity, is therefore not a meaningless concept and must be considered as the potentially most satisfactory concept to do justice to the greatest number of facts. Thus religious language is not irrelevant, even when most true to its own category, but constitutes a dimension of meaning which puts the more obviously human activities and concepts in the most viable position. No limit is therefore to be set to human reason in its investigation of the meaning of words or the realities they represent, except to deny their final completeness. Equally religious language must not evade investigation by such means. We are now ready for the next step.

3 Compiling the agenda

'For it was fitting that he, for whom and by whom all things exist, in bringing many sons to glory, should make the pioneer of their salvation perfect through suffering. For he who sanctifies and those who are sanctified have all one origin. . . .' (Hebrews 2:10f.)

WE have now surveyed the scene in general and noted the participants in the talks. We have also examined and explained as far as possible the meaning of the terms used in the discussion. Now we must compile the agenda of the meeting, the list of items of business to be considered, issuing in decisions about what needs to be done.

Order of business

There is great skill in drawing up an agenda so that the business is dealt with in an orderly manner, each stage contributing in a natural progression to the next. The first meeting begins with the election of a chairman and a secretary, receives any apologies for absence, proceeds to courtesies, congratulations, condolences, appreciations, and then hears a statement of the purpose of the committee or organization. Thereafter an analysis is made of the position to be faced, the steps to be taken and the people to take them, the estimated cost of the proposition, with a place for any other business which may be relevant but not realized previously. The meeting concludes by fixing the date, time, and place of the next meeting. The secretary makes a record of all decisions taken, though not necessarily of the arguments used, except in special circumstances. If the debates are in public, a transcript may well be made of the various speeches, as in the Hansard publications of the British House of Commons.

Relationship of members

Just such a picture we are using as an illustration of the internal debates of the Godhead. Naturally not every detail can be pressed, and a sense of awe descends upon us lest we appear over-familiar in our approach. We are certainly not encouraged to believe that there is ever any dissension in such circumstances. The unity of the Godhead is part of the holiness to be imparted (John 17:20–25). There are no apologies for absence because Father, Son, and Holy Spirit are everywhere and always present. In so far as the Bible and our human thinking is concerned, pre-eminence is always accorded to the Father (1 Corinthians 15:20–28), but this does not intend to convey the idea of superiority, only that for the sake of invaluable model-language in a tripartite pattern of personality, one partner must be representative of initiative, the original momentum, idea, energy, even though in terms of time the reactions of the other two parties are immediately identical and participant. The Son represents the potentiality of form, shape, medium of expression and transmission. The Spirit represents the potentiality and actuality of energetic idea in action through the specific form, especially in continuous impartation, whether of ideas, relationships, processes, or forces.

Running the film backwards

The purpose of this particular set of top level talks is to visualize the creation of man in the context of the whole creation, and to consider the possible results with preparations for each. We are of course reading back the course of events and their Biblical interpretation into the mind of God, rather like running a film backward as previously described. We are surveying the meeting from the point of view of such startling statements in Scripture as '. . . according to the definite plan and foreknowledge of God' (Acts 2:23). This does not necessarily mean that God predetermined everything that takes place in the world, but that given certain circumstances arising from man's use or misuse of his limited area of free will events would take place as they did. God committed Himself to certain courses of action in certain circumstances, without determining the total circumstances in detail.

The purpose of the meeting

First, then, the purpose of the summit meeting must be stated. In the nature of the case (and who would have it otherwise?) there must always be a penumbra of mystery. The power, the purpose, the purity, the personality of the Godhead by definition eludes man's complete understanding. We are dealing with the supreme self-awareness of the universe, the 'I AM THAT I AM' and the 'I WILL BE WHAT I WILL BE' (Exodus 3:14), and 'great is the mystery of godliness' (1 Timothy 3:16). Nevertheless one of the main themes of Christianity is that at the central and most important point so far as man is concerned the mystery has been unveiled: 'for he has made known to us in all wisdom and insight the mystery of his will, according to his purpose which he set forth in Christ as a plan for the fulness of time, to unite all things in him, things in heaven and things on earth' (Ephesians 1:9-10). Some kind of constructive harmonious energy is envisaged with an inter-relationship of personal wills to accomplish a purpose. Since creative and responsive love is of the essence of the operation, freedom of some kind must be posited. Such freedom is unreal unless the possibility of misuse is allowed. Possibility may become actuality, which means that there could be a breakdown. The supremely unfortunate eventuality (to be guarded against on the one hand and the repair department prepared for on the other) is just such a rupture of relationships.

Continuous session: full appraisal

The meeting has now commenced, though it is important to remember that it is in continuous session, 'for he who keeps Israel will neither slumber nor sleep' Psalm 121:4), while at the same time inherent in the system is the Sabbath rest, the silence in heaven (Revelation 8:1) 'about the space of half an hour', which saves the incessant activity from a kind of celestial St Vitus's dance. There has to be an unhurried, calm appraisal of the total situation, with alternative Plan B prepared if Plan A[1] is interrupted.

[1] At Cliff College Whitsuntide Anniversary Plan A details programmes for each of the seven meetings. Those held on the Terrace are in the open air. In case of rain a detailed Plan B is arranged to disperse the Terrace group to cover.

Creation; man; first steps

The first eight chapters of the book of Genesis (or Beginnings) well describe the line which God took and the actual consequences which brought Plan B into operation together with the detailed elements which inevitably arise under such circumstances. Within the short space of this piece of writing *creation, man, sin, law, judgement, penalty, death, covenant, blessing* all appear. Creation is seen as an act of God's love and fraught with His nature. In one sense we have to take the creation as a going concern, and many are prepared to leave the matter there. Some, however, cannot suppress their curiosity about the how, the why, the wherefore. Once such questions are asked our immediate theme is launched, and it is acting too much like a parent embarrassed by a child's query about birth to brush them on one side as meaningless or unanswerable. Incidentally theories about evolution and astronomy have little to do with this matter. Their concern is with the universe as already existing, and the examination of its processes. There must be some relation between the processes and the purpose, but each can be clearly distinguished from the other. The specific point at issue is the significance of the facts as well as the original aim of creation at all. It is reported of Albert Einstein that when he began to examine a scientific theory he asked the question whether if he were God he would have made the world in this way; if not the theory must be inadequate.

Personal activity and the measurable universe

The Hebrew word for creation is *bara,* used exclusively in the Old Testament for the divine activity. The world is seen as itself the work of God and as a stage for the drama of human history. God is throughout the sovereign Lord, whose will and power are expressed in the impersonal measurable world as well as the immeasurable dimension of the personal: 'it is I who by my great power and outstretched arm have made the earth, with the men and the animals that are on the earth, and I give it to whomever it seems right to me' (Jeremiah 27:5). When God speaks things happen; word and deed are one with Him. The mode of creation remains unknown or ultimately to be known by scientific investigation, though the latter can never really reach the full truth so far as personal thought and will are concerned. The point is that personal activity is involved in the process of creation of the cosmos and of mankind, who is related to the material universe though not exclusively determined by it. 'He who forms the mountains, and creates the wind, and declares to man what is his thought . . . the Lord, the God of hosts, is his name' (Amos 4:13).

Man's likeness to God

The climax of the process is the creation of man (Genesis 2:26f.), though here the Hebrew word used is *asah*, which means to make with the idea of using the material base while infusing spiritual life. Man is made with similarity to God: 'he who oppresses a poor man insults his Maker, but he who is kind to him honours him' (Proverbs 14:31). Man has the same qualities of self-awareness, rational thought, moral choice, sensitive appreciation, social relationship. The core of all the qualities is righteousness, or the will and power to be enduringly loyal to disinterested justice until and including the final vindication; without this steadfastness and responsibility relationships break down.

Patterns of energy

It therefore appears that creation of matter and personality is the main subject on the agenda. The two must be related though distinguishable. The same mind and will must operate from beginning to end, all through and all round. The constitution of the universe appears to be that of an intricate series of patterns of energy, assembling, interchanging continuously, but all responding to a mental message of some kind. The ultimate constituent to date appears to be the particle known as Omega Minus. It is fatal to rest theories of meaning on contemporary scientific fashions, but it may be permissible to point out a possible interpretation of this mathematical symbol. Omega is the last letter of the Greek alphabet as Alpha is the first. Matter, space-time, or impersonal energy, is the final measurable constituent of existence, but of itself it does not account for all the elements in existence; the missing

41

factor is the selfsame elusive entity known as personality, wherein lie the powers which make scientific discovery and social and cultural relationship possible. Jesus Christ is known, among other names, as the Alpha and Omega, without any minus, nothing lacking, and one reason is that personality finds its completest expression and fulfilment in Him. Hence He is the message 'without which was not anything made that was made . . . In the beginning was the Word, and the Word was with God, and the Word was God' (John 1:1ff.). Again, 'in him all things cohere' (Colossians 1:17), for the simple reason that 'he is the image of the invisible God, the first-born of all creation; for in him were all things created, in heaven and on earth, visible and invisible, whether thrones or dominions or principalities or authorities—all things were created through him and for him' (ibid. vv. 15f.).

Interaction of process and decision

The totality of the Trinity is at work in the creation. God the Father is the potent generator of controlled energy; God the Son is the potent shaper of the energy; God the Spirit is the potent driver of the energy, both as external director and also as coordinator and inward momentum, which is why the Spirit can be referred to on different occasions as an almost impersonal force and as a personal agent. Since personality in relation is the ruling factor in the situation the creation must so take place as to prepare for, achieve, and sustain its existence, function and purpose. The opening chapter of the Bible describes the stages as they appeared, and with reasonable similarity to what are called in biology theories of evolution, which in simple essence conclude that the steps of development are continuous from the simple cell to the complex organism. This method is well exemplified in our Lord's parable of the seed and the earth developing from its own internal impulse, 'of itself', automatically, self-propelled (Mark 4:26–29). The interacting and necessary element of personal action appears in the climax of the story where the farmer assesses the ripe time, decides to intervene, and thrusts in the sickle to gather the harvest, which otherwise, if the process is left to itself, goes on to rot. Hence man is directed to subdue the earth, care for it, and enable creation to fulfil its purpose for man's well-being (Genesis 1:28–30).

A reasonable, good, beautiful world

The Scriptures throughout assume that the whole creative process bears the mark of its divine origin and speaks of dimensions greater than itself through its own limited dimensions. 'Speak to the earth, and it shall teach thee' (Job 12:8). 'Even the stork in the heavens knows her times; and the turtledove, swallow, and crane keep the time of their coming; but my people know not the ordinance of the Lord' (Jeremiah 8:7). The teaching of Jesus is crammed with such parallels seen in the context of the eternal; 'behold, keep your eyes open for the hidden meaning, a farmer went out sowing seed', and as the results appear each unfolding of the story strikes home the truth about the creation and its possibilities (cf. Mark 4:1ff.). The total human situation, which is the subject of the sanctifying work, needs to be seen perpetually against this integrated background of the world known to science, to art (for again the Scriptures are full of the breathtaking beauty of the heavens, the countryside, the shapes and sounds and scents of both God's and man's devising), and to morality in society. The world as created is good in its stages and supremely good in its totality and coherence (Genesis 1:1–31). God gave man 'all things richly and freely to enjoy' (1 Timothy 6:17). When the world appears as hostile to God's purpose what is in mind is human society organized apart from God in distrust and disobedience. It is vital, especially when considering holiness, not to confuse the two uses of the term *world*. Immense damage is done, especially to family life, when this disastrous error is perpetrated, though it is true that the corruption of the sin which has entered the world can spoil the most innocent and beautiful experiences and enjoyments.

Restoration of coherence

This coherence and interdependence which we have been describing is a projection of the innermost unity, knowledge, goodness, beauty, relationship of the Godhead. Wickedness, however, whether celestial or mundane, by the misuse of personal freedom may in part disorganize the divine plan, and to that extent inflict wounds on the Godhead, though not such wounds as that same Godhead does not already potentially bear: 'the Lamb is slain from the foundation of the world' (Revelation 13:8). Attention must be given to the restoration of coherence, which means the necessity of reconciliation and reintegration. Whatever person or persons carry through this project must know what to do, and why, how, when, and where. Now we begin to see how the agenda must be compiled.

Distortion in abstract thought

The aim is the creation of beings who, in society, can have fellowship with each other and with their Creator. The material with which the operation is to be carried through is measurable energy in terms of time and space, which are two aspects of each other and of the basic energy which is the stuff of creation. Time is the extension of the energy in terms of motion, and space the extension of the energy in terms of mass. The simultaneity of the inherent energy which is God is called eternity in relation to the motion of time, and infinity in relation to the mass of space, which is finite though unbounded. All the way through any thought about ultimate matters runs the tension between these concepts. Abstract thought is inadequate to contain the total truth; it inevitably distorts spatial and temporal language and concepts because it arbitrarily isolates and immobilizes the total reality of any moment or area for the purpose of drawing out the general principles inherent in them. This is a legitimate activity provided it is done deliberately, with full understanding of what is happening, and the element of distortion is declared. Geographers will be familiar, like travellers generally, with the various projections used by map-makers, which make identical land-masses appear vastly different, because each particular projection is required for a different purpose. All instructed persons know how to make allowances. So it is with thought about God, especially at the point of relation between eternity and time, infinity and the finite. Hence apparent contradictions will appear all along the line at every point, but they will be the same in essence though different in guise. Once this fundamental point has been realized and accepted it is possible to push ahead with the argument; otherwise there will be stumbling and grumbling at every point.

Is the measurable world self-contained?

The real point of divergence between those who believe in the existence of spiritual reality, such as we call God, and those who do not, appears here over this issue at the very beginning. Is the measurable and predictable world known to science complete in itself, apart from the actually unfinished nature of time, or has it in fact cradled elements which are not by their very nature confined within such limits? Our claim would be that such phenomena exist, and that their existence implies the potentiality of their existence from the beginning in the cosmos as a going concern. These elements are inextricably associated with consciousness, in particular the human consciousness. Reading back, therefore, into the potentiality from which such elements became actual, we infer that the original self-consciousness was responsible for this situation. Hence we accept that God made man in His own image, though we acknowledge that those who choose so to do are at liberty to suggest that the process is really in reverse, and man has made God in his own image. The difficulty is that man's image is contradictory and mixed-up, while God's is consistent and straightforward.

Indivisibility of health

The first item on the agenda was the creation of the world, and the second the creation of man. At this point we may well remind ourselves of the astonishing similarity between the Biblical and the contemporary view of human nature as a psychosomatic entity, i.e. a body-spirit unit. The two elements cannot be separated, though in thought we can, indeed must, approach man from both points of view, the first being 'that which is natural' as Paul put it, the measurable, and the second being 'that which is spiritual', or immeasurable. For a full estimate of man both are needed. Life in its unicellular beginnings strives to survive and perfect itself through an internally cooperative interaction. Thus mankind's health is indivisible.

Dealing with breakdown

Once such beings have come into existence, should they in fact deviate from the norm (which is what in part is meant by righteousness) confidence will be broken. Thereafter follows separation, uncertainty, fear, guilt, enmity, and all the rest of the destructive and dismal brood of sin, which is essentially a wrong relationship with God, who will then appear as Judge. The supreme question then posed is whether anything can be done to put matters right, or whether the whole experiment is irreparably spoiled. Certainly it must be made clear beyond doubt that the will and power of the Creator are final, and that the parties involved understand the position. The Creator Judge must both punish the offenders and indicate to them how they ought to behave, which means some form of law, though this must be seen as reasonable and not merely arbitrary. It must be an expression of personal mind, will, and power. Punishment may well have to be progressive, with some aspects of crudity to begin with. An elementary moral stage may need an elementary treatment. Thus Noah's flood served a purpose, even though, like the thunderbolts recommended by the Angel Gabriel in *Green Pastures* they 'don't do no good; dere dey (mankind) is, jes' as bad as ever'. Whatever is done will almost certainly have to be phased both as penalty and rehabilitation.

Restoration and covenant

If there is to be a restoration of relationships a *covenant* or binding agreement is required, and here we come to one of the supremely important items on the agenda. The documentary evidence of the business to be done by the Triune God is to be found in the Bible, which is divided into two sections, each about a covenant, with continuity between the two as well as vital differences. The basic idea is of mutually controlling agreement between two or more parties with a legal core of public commitment surrounded and suffused by personal relationships of loyal devotion and loving service. Steadfastness and warmth mark the covenant, with a profound sense of responsibility and obligation. It is essentially moral and personal.

Covenant, initiative, grace, and maintenance

Somebody has to take the initiative in proposing such a covenant relationship, and in these particular circumstances no one but the Creator of the universe is in a position to do so. According to the Biblical transcript God acted by choosing a particular people to be the first partners in this work, though it is stressed that the choice lies in the sovereign will of God and not in either the size or the wealth of the parties concerned. This election-love requires trust and obedience as its response, and offers provision and care as the divine part of the promise. Failure to discharge the appropriate obligations by one party releases the other. Since it is axiomatic that God will not deviate from His share, the possibility of an initial breakdown in relationships is confined to mankind. In such case any perpetuation of the covenant will be an act of grace, of free pardon and maintenance. The Authorized Version usually describes this attitude as mercy, but the Revised Standard Version more adequately translates as steadfast love, though even this misses the element of ardour which suffuses the creative and restoring spirit in which God seeks to maintain the covenant.

Vindication of the divine will

The danger with such long-suffering loving-kindness is presumption and exploitation on the part of the recipients. Since the ground of confidence throughout is the absolutely reliable will of God it must be made plain that there is no favouritism or weakness which weakens the holiness on which all else depends. Whatever is done must establish beyond cavil the unswerving holiness and righteousness of God, the penalty due to sin, and the necessary trust and obedience in performing the will of God. Thus His kingdom or rule is done on earth as in heaven. The essential elements of the law must be vindicated and a thoroughly adequate satisfaction of its demands enacted. The law itself must be seen as an expression of the power and will of the Creator-Judge-Saviour. Somehow the gracious act of pardon and any rescue operation must be realized as furthering the establishment of the will and rule of God on earth as in heaven.

Guilt and justification

At this point we take up the pictures suggested in the preceding chapter on terminology. The law-court is the first of the dramatic scenes as the theme of justification is approached: the defendant has to be given the right status before the law. Where such an intimate and binding relationship as a covenant has been broken the responsible party is put in the wrong, and is guilty as a matter of objective fact. In so far as the party or parties concerned are properly aware of the situation, there will be the complication of a sense of guilt, shame, personal disloyalty and offence. Three actions at least will be necessary if the defendant is to be transferred effectively into a satisfactory state for a new start. It is assumed that his guilt is proved and acknowledged, and that punishment is due to him. He must be pardoned for the past, given a new access of energy for the present and the future, and also totally released and cleansed from any clinging aroma and suffusing alien influence from the past. Justification affects the first of these stages: the delinquent must be put in the right before the law. In terms of the law this means the apparently contradictory judgement of acquittal after sentence of guilt. In the Old Testament the judge who acts thus is characterized as unjust, whereby the very foundation of confidence is undermined. In the New Testament the paradox is boldly affirmed of justifying the unjust, but always with the assertion that the Creator-Judge Himself accepts the penal consequences.

Redemptive cost

At each point in the process cost will appear. In any meeting where practical problems are discussed, inevitably and properly the question of price is raised. The creative element in every case lies with the people in charge, since they alone possess the resources. The typical Biblical term for this element in the process is redemption, which emphasizes the activity involved in creative release. People and things are brought and bought out of whatever frustrates freedom, e.g. prison or pawn, by the initiative and expenditure of status, energy, and prospects of those with the ability, training, efficiency and willingness to devote everything, including life and reputation themselves, to the task.

Verdict, separation, price

So far as this first picture of juridical status is concerned the Godhead is prepared to suffer, 'the just for the unjust, to bring' mankind back to the right relationship after downfall, capture, and adverse verdict. The consequence in this ultimate relationship is separation from the source of life, status, dignity, and destiny itself. Such a verdict is not arbitrary but in the nature of the case. The verdict merely states specifically what is true essentially, and thereby clarifies the position beyond cavil. The price, therefore, to be paid by the would-be saviour-judge is to accept the penal consequences of these responsibilities on behalf of the condemned felon. *Physically* the penalty for rebellion is death; *emotionally* it is separation from home; *morally* it is a guilty conscience; *mentally* it is the removal of the foundation of rational confidence; and *spiritually* it means isolation from the approving sovereign presence of God Himself.

Full account taken of possible cost

In one sense God cannot be subject to any of these dire results, but the very clear hint of Scripture is that the Godhead was willing to enter such a situation. One element must inevitably be absent, namely *merit of such treatment;* but in all other respects God's omnipotence includes the capacity to be Himself within such restricting confines, though only with the inherent provision that such restriction in terms of time could only be temporary. A bursting of the cramping bonds cannot be prevented: 'it was impossible that he should be holden of death' (Acts 2:24). Even God Himself could not be actually guilty or deserve the penalty or be permanently killed, but He could bear the consequences which His children would deserve should they in fact prove disobedient. Hence there might prove necessity for such a work at such a cost, and the Godhead was prepared for such works-costing, which involved a representative with full divine authority identifying Himself with the sinful situation and the guilty race in its ultimate predicament. The total cost to purity of such involvement in sin is beyond the grasp of human imagination, though fragmentary glimpses of vicarious suffering are frequent in human experience. The main point is that at the summit meeting and in the top level talks full account was taken of the greatest possible defalcation on the part of mankind and the greatest possible liability on the divine resources at this and all other possible stages of rescue and rehabilitation. Since the accused is bankrupt only a free gift will suffice, but obviously somebody always pays. What is free to man is infinitely costly to God.

Regeneration

Once this work of reinstatement as an innocent citizen is established the problem will arise of enabling the released prisoner to take actual advantage of his miraculously donated technical freedom by walking out of the open door of the dock, and acting like a man with the freedom of the city and the key to the home door. The nervous system adjusts itself to the conditions of captivity, and both the will and the energy to escape tend to atrophy. In fact a new lease of life is required; there has to be a blood transfusion, a new birth, a new creative deed, which is known as regeneration. Just as man cannot live physically unless life is given to him in the first place, so neither can he live as a truly human person unless the capacity for such nature is implanted within him. If this total life were to be damaged drastically a restorative impartation of new life from the original source would be required. The illustration of the law-court is totally inadequate here and must give place to the maternity-ward. Man will in such circumstances need to be born again from above (John 1:12f.; John 3:3–8), to be begotten again (1 Peter, 1:3) 'born again, not of corruptible seed, but of incorruptible, by the word of God, which liveth and abideth for ever' (1 Peter, 1:23). Such new life cannot be imparted without effort at least as great as the original impartation. Anyone who has tried to insert a fresh and vigorous spirit into another person weighed down with past associations knows what expenditure of nervous and spiritual energy is required. We have to give ourselves for their renewal. The Godhead is prepared for this situation. God's own life is available for the purpose, though to be fully effective such life must operate under existing human conditions, and such self-giving must include willingness to give to the uttermost, in death if need be. The works-costing or redemptive element in the saving act must be ready to include the emptying out of the pure, creative, and hence recreative, life. Henceforth the beneficiary under this precious legacy is able to profit by his technical inheritance of justification, whereby he is put in the the right before the law and the ruler-judge, because he also possesses the necessary energy from above to start again like a newborn babe, learning to walk, and in general becoming that growing child of God who is always hungry for the Bread of Life, and thirsting for the pure milk of the word, the inner spring-water of eternal life, and the wine of the Spirit.

Miracle of atonement

Such a reversal by free grace both of status and state would be a marvellous and infinitely costly work of compassion and mercy, which is what is meant by a miracle. God would be keeping His part of the covenant, even though man had broken his part. Such steadfast love alone could make rescue possible, and all along the line it must manifest and vindicate the holiness on which alone everything else depends. The key to the whole problem from the divine point of view, so far as human beings can discern it, is a work of atonement, both as dealing with the past, the present, and the future, once the space-time continuum has come into existence.

Sanctification

The two scenes so far imagined help us to visualize the meaning of the first two stages of the work, but each exhausts its usefulness in turn. Further scenes are required of which one is the cleansing-department, and another the training-school. The most elusive and resistant element in man's nature, once corrupted, will be the stain and the smell. The two are as intimately related as the olfactory and optical senses. Both soak into the remote interstices and fabric of the construction, and can only be removed by some detergent flood which breaks up the tiny globules lurking in otherwise inaccessible hide-outs. Thus a sanitary work of decontamination is required, a fumigating, antiseptic operation. The whole nature has to

51

be renewed and rendered suitable for the presence and use of God, trained, disciplined, with all faculties at a pitch of fitness required for the service of the Kingdom of God. Such a work is implied in each stage and in each picture, all contributing to this same end, and each fails of its purpose unless the end-product appears. Here the specific work known as sanctification is seen both in its separateness from and its identity with the parabolic scenes and processes.

Creative expenditure of energy

Equally here an agonizing expenditure of energy is called for. The life-energy imparted is both the pure blood or life of God 'which cleanses from all sin' (1 John 1:7) and the work of the Holy Spirit, who proceeds from the Father and the Son, applying, inserting, extending, and continuing the total productive enterprise. Behind the terms agony and tribulation lies the picture of the torture implied in being impaled on three stakes, but the specific idea conveys the sense of painful gasps as an athlete or a mother in childbirth throws everything into the final concentrated effort which produces the desired results. Pain, price, effort is therefore written into the creative process. Its whole purpose should be creative and recreative. Where such a creative element is missing there is wasted and pointless suffering, the final absurdity in the universe, and the one obstacle to wholehearted faith in God which defies complete solution in terms of reason. The only conceivable answer, once the amount attributable to human folly and wickedness has been eliminated, is the necessity for an impersonal, measurable base in the created structure in order that creative suffering and personal beings should exist at all (cf. Romans 8:18–23).

Total possible consequences

Once the idea of creation, both of the universe and man, was mooted, God being what He was, the total possible consequences had to be thought through and out. It has now been shown how the divine mind measured the possibilities of the experiment. There are refinements of analysis and elements of synthesis which fill out the broad structure of the total work of salvation if required, but the main outlines are

52

now visible, and strangely familiar to mortals as they overhear the internal debates of the Godhead.

Priesthood and intercession

There remains the linking of the ideas with actuality, the mediating or relating of the divine scheme to the human situation. Both the work and the cost will become precise and actual once creation is in being. The whole problem thereafter is the linking of the two. It is here that the concept of priesthood comes into its own. The priest is the linkman or liaison-officer, where contact, explanation, communication backward and forward are made. In the liaison-office there is usually the counter or the table, across, through and around which the total benefits are mediated. Since the heart of the work is sacrificial trust and obedience the priestly function will as it were ferry backwards and forwards between the divine and the human, though for a fully effective work God Himself must be the priest and the sacrifice, and do all works at once in the same deed and with a total continuity in time and space. Since the work includes justification, regeneration, sanctification, and redemption at each point, the priestly work includes each and all in the full work of atonement both in the historic deed and the continuing application. The heart of this work is intercession for the transgressors (Isaiah 53:12). The actual setting forth of the divine is the prophetic task; its mediation and the representation of man is the priestly. Since the simplest picture of such intimate relationship and common sharing is the meal it is not surprising that God uses such elemental material for His as bread and wine, broken and poured, as the symbolic means of imparting His grace.

Associated division of Trinitarian tasks

In one sense every member of the Trinity is involved in every activity of the Godhead, yet for economy of action specific aspects of the total work are associated with one or other Person of the Trinity. Thus the Father remains in sole control of the universe in all its aspects, including creative, juridical, redemptive, and sanctifying, yet both the Son and the Holy Spirit are recognizable in each of these aspects.

53

Nevertheless the Son is especially associated with the redemptive and saving work, and the Spirit with the sanctifying work. The Spirit is the elusive element in personality which hovers between the measurable and the immeasurable, the impersonal edge of personality and the personal edge of impersonality, the decompression chamber between the two pressures of reality, the celestial and the terrestrial. The Spirit above all else witnesses, offers convincing evidence, that those who believe are children of the Father and can address Him thus (Galatians 4:6), that the incarnate Son is Jesus the Lord and Saviour, and that love reigns in the heart and the fellowship, thus creating peace and ordered community.

Limitation to particulars

While such a plan is adequate in principle it involves actual creation, with its characteristic limitations of space and time. Both of these will therefore have to be taken into consideration. While the basic construction will be present throughout so that glimpses of light will be available to all everywhere, particularity is of the essence of the project. Therefore God will choose people to be His messengers and interpreters, who must themselves be made fit to hear, see, understand, and transmit. Since the work is corporate as well as individual the choice will fall on a particular people as well as particular individuals. The area to be specifically chosen needs to be at the crossroads of civilization, and this is found at the eastern end of the Mediterranean Sea in what is later called the Middle East. As the people and individuals appear God will choose, call, and direct in a continuously adjusting pattern of saving activity, related both to the actualities of the situations as they are and to the final plan in its stages and its completion.

Trinitarian blessing

The responsibility of the Father is mainly to eternity, of the Son to history and geography, of the Spirit to personality and community in their inner drives. Yet when this has been said it remains true that each is in, through and with each at every point. The beginning and the end, and all in between, is summed up in the Trinitarian blessing, both in its formal and logical presentation as 'in the name of the Father, and of the Son, and of the Holy Spirit' (Matthew 28 : 19) and in its practical and informal presentation as 'the grace of the Lord Jesus Christ, and the love of God, and the fellowship of the Holy Spirit be with you all' (2 Corinthians, 13 : 14).

Extensions of saving health

The agenda in general is now complete, and the decisions made. There are many glimpses of the glory of the divine mind and plan in creation, in Scripture, in history, in the Church, but perhaps 'the inmost shrine of revealed religion' is the seventeenth chapter of Saint John's Gospel. The unity of the Divine nature, will, and plan is there disclosed as an inspired imaginative glimpse into the prayer-life of the Son now incarnate. The aim is that none should be lost or wasted, as none is except sons of perdition or waste, like Judas who asked of a typical act of divine bounty, 'to what purpose is this waste?' (Matthew 26 : 8). The Godhead, holy, righteous, loving, is totally the saving reality, and therefore the nature of God to be imparted to man, the image to be restored when broken and marred, is a saving nature with all the constituents mentioned. To be holy as God is holy, to be distinctively divine, is to be a saving person and to belong to a saving community. Such sharing in the health-producing community involves the redemptive cost of being a justifying, adopting, regenerating, sanctifying person, and extension of the Incarnation, the Atonement (of which it is a postulate), the Resurrection (which is the inevitable consequence), the Ascension (or return to heaven, above where Christ is (Colossians 3 : 1), in prevailing intercession for the transgressors), and of Pentecost. Thereby we become part of the growing-points or cells of the Body of Christ, communicating health of nature, motive, and purpose. This is to be a partaker of the divine nature. Such a community is the temple of the Godhead, a health-giving nation, a priestly people especially God's own (possessed, purchased, and preserved by Him), the household of the Father, the Body of the Son, the fellowship of the Holy Spirit, the One who comes alongside to help as the strong standby or Paraclete in every way required. In separateness the Church is seen as the Bride, who is to be pure and spotless, unwrinkled with senility and care, adorned with every scintillating gem of the Godhead, like a crystal sea or a jasper wall.

Continuous creation and salvation

The top level talks at the original summit meeting are not concluded. Any other business is perpetually on the agenda. In one sense the meeting is still in session; the creation, the judgement, the salvation, the justification, the regeneration, the sanctification are both initially complete, currently continuous, and finally to be concluded. Nevertheless the basic decisions were made before time was, and all that appears now is within the total context of the divine plan, even though the random element of the creation once embarked upon will raise inscrutable problems for the limited human mind, which observes and experiences only an infinitesimal part of the vast concerns of God. Hence the important thing for man will not be that he knows God, but that he is known of and by God.

Perfect mediator

Inevitably this whole picture appears in a hazy mirror to the unaided human eye, but the divine aim is to produce a perfect mirror, as in the floor of Saint Peter's at Rome, where the glorious picture on the remote ceiling is perfectly reproduced at a level human beings can examine. As they bow head and body low to the ground they come where God is earthed, and from this lowly posture see all the glories above. It will be through Jesus the Son that men come to the Father, and from Jesus the Son that they receive the Holy Spirit, and themselves reflect, as in a mirror, the glory of God. This Jesus will be seen to be the centre and sun of every sphere, as well as near and dear to every believing heart, the pioneer and confident exponent of man's salvation, both related to us and distinct from us.

Other possibilities

What has been so far said takes no account of the possibility that man might never have deviated, and therefore Plan B never have been brought into operation. It would still remain true that God was as described, and had made decisions anterior to creation in precisely this way. The question is sometimes raised in this form in relation to possible conscious life on other planets now in course of visitation. Has there been an incarnation elsewhere? If so, was atonement found necessary? Alice Meynell speculated that God might have other Words for other worlds, but rightly recalled that for this world the Word of God was given in Christ and Him crucified. Whatever variants there may be will not contradict Christ, and in whatever circumstances God gives the personal revelation in finality and fulness the incarnate One will be seen as the clue to universal meaning and the Saviour in the form required by the existing situation. Alice Meynell takes up the theme again in her poem 'Christ in the Universe', which perhaps prepares us for the revelations of the space age even before the final vision of comprehensive truth she envisages in heaven:

> *With this ambiguous earth*
> *His dealings have been told us. These abide:*
> *The signal to a maid, the human birth,*
> *The lesson, and the young man crucified.*
> ....
>
> *Nor, in our little day,*
> *May His devices with the heavens be guessed,*
> *His pilgrimage to thread the Milky Way*
> *Or His bestowals there be manifest.*
>
> *But in the eternities,*
> *Doubtless we shall compare together, hear*
> *A million alien Gospels, in what guise*
> *He trod the Pleiades, the Lyre, the Bear.*
>
> *O be prepared, my soul!*
> *To read the inconceivable, to scan*
> *The million forms of God those stars unroll*
> *When, in our turn, we show to them a Man.*

Agenda completed

Meanwhile, the main items of the agenda have been completed, and we know that sanctification is the will and work of God which He undertook for the establishment and maintenance of glory, which is the true manifestation of the worth and power of God, revealing His nature and purpose that all may recognize, evaluate, and acknowledge the holiness which is His alone. God, the world, and man are embraced in a common unity of effort. The divine energy is fully employed to complete the divine plan. The suffering involved is the discipline of directed dynamism, and is condensed in concentrated energy in Jesus Christ. Man's holiness will consist not in achieving some Stoic or Pharisaic righteousness, however refined or Christianized (or valuable within its limits), but in receiving God's total grace, Himself in saving deed and relationship, concentrated in the historic Jesus, setting him apart for saving service, removing every kind of hindrance, whether as dirt or clutter, and flooding the inward self with the overflowing Spirit. Everything depends therefore upon God's faithful intention, promise, and performance. The upshot will be the glory of God: 'then shall the heathen know that I am the Lord when I am sanctified in you before their eyes' (Ezekiel 36:23). Men will 'see your good works, and glorify your Father which is in heaven' (Matthew 5:16).

4 Outlining the programme

'This is the word which by the Gospel is preached unto you.' (1 Peter 1:25; cf. vv. 10–12.)

THE scene has been set, and the main participants introduced. The language, we hope, has been mastered. The agenda, the most important part of the whole proceeding, has been compiled and dealt with. The decisions have been made, and it now remains to let all interested parties know what has been and is to be done, in order to inform, persuade, instruct, train, warn, encourage and guide them in respect of the overall plan and particular details. The programme must be outlined so that the intention of the summit powers can be understood and followed. The main emphasis will be on what God proposes to do, indeed has already done, and how man is expected to cooperate in response. We are to work out our own salvation with a great sense of the sacredness of what we are doing, because God Himself is at work at the same time (Philippians 2:12f.). There is to be a divine and a human side, both working together, with the initiative originally with God, who nevertheless often allows man the privilege of apparently starting the process.

Two main stages of this programme-outlining may be noted. First there is God's revelation, with the necessary inspiration to grasp its content and significance; second man's proclamation of God's revelation and the necessary faith to receive and profit by it.

God's own outlining

We turn therefore to God's own outlining of the programme based on the decisions and plans made in the top level talks at the Christian summit meeting. The technical phrase for

59

this activity is revelation, which means a making known, an opening up, a disclosing of what was previously unknown and hidden, so that others apart from the revealer may know for themselves. Knowledge usually comes through a combination of observed actions and words, either spoken or written, and preferably both. If there is conflict between the two then automatically priority is accorded to action, as in the case of circumstantial evidence, unless there is an overwhelmingly convincing explanation to the contrary. On the other hand mere description of events without some measure of interpretation leaves man's mind unsatisfied. Man wants to know not only what, when, where, but also how and why. We are most convinced when deeds and words fit each other exactly.

Deed and word

So far as Christianity is concerned the Bible is accepted as the authentic record of the way God has revealed His plan by word and action. With Him indeed the two are so much one that the phrase 'Word of God' includes both. When He speaks things happen. 'In the beginning God created the heavens and the earth . . . And God said, Let there be . . . and there was . . .' (Genesis 1: 3, 6, 9, 11, 14, 20, 24, 26). 'In the beginning was the Word, and the Word was with God, and the Word was God. The same was in the beginning with God. All things were made by him; and without Him was not anything made that was made' (John 1:1–3). The Word of God is God's revelation of Himself and His purpose in 'mighty acts' (Psalm 103:7; 106:2, 8; 145:4–12), and a special integrated interpretation of those effective deeds.

Evolution and natural religion

These saving activities, recorded in Holy Scripture, exemplify the principles on which God has constructed His universe of time and space, and how He has imparted the understanding of them. Since process or continuous evolutionary development is one clear element in the structure of the universe we shall expect some hints within the natural order of God's regular method of activity, and so it proves. There is a form of natural religion which recognizes gift, use, and purpose in the fructifying purposes of the world, with which men can cooperate for the common good. The Harvest Festival recognizes this natural religion with its appreciation of usefulness, dependability, and beauty. It is not surprising that there are a variety of religions in the world, with features in common, each laying hold of a part of the truth, and with much to teach each other. Each recognizes the need of man's salvation, though the difference between them is largely determined by their concept of the final power and satisfaction in the world, and the consequent diagnoses of man's specific need. Each therefore has its own conception of sanctity and distinctive type of saint. Natural religion is not of itself a full revelation; it is capable of diverse interpretations, even of a merely naturalistic religion, which means a worship of the processes, in certain sophisticated circumstances amounting to a humanistic religion, where man is worshipped as the measure and master of things. In effect, this usually means some form of Vitalism, worship of the impulse of life and its increasing complexity and fertility. George Bernard Shaw with his Life Force and, at one time, Julian Huxley with his Divine Urge, have been prophets of this religion in the present century. The witness, however, of the creative process is ambiguous. It leaves man as the Great Amphibian, capable of living in two worlds, one measurable and scientific, the other immeasurable and spiritual, but without a clear reconciliation between the two.

The clash of history

The Bible recognizes the evidence of the natural order towards God, but considers the scene of human history as a more useful and potent clue to the divine activity (cf. Isaiah 61:11), precisely because it deals with human wills and plans, their clash, their reconciliation, their frustration, their fulfilment, both in relation to each other and to the raw materials of the actual situations in which they find themselves at different junctures. Physical events, like Noah's flood, the crossing of the Red Sea and the River Jordan, the sun standing still in Gibeah, are seen as happening at uniquely providential times for the progress of the community God had chosen to be the special vehicle or revelation of Himself to mankind. This people, variously known as the Hebrews, the Israelites, and the Jews (roughly corresponding to three stages of their history, divided by the two catastrophes of slavery in Egypt and captivity in Babylon) received the clearest indications of a purpose at once providential, saving, and redemptive, which was for the benefit of all mankind. The farthest islands were to wait for the true religion at their hands (Isaiah 60:9), and it all began with a series of selective covenants through Noah, Abraham, and Moses, summed up in the first five books of the Bible, known as the Law or Torah, to this day the centre of Jewish religious life, and fundamental background also for the Christian religion. The Torah is the supreme pre-Christian instance of divine revelation, emphasizing both deed and word. 'I am the Lord thy God which brought thee up out of the land of Egypt . . . therefore ye shall have no other gods before me' (Exodus 20:3).

Story of beginnings

The earlier events in the dim dawn of time, before men had developed recording facilities, are inevitably less easy to verify by acceptable historical apparatus. The earlier ones bear the marks of a mixture of actual events with a large element of parabolic interpretation. Herein lies the true meaning of what is so often very misleadingly called myth, which in everyday language (as distinct from academic technical jargon) means mere phantasy, a mingling of children's fairy stories and Christmas legends, to be outgrown by the mental age of between five and eight. The truer interpretation is to admit the present lack of adequate criteria to verify unmistakably every detail (while cherishing the legitimate hope that archaeological research will continue its successful pioneering probe into the interior of antiquity), and discerning the profound truth conveyed by this perfectly legitimate method of parable, metaphor, and simile. There is no doubt that the relationships, motives, reactions described in the very earliest chapters of the Book of Genesis, as well as in the developing story of the Bible in general, reveal to us genuine human beings in recognizable situations. Nobody need be ashamed of accepting the flash of supernatural insight therein given to straightforward minds capable of accurate observation of other folk and clear-sighted self-analysis.

The background setting

The most significant stories are introduced immediately, and constitute the background and context of all that follows, even if there are not many further specific references. The first chapter of Genesis describes the recognizable stages of evolutionary progression, in a manner both intellectually and aesthetically satisfying, with the climax in man made similar to God, with delegated powers of control over nature for the benefit of all. In the next chapter a quite different style appears, less abstract but much more typical of the odd mixture of happenings, motives, and consequences in ordinary human life. The relationships of men and women to each other and to the limitations and possibilities of the world they find themselves in are described in the setting of the fertile land between the Tigris and the Euphrates rivers, described in terms of an ideal parkland, the Garden of Eden. Another name for this original state is Paradise, which is related to the Persian Firdausi, the King's court garden, equivalent to the square next to the King in chess. Man is seen in the presence of God with the mixed sense of intellectual and moral discrimination requisite to exist in harmony with the divine will, but with clearly defined limits. The fundamental problem of man is here set forth: shall he remain in this idyllic innocence or shall he learn the distinctions which could lead him to the illusion of complete independence and mastery of the creation, eliminating mystery, worship, and any holiness beyond his own power and will? The main point is that he is called to recognize natural limits as a creature, while exercising supernatural possibilities as one into whom divine life has been imparted. He is expected to trust and obey his Maker even while he exercises supernatural quasi-transcendent rights, authorities, and powers.

Origin of temptation

At a very early stage appears a further party to the proceedings, who appears to be the main source of trouble, the serpent, who represents in Scripture, in mythology and psychology, the original drive of life apart from moral and spiritual control. Silent, sinuous, twisting, wriggling below the threshold of observation, it makes its initial approach, and has sufficient of the characteristics of consciousness to pour its poisonous suggestions orally in superficially attractive form, directed at man's weakest point, his sense of creaturely finitude and limitations which affect his confidence and status. He desires immortality, perpetuity, for he has tasted eternity, the simultaneity of consciousness above the flux of time; he also desires to know enough to be independent of any other power, and to experience uninhibitedly the ecstacy of beauty and pleasurable sensations generally for himself (Genesis 3 : 4–6).

Misuse of freedom
In the limited freedom loaned to man lies the potentiality of good and evil. The choice whereby Eve (the Hebrew word for 'woman', or 'life-giving wife') listened and succumbed to the blandishments of the impersonal drive of human nature (when linked with personal consciousness, with sex as the type of the basic instincts because the continuation of life depends upon it), and persuaded Adam (the Hebrew word for 'man', 'of the ground', 'firm', 'made of the same cells' or 'dust', as the rest of creation) to share in distrust and disobedience, constituted man's downfall. One great early thinker of the Christian Church expounded a line of interpretation which should satisfy all, even though some would want to go further. He pointed out that the human personality goes through the stages of the human race as does the human body in the womb, and each individual recapitulates what has become universal for mankind, whatever the original cause. There is a bias in human nature, through heredity reinforced by environment, which constitutes all men liable to sin, which is a distrustful, and consequently disobedient, relationship with God. The whole human race is both affected and infected: 'God hath concluded all under sin' (Galatians 3 : 22).

Man goes wrong
Man is therefore driven in the nature of things out of the Garden of Eden. Were he physically to remain, the change in

his nature and his relationship to the King of Kings would make the place and the presence of God too uncomfortable and unappetizing for him. He both plays truant himself and is also turned out of house and home. He has tried to make himself too big and therefore there is no room for him and His Father under the same roof. He has a guilty conscience, a sulky defiant attitude, a loss of trust and love generally, and soon there is jealousy, conflict, deceit, violence, death; 'the blood of Abel thy brother cries from the ground' (Genesis 4:10). The mark of Cain and murder appears on the earth. Mere physical destruction does not act as a sufficient deterrent; despite the great Noachian flood and the survival of one family, the vicious entail continues. Soon man's independent skill erects one of the wonders of man's engineering capacity, the tower of Babel, the Babylonian ziggurat, the man-made temple-mountain, where God made only level plains. The result of every attempt by man to act as his own divinity and establish his own security proves a threat to his fellow man, and thus the result is division, symbolized by the greatest hindrance to human communication, the barrier of different languages. There is a clamouring babel of speech, but no mutual understanding.

Haunted by home

Yet since man still has also the mark of the divine upon him he can never quite forget what and where he was meant to be. He is haunted by a passion for his original home, where he could be his real and best self in perpetuity. He has an unappeasable hankering after the conquest of death and of the consequences of sin, which two factors in the satanic pharmacopeia constitute a lethal mixture of poison. Thus the law which was meant for man's good becomes itself his enemy: 'the sting of death is sin, and the strength of sin is the law . . .' (1 Corinthians, 15:56). Marxist Communism shares this Jewish-Christian framework of an original Paradise with hope of an ultimate Millenium, a thousand-year reign of the original happy spirit of sharing in the Kingdom-family, where man in community of partnership is his true being. All the various cravings, refined or vicious, of mankind are variations on this single theme. Here is the root of moral and spiritual evil, which invariably spoils any party, however well-meaning, unless radically dealt with. Man fell because he overreached himself in his attempt to make himself more invulnerable than he was meant to be for his own good. Jesus described the wealthy moral moron who had such security so well invested that he thought he could evade the basic disciplines: 'this night your essential self will be summoned to account; then what use will be those things in which you trusted?' 'What shall anybody give in exchange for his genuine unadulterated personality?' (cf. Matthew 16:26).

Use and abuse of law

The Law has now appeared, partly affirmative, partly negative, and is built up around covenants, such as those with Abraham and Moses. Trust and obedience on man's side, provision and control on God's side are the main elements involved. The remainder of the Bible really revolves around these basic concepts. The purpose of the commandments is to give fundamental guidance about attitudes required. More than mindless toeing of the divine party-line is called for. The commandments give specific practical content to a much profounder attitude best described as a covenant-relationship. At every point they are based on worship, the acknowledgement of the holiness of God. Hence no earthly or heavenly object whatever must be given equal adoring trust and obedience, otherwise they become idols. The remainder of the ten-point manifesto of requirements have to do with different aspects of proper respect for the God-given factor of personality in community. Murder, adultery, theft and the like, including the covetous attitude in general, are expressions of a destructive attitude to life.

Relative revelation

It is important to remember that the Bible relates to changing and developing historical circumstances, and God's full revelation could not be given all at once or too soon. Thus detailed laws which are outmoded or even contradicted later on are not therefore any the less revelatory and inspired at the point when they appear. The capacity for moral comprehension of a child-race has to be kept firmly in mind: 'When Israel was a child . . . I called my son out of Egypt . . . I taught Ephraim also to go, taking them by their arms' (Hosea 11:1ff). As Calvin put it, 'In Scripture God treats His people like a nurse; when talking to a little child He babbles.' Likewise a child has to learn, and relishes learning, the principle of equal justice, one eye for one eye, statistically equivalent, instead of two for one; one tooth for one tooth instead of an unlimited number in revenge. Just as justice has always to be tempered with mercy to be complete justice so mercy cannot be appreciated without a core of justice; otherwise mercy soon degenerates into chaos, favouritism, envy, and frustration all round. 'The law therefore is holy . . . and for our good' (Romans 7:12), a guardian to train us up in the way we should go till we are capable of discerning for ourselves and entering into a new covenant, with the will and methods of God inwardly written into our constitution (Jeremiah 31:31ff).

Adventure of faith

The remainder of Old Testament Scripture revolves around certain outstanding events and personalities, of whom Abraham is the model of faith and obedience exemplified in his leaving the settled security of civilized Ur of the Chaldees for nomadic wanderings in a strange land which nevertheless was promised as an inheritance; in his waiting for a son by his hitherto childless wife Sarah when she was past the age of child-bearing; and in his willingness to let this precious only heir, through whom alone the promise could be fulfilled, be a sacrifice of trust and obedience, if required. He bound his Isaac to the stake, as God had already been willing to do, but the sacrifice was not required of him as it was later of God. The act and spirit, however, were of the absolute nature to which holiness is entitled. There is an element of ruthlessness in the ultimate, which acts at the last irrespective of man's self-will. This constitutes the holy, before which men fear and tremble or utter defiance. The beginning of their wisdom is to realize a reverence proper to the ruler of the universe. 'Behold,' said Abraham, 'I have taken upon myself to speak unto the Lord, which am but dust and ashes' (Genesis 18:27). Again he says, 'shall not the Judge of all the earth do right?' (Genesis 18:25): holiness and righteousness belong together. Again he says, 'the Lord will provide' (Genesis 22:8), though it is vital to note that the providence he mentions is relative to sacrifice; the Lord provides the offering, which again is a foreview of the final revelation of holiness as not only requiring but also providing the offering.

Programme unfolds

So the story proceeds, each page adding something to our knowledge of the line taken by the supreme programme-controller. Jacob represents the choice of the unlikely brother whose unpleasant characteristics could never hide from him his faults and needs of mastery by God, as in his wrestle with the impalpable spiritual energy at the ford Jabbok, where God the emptiness became first God the opposer and then God the companion. Perhaps also the fact of his curious combination of worldly astuteness and occasionally sensitive conscience taught him the need of a higher and watchful power as the only final bond of community. For his sins and weaknesses he paid dearly, but his offspring founded the twelve tribes through whom the plan was to be worked out, despite their manifold and manifest faults. Joseph had a double stake because he at once suffered and triumphed more than his brothers in the recurring pattern of providential death and resurrection, down the pit literally and later metaphorically in prison unjustly, but at last emerging as the practical statesman through whom his own people found a home in distress.

Breaks in continuity

The continuity is ever in danger of breaking; 'there arose a new king which knew not Joseph' (Exodus 1:8), and apparently the plan was lost in the sands of Egypt. Nevertheless the people learned what slavery meant, with its loss of status, dignity, and destiny. At this point another towering figure of history, Moses, looms up out of obscurity in the bulrushes of the Nile, born among the dispossessed, but early translated to the seat of training in the skill of government. The second long haul begins with a mighty deliverance which became the model of salvation, dying and rising, crossing the apparently insuperable barrier in that breath-taking epic of escape, the Exodus. Thereafter followed the generation-long period of wearing out the scene of slave-mentality, toughening-up the new generation for freedom with the wisdom learned from existence under the menacing conditions of the howling wilderness, whose lonely silence and sudden unpredictable hazards remain as a close margin affecting the life of God's people from then to now. In particular they learned the close connexion between holiness and careful community planning. The book of Numbers is crammed full of statistical holiness; Leviticus is largely concerned with sanitation and the hygiene of holiness, while Deuteronomy stresses the necessity for statutory and legislative holiness.

Each book adds a characteristic of holiness

Indeed, each book of the Bible has its own variant application of the constant theme. Genesis keeps us close to the creative primeval origins of holiness as the raw material from which later refinements are introduced. Exodus describes the adventurous and rescuing element, Joshua the element of invasion, conquest, and possession of an inherited and promised territory. Judges shows the pioneering element under harshly adverse conditions. Samuel and Kings show holiness at work in the processes of governmental history. Chronicles brings out the liturgical streak, Psalms the prayerful and choral aspect, Ecclesiastes the moderating expression and Proverbs the common-sense application in mundane settings. Esther is political, without even mentioning the name of God, yet breathing devotion to His people's cause in every line, with Mordecai's devotion absolute. Ruth illustrates the unbreakable element of loyalty in human relationships. The Song of Songs illustrates the place of romance in the theme. Suffering in Job and grief in Lamentations are required for a full picture. The prophets in diverse manner relentlessly harp on the theme of proper citizenship and government, and so confident are they of the constitutive pattern of the stuff of history that they even dare to hazard predictions of the future course of events, and with such dedication as both spares no authority and is prepared to accept the penalty of unpopular views before events have vindicated them or otherwise. In every case the particular emphasis is related to absolute trust and obedience towards the holy God.

So also in the New Testament

In the New Testament the four Gospels each bring out a different trait in the holiness of Jesus. Matthew is didactic, Mark dramatic, Luke human, and John dominant. Acts is dynamic, Romans theological, Corinthians ecclesiastical and disciplinary, Galatians liberating, Colossians speculative, Ephesians comprehensive, Philippians mature, Thessalonians final, Timothy pastoral, Peter hopeful, Jude and Titus admonitory, the Johannine epistles moral and personal, James practical, Hebrews priestly and sacrificial, and Revelation celestial and morale-stiffening. Obviously such a list must be very general and capable of many modifications of description, and yet it should be found not entirely wide of the mark. The programme has many sub-titles and each a deal of small print to contribute to the audience's knowledge.

Different summaries and applications

The early Christian preachers regularly summarized these events in different ways for different purposes. The most comprehensive summary is possibly the one by Stephen before the Sanhedrin, or supreme Jewish court, (Acts 7:1-53), which should be read together with the summary from the point of view of the type of faith involved in the letter to the Hebrews (chapter 11). Joshua led the children of Israel across the decisive River Jordan, and many were the experiences of victory and defeat through which constant lessons were learned, as at Jericho and Ai, where the valley of Achor or humiliation became the door of hope. All the time the programme was being both outlined and put into effect. Almost every conceivable type of social existence is depicted in essence as the lot of this people. In Judges we see the rough justice of pioneer settlements, where everything depends on the personal stature of the contemporary strong man, rather like the sheriff in the

Wild West cowboy stories. Then follows the move to central
government under Saul and David, with Samuel, the unwilling
king-maker, seeing both the advantages and disadvantages of
the system. Prophets like Amos, Hosea, Isaiah, Micah, and
Jeremiah ceaselessly identify holiness with personal and social
righteousness, fair dealing, and concern for the exploited
underdogs.

Attempt at codified separatism

As a small power between the two great millstones of East
and West the tiny kingdom, itself soon divided into two, was
inevitably ground to powder, the northern, more exposed and
wealthy, section first. The interbreeding which followed produced the half-breeds or Samaritans, and the consequent fierce
hate of hostile relatives, yet at the same time a link between
Jew and Gentile which was eventually itself to be built into
the programme in the time of our Lord. Meanwhile there
developed the protective separatism which, despite its necessity
after the Babylonian exile, led to one of the greatest distortions
of holiness in the most concentrated attempt at it on codified
lines which the world has known, and which still rears its head
in a revised form within Christianity, especially in movements
devoted to holiness, namely Pharisaism. It was as if, even with
the People of God, the various human attempts after the
holiness which God required, had to be pushed to their presumed logical conclusion before the true holiness could be
unmistakably seen. Self-righteousness is the last hindrance to
God's righteousness, and is so intricately embedded in the
human heart that the greatest saints have besought God to
reveal and root it out of even their holiest moments (cf. the
Methodist Hymn Book, No. 743). It proved to be the despised
customs-officer crying for mercy who was nearer to holiness
than the consciously moral pedant and acme of scrupulosity,
in our Lord's story of the Pharisee and the Publican.

Written word and humble prayer

During the Babylonian captivity this pupil people began to
learn through bitter suffering, at least through a few sensitive
souls who had the perceptive qualities of the butterfly's anten-

F   71

nae, the profoundest secret of the divine plan. Deprived of all the outward signs of self-identity and self-respect in territory, capital city, temple, ritual, and compelled to live amid the pressures of an alien and technically triumphant civilization, which contemptuously or patronizingly commented on their folk-songs (Psalm 137:3), they had nothing but memories, teaching, and hopes to encourage them. During this interval the written record inevitably assumed pre-eminence among them, and holiness revealed itself in devotion to the sacred writings and in the dedicated professions of scribes and rabbis, or interpreters and teachers of the written word. The typical figure in public circles was Daniel, who though by ability he rose to the top in the seat of government and was subject to all the pressures and suggestions to conform to Babylon ways nevertheless kept his Jerusalem loyalty undimmed by means of the open window in his home towards Jerusalem (Daniel 6:10). Thrice daily, like the humblest Jew, he resorted thither to gaze into the empty distance towards the ruined holy city he had never literally seen. Reverence towards his God and faithful obedience to His will were the secret of his resistance and triumph.

Forward-looking few

Among the abiding pictures of this period is that of the Son of Man, (which became a favourite with our Lord Himself) an elusive concept who appears to be the incarnation of true humanity as divinity meant him to be, who would be manifestly of heavenly origin, coming 'with the clouds of heaven' (Daniel 7:13). Various idealized forms of the divine agent of salvation and vindication appear during the period of the pre-exilic and exilic prophets. The First Isaiah had projected on to the future the model king, anointed to his divine task on earth, the Messiah, who would apply God's will on earth among His people. The vision came out of the death of an illusion centred on one of the best of human kings, Uzziah, who nevertheless overreached himself in by-passing the laws regarding temple behaviour. As the foundations of his faith rocked, the prophet saw the Lord 'high and lifted up, whose glory filled the temple' (Isaiah 6), and consequently he realized his own sinfulness at the point of his greatest strength in oratory (just as David took Jerusalem at the point of its greatest natural invulnerability where the least defence was made), and his identity with his people in their corporate sinfulness. Hope came through the initiative of God whereby the purgative fire was transferred from the altar to his point of corruption, and he was justified and cleansed. Immediately the call to saving service came with the realistic knowledge that only a few would care, the remnant, the severed tree-stump of God's people, who nevertheless were those nearest the roots, the ground, and the source of nourishment.

Suffering for the world

During the exile the Second Isaiah saw the universal sweep of God's plan and the saving service through vicarious suffering for which the people were called. The close association between these themes and the interpretation of the death of Jesus can hardly be resisted, even though their integration depends rather on being cuts as it were from the same cloth than clearly deliberate sewing together either by Jesus or the early Church. Something of both may well have taken place, though the antiquarian problem of delimiting the relative importance of the two may well be left to the inconclusive and interminable debate of scholars, 'the agonie of pious wits, disputing what distorted thee' (John Donne).

Transference and substitution

The main point is that in such chapters as the fifty-third of Isaiah the purpose, plan, and processes of salvation are concentrated into greater clarity than possibly anywhere else in the world before Christ came, both as slotted into the existing picture and also as enlarged, modified, re-sorted, and applied in practical effect. A detailed analysis of the factors and attitudes involved requires a dissertation in itself, but the heart of it is the positive, creative elicitation and bearing of the total hatred and perversions of the distrustful, disobedient human race by intercession, identification, transference or substitution, without ceiling of price, with the intention of winning trust and love, leading to the dominant impartation of the life of the saving agent in the interest of the harmonious rule of God for man's benefit. All the detailed series of picture-shots of the elements in salvation are seen simultaneously in this one process, which humanly speaking has its clearest analogy in the personal relationships involved in sincere psychosomatic therapy.

Meanders of providence

It is true that this preliminary flash of final truth appears to have made singularly little impression upon the writer's contemporaries, or indeed until the fulfilment came in Christ centuries later. There is a stereoscopic multi-dimensional perspective necessary to perceive total truth in depth, additional to height and length and breadth. After the return home, apart from a brief century and a half under the Maccabees, the Jews had to soldier on as a religious and economic community without political independence but suffering a variety of imperial overlords. From each they took some spoils of thought and practice, and learned much of the vagaries of human tyranny. What a case-book is the Bible, both of individual and small-scale psychology and also mass sociology! Yet all the way through is the context, the penumbra, the suffusing of an elusive but directing will, bringing pattern out of frustration, and working out a sovereign will through what Sir Thomas Browne called 'the meanders of providence', and, he might have added, of salvation.

Recuperative resilience

The hero of the rebuilding period is Nehemiah, who surveyed the devastated site of Jerusalem, salvaged usable materials from the débris, indented for fresh supplies from a favourable overlord, enheartened and organized the chosen people, rebuilt the fortifications, outwitted those sappers of confidence, Sanballat the Horonite, Tobiah the Ammonite, and Geshem the Arabian, manipulated preposterously inadequate resources, and all in all exemplified once more the recuperative resilience of divine holiness. His book illustrates the reconstructive element in holiness. Alongside him Ezra concentrated on the detailed application of the law as codified, and the necessity for the negative insistence on separation to keep pure and concentrated for the divine purpose the saving people. Most separatist doctrine is traceable to Ezra, both in its strength and weakness.

A long wait

During the following four hundred years there was little opportunity to learn the more positive lesson of the purpose of separation, not for itself or mere preservation, but for fitness in saving service. It is hardly accidental that the intermediate writings contained in the Apocrypha have never gained a full acceptance as Holy Scripture on the same level with the Old and New Testaments, though the Roman Catholics include this section. A special development during this period was apocalyptic literature, which used bizarre and elaborate symbolic pictures of ultimate triumph for the humiliated people of God. All these various developments were both expressions of and help towards the hope of a coming Day of the Lord, and a suitable agent thereof through whom the saints of the Most High would exercise supreme influence in a renovated universe, so that carnivorous and herbivorous beasts would live constructively together, and the world should be safe for little children (Isaiah 11:6–8). The fulness of sanctification is that 'the earth shall be filled with the glory of God as the waters cover the sea' (Isaiah 11:9); it includes neutralizing the effect of the sin of man on the created universe. To this end the people of God were to be led by a Man of destiny provided by God for the vindication of His holy will of love, with its public form of righteousness.

Bible and scholarship

Some such scrappy survey of the Old Testament is required to observe how God outlined His programme to mankind by the project method. Revelation is both the potent deeds, personalities, events, and also the inspired interpretation of them by God's own people, and especially by certain more spiritually sensitive personalities therein. The sense of the sacred profoundly controlled the scribes, the recorders, the copiers, known as Massoretes, with their meticulously careful system of checking and rechecking to reduce human error to a minimum, a technique which was itself the product of the emphasis on holiness, so that even the jot and the tittle, the i and the t were duly dotted and crossed. Herein lies also the justification for critical scholarship, both as the investigation of sources (known as Higher Criticism) and of the manuscripts and the like (known as Lower Criticism). Their function is not to stifle inspiration, but to deal faithfully under disciplined care with the forms it has taken, so that each generation can discern for itself what is speaking to its particular need as well as what is required to be safeguarded for future generations with different needs. The same Holy Spirit who controlled the creative processes breathed into the men who interpreted God's message and those who recorded it. They were breathing the same atmosphere of ordered energy and loyalty to truth and appreciation of beauty in each case. 'He who forms the mountains . . . declares to man what is his thought' (Amos 4:13). The possibility of human error or inadequacy of reception is not excluded, but substantially the Bible stands or falls by the accuracy of its apprehension, recording, and interpreting of authentic events. The Bible is the sample slice of human history. When Cheshire cheeses are exhibited the trained tester knows where and how to extract the significant sample which indicates the quality of the product. So the Bible is the significant sample of human history. The large-scale principles and forces which work too massively for human knowledge are discernible here on the model scale where they can be examined microscopically, and applied at any point required. The element of inspiration is the breathing of the pure atmosphere of the heights of insight which makes for the total existence, survival, and effective living of mankind. In a sense trial and error are the only ways of finding out, yet a certain innate appropriateness of reaction may be expected since both environment and organism are of the same substantial origin, 'for he who sanctifies and those who are sanctified have all one origin' (Hebrews 2:11).

Apostolic message

With the inspired and authoritative record of revelation in man's hand a base is established for man's relaying of the message from beyond which gives momentum and direction to the activity of the people of God, especially in propaganda and persuasion. Preaching has been from the beginning of the Christian era the main means of outlining the programme from man to man, especially in the aggregate. Unless men know and understand what they are doing, their work is liable to be at the mercy of mood and circumstance. The Church from the beginning centred on the apostolic message, which included the Old Testament in the Greek translation, and such writings as had already fallen into the hands of the early compilers, together with the spoken account of Jesus' work, life, teaching, used in instruction for a generation until the passing away of the first authorized expositors rendered an authoritative written account imperative. The rest of the New Testament books emerged more or less haphazardly as need required. The significant sample of the career and impact of Jesus Christ comes first as fundamental to all else, and is providentially supplied from four points of view—the civil servant and pedagogue in Matthew, a natural dramatic script-writer in Mark, a humanly large-hearted medical correspondent in Luke, and an aged seer, once an explosive firework of a man, for whom the mellowing influences of time have translated the spurts of flame into a glow of glory, reflecting the profoundly majestic significance of Jesus and His work.

Ripe time
Before proceeding to the rest of the New Testament it may be well to recapitulate a little, and draw together the Old Testament and the Gospels. The various stages of the educational process already outlined are only fully grasped when the end is reached. Individual items may well appear haphazard and isolated, and the whole process be appreciated with varying degrees of coherence and clarity at different epochs. There are longish periods of apparent sterility, or at best wearingly slow and patchy in progress, followed by short epoch-making bursts when the time is ripe and the cup overflows. The coming of Jesus is at just such a 'fulness of the time' (Galatians 4:4f.). In Jesus the various threads and otherwise apparently unrelated items are drawn together; 'in him all things cohere' (Colossians 1:17) for 'God, who at sundry times and in divers manners

hath spoken unto our fathers by the prophets, hath spoken unto us in these latter days through his Son' (Hebrews 1:1f.). The programme became focused in (and fanned out from) a human individual, who mixed with spoiled humanity from the inside. The potential shape of the original idea and momentum became actual, and through the Son the Father became available in a unique manner: 'in him dwelt the fulness of the godhead bodily' (Colossians 2:9). All the way through, the message and the programme were becoming incarnate: even in the Mosaic wilderness-wandering was living water obtainable from the spiritual rock which followed the chosen people in their arid trek, 'and that rock was Christ' (1 Corinthians 10:4). Now the process was sharpened to its finest point of insertion and culmination. Jesus is the Christ-Messiah, the Lord, the Saviour, Master, Teacher, Just One, Son of God, Son of Man, Suffering Servant, the Holy One of God. He is at once the finest flower of humanity and the purest deposit of the divine nature. His name is above every name, as His nature is above every nature, and therefore before him 'every knee shall bow' (Philippians 2:10).

Climax of outlining

His birth, life, teaching, worship-inspiring activities, death, resurrection, ascension all proclaim the one great truth about the self-giving, other-creating, dynamic love of God that Jesus is Immanuel, the One who comes to live in the midst, and insert and release the fresh ever-youthful life of God within the complex prison-chains of humanity, and break them from within, carrying the prison-governor captive, shattering the dungeon of death and sin, 'openly triumphing over' (Colossians 2:15) the ogres which haunt and chill man's blood with their braggart threats and brazen grip. He achieves all by the trustful obedience which re-establishes the divine will and rule under the conditions of mutiny. Such creative, trustful obedience in a distorted, destructive, disobedient society must inevitably suffer and die violently, though by perfect endurance to the bitter end—tasting death for every man (Hebrews 2:9)—He wins through because the spirit of incorruptible holiness must prevail (Romans 1:4). He rises from the dead, appears to those who are able to recognize Him creatively, points out the former clues, and the way the Old Testament and His work throw light upon each other, and finally re-ascends His native heaven with the added experience of humanity from within.

Initial impact

The historic programme-outlining is now done; the clue to interpretation is given, and the conditions are right for the first instalment of the full consequences. The Holy Spirit appears with a fresh fulness of power, insight, community and guidance because now known with all the content of the person and work of Jesus Christ. The second chapter of the Acts of the Apostles is from this point of view the supreme clue to God's outlined programme and man's propogation of the same. The immediate result was an access of power in communication and victorious living. Fire is a traditional symbol of the divine presence, purifying and brightening. The violent wind is the symbol of the impalpable driving force of the Spirit. All were affected by the latter, and each received the former. The experience was both corporate and individual. Tongues appeared in two forms inextricably intertwined, glossolalia, a psychic state of ecstatic utterance, and also the faculty of translation into the various languages those present could understand. It was indeed the language and work of divine love. The traditional barriers associated with the tower of Babel were swept away, and the believers together became such altered personalities—expansive, sociable, jovial, courageous, uninhibited—that the more hostile and therefore less perspicacious observers attributed the phenomenon to alcohol.

Initial response

It is important to analyse carefully the course of events because here only do we see the initial impact of the full combination of revelation and inspiration without any later complications, accretions, or blurrings of outline. All the elements in God's design for rescue had been historically completed. A brief interval had elapsed for absorption of the final shock of losing the tangible presence of Jesus in any form. In trustful obedient fellowship and prayer the little surviving group had waited in the Upper Room. Suddenly the awareness arrived of all the long series of events in God's programme, and the Christian Church became aware of itself as indwelt, directed, and empowered by God Himself. The Church had already been conceived in eternity, gestated in history, born with the Lord Jesus at Bethlehem, Calvary, the garden tomb of resurrection, and on Bethany Mount, but now it achieved the vital and miraculous gift of self-consciousness.

Alternative explanations

Immediately remarkable phenomena appeared which attracted public attention and curiosity. The first question was the technical one, '*How* do we hear in our own language?' Soon there is widespread acknowledgement that the events are miraculous, wonderful works of God, and the second question concerns the implications of the fact: 'What does this mean?' When a measurable alternative explanation, such as alcohol or brainwashing, is inserted by hostile critics, Peter patiently disposes of the allegation by evidence that the requisite material conditions are not available since it is not opening time yet; in other words Peter uses human reason and apologetics as part of the inspiration of the Holy Spirit. Thereafter he gives the first example of typical Christian preaching.

Explanation and challenge

Peter begins with the facts before everybody, and sets them in historical context. The assembled crowd are like people who have come in half way through the drama. He selects a passage from the prophet Joel describing the coming day of God's revelation and vindication, and lets it be seen how the forecast and the present phenomena coincide. The explanation is to be found in the person of Jesus, unjustly executed though vividly alive, the long-promised divine deliverer of God's people. Here is the day of opportunity to be seized avidly. Many of those present then ask the third and practical question for responsible people: 'What shall we do?' They ask the preacher to make the challenge, the offer, the invitation and appeal. Peter hesitates not at all, but begins where Jesus began, 'Repent, change your attitude, direction, inner motivation.' He does not actually mention faith at this point, but it is implied in his directive to action, 'be baptized every one of you, in the name of Jesus Christ of Nazareth.' Baptism meant complete immersion in Christ, dying to the past which is washed away, and rising to the new clean kind of life naturalized by the Holy Spirit.

New community

The immediate result of the day of Pentecost was the unmistakable emergence of a distinctive community destined to affect decisively the course of human history, and it fanned out as a spreading and contagious society, a missionary body, an evangelizing agency. Its internal marks were this same programme, outlined now by the commissioned messengers of God, the apostles, together with a consequent intimate partnership, corporate and private prayer in the name of Jesus, meal-sharing, common participation in material resources, and multifarious worship-provoking deeds of divine compassion. Soon these community-members were involved in the conflicts with the surrounding society organized on the basis of self-interest and self-righteousness which crucified its Lord, but their courage, hope and love were unquenchable. The whole Church looked forward to the final return of the Lord in judgement and vindication, and to the ultimate realization of the heaven where the top level talks took place. The end of their journey was the very summit where the whole experiment began. Incidentally heaven is a spiritual, not a geographical elevation. Heaven is a state of relationship to God rather than a place. As St Augustine put it, 'There is no distance from God except unlikeness to Him.'

New literature

Central to the movement was the constant reiteration, explanation, and application of the outline programme in the Scriptures, which at first were the Old Testament with Christian interpretation. Naturally the preaching of the first Christians had certain common themes, structures, and illustrations about the Father, the Son, and the Holy Spirit, especially the more readily graspable stories by and about Jesus. These eventually appeared as Gospels, the selective and constructive journalism of God. Their own history, in its early stages appears in the

Acts of the Apostles, the one unfinished book of the Bible. As need arose various theoretical and practical matters called for more detailed consideration, and a collection of correspondence built up in the churches which gradually achieved revelatory authority by a kind of spiritual survival of the fittest. The continuing need for faith and hope to be sustained amidst the same wicked world is still stressed in the programme, this time with a magnificence, a perspicacity, a coherence without parallel in the literature of the world, namely in the Revelation of St John, imparted under the extreme isolation and earthly hopelessness of the island concentration camp of Patmos in the Aegean Sea. Among the means of revelation, inspiration, and expression of ultimate insight are the doxological songs of the communion of saints in heaven, whose waves of praise beat ceaselessly on the shores of time, and whose theme is the Lamb slain from the foundation of the world as a trustfully obedient sacrifice to break the power of the past, clean up the present, and enliven the future.

Pattern of instruction and exhortation

When analysing the correspondence of the main figures, of whom the outstanding is Paul of Tarsus, the converted Pharisee who devoted the whole passion of his thrusting nature to the achievement of Pharisaic holiness before becoming the classic case of its breakdown, we find a fairly general pattern of instruction and exhortation. There is the dogmatic initiative, the devotional transmission, and the disciplined outworking. All three are important. Hitherto we have concentrated on the dogmatic initiative because nothing happens unless there is a beginning powerful enough to carry through to the end. The devotional transmission naturally finds its place when we are dealing with the conduct of the operation. In the remainder of this chapter we must glance at the disciplined outworking, and in the next chapter describe the warning signals which reveal the presence of dangerous deviations.

New morality

The end-product of this vast activity is character in community, a kingdom-family where the glorious variety of life at all levels can be lived to the full. Glory is the final word, and it is revealed in the godlike qualities of Christian living, which has to reflect itself in the individual, the family, work and play, and worthy citizenship. There is discernible in the New Testament a fairly consistent pattern of instruction to Christians in the kind of life holiness demands . . . 'You have received from us how you ought to walk . . . for ye know the commandments we gave you through the Lord Jesus Christ' (1 Thessalonians 4:1–2). In other words an elementary code is required to act as a kind of set square or copy line in addition to the teaching and example of 'the measure of the stature of Christ' (Ephesians 4:13). Our Lord certainly exhorted men to be of the same nature as the Father, 'perfect as the Father is perfect' (Matthew 5:48), and emphasized that the spring of motivation in the heart must be renewed, because therefrom came things evil and good (Matthew 12:34f; 15:19). To see and know God in the most intimate sense of uninhibited intercourse known as blessedness requires purity of heart, concentrated concern, and commitment such as is seen in technicians totally devoted to the task in hand, as in a television programme. Inner cleanliness comes first. It is a more godlike and satisfying attitude to give than to grasp (cf. Acts 20:35). In the Sermon on the Mount our Lord offers devastatingly surprising stories and sayings to illustrate the general principles of his interpretation of life, as with the willing and joyous initiative in offering to double freely the conscripted service exacted by the nauseating agents of a hated foreign power by going a second mile, but some things can only be elicited by circumstances drawing out later implications. The Holy Spirit was to lead the disciples into all truth, and greater works should the Lord's followers do. It is to the more detailed and codified material that we now turn.

Negative and positive guidance

The catechisms emphasize the necessity for the sharp break of baptism and then the necessity for unconquerable endurance under persecution to the end. Obedience to the existing order so far as may be without ultimate compromise and grievous damage to conscience is added, with special reference to the natural groupings of family, employment, and the state, where the emphasis is on mutual subordination for the common good. Thereafter two groups seem to be in mind, first those who have been brought up within the influence of the saving community, and second those who have been brought in from outside that context. The equalizing principle is that 'to whom much is given of him much will be required, and to whom little is given of him little will be required' (Luke 12:48). Each has its advantages and disadvantages, its special opportunities and temptations. The moral instruction is both negative and positive. Believers need to hear such words as 'Do not touch'; 'Keep out and off'; 'Danger—thin ice, live wire, dead end, this road leads to subsidence'. There is to be no conformity to this world, which is twisted out of its true pattern. They are to abstain from every form of evil, either as appearance or pattern (Romans 12:2; Philippians 2:15; 1 Thessalonians 5:22).

Word to insiders and outsiders
The insiders are to abstain from fleshly lusts, cravings, violent breathings, fornication, covetousness, and the greedy desire to accumulate for themselves. Perhaps they are less immunized against these elementary ingurgitations by the very fact of their protected upbringing. It is the whole vortex-attitude, like the Scandinavian maelström, which is under condemnation. It might be called the bathroom plug-hole attitude to life. Positively the reborn insiders need to express their holiness as kindness; it is so easy in the limited social grouping for the imaginative sympathy about how others live to contract. The reborn outsiders, who often have a more dramatic conversion, need stability, clothing with a new kind of moral life, straightforward, compassionate, longsuffering, forgiving. Their virtues need to be based on truthfulness, humility, and love. Psalm 34 and Proverbs chapter three seem to have influenced this approach. A huge act of renunciation is called for from the type of custom which has conditioned them hitherto. Evil must go, especially in speech and temper; malignity, ill-will, the desire to injure people or indulge in shameless law-breaking, must be jettisoned. In some ways it may seem rather elementary. Lord Elton had to revise his prejudices against village noncon-

formity when he saw for himself that the chapels were not full of unctuous hypocrites; they were little lettered with little dogma, but with enviable success living up to two ethical precepts, 'Be kind, and eschew the sins of the flesh.' For a minister to be sure that every member of his congregation lived by such a standard would make him think the Kingdom of heaven was at hand!

Spirit of love transcends code

However valuable and necessary such codified instruction may be the Christian knows instinctively that no final detailed code is possible. Jesus did not provide one, and if he had done so it would have shortly been out of date. The first name for the Christians was 'those of the Way' (Acts 9:2; 19:2; 24:14–22). It is not so much a programme, more a way of life, an attitude, an approach, a Spirit identical with God's, i.e. constructive compassion without demand of merit, though with expectation of trustful and obedient response, and prepared to give beforehand and help to the uttermost, even to the extent of redemptive outpouring of the self in saving service. This is the principle of Incarnation, Atonement, and Pentecost, all three vital to a total and lasting work. The Spirit is the root of fruit and gifts, and the supreme in both is faith working by love (cf. Galations 5:6), spontaneously generated, effectively executed, freely offered, tightly binding, eternally seeking and growing. The fruit of this Spirit is love, joy, peace, long-suffering, kindness, and the like (cf. Galatians), though these should not be seen as separate items which can be plucked apart from each other. They represent aspects of the total bloom produced by the Holy Spirit. 'By their fruits ye shall know them' (Matthew 7:16) and Him. 'Do men gather grapes of thorns, or figs of thistles?' (ibid.). The unity of the natural and the supernatural, the evolutionary and the revolutionary, the common and the uncommon sense all combine. The summary of the whole programme in model concentration is in Paul's Christian love-song, the thirteenth chapter of Paul's first letter to Corinth. Love builds up the Body of Christ (Ephesians 4:2), casts out fear (1 John 4:18), carries everything, and outlasts all opposition and contention.

Degeneration or regeneration

Here is the outline of the programme, the revelatory authority of Holy Scripture, the original preaching and teaching, and the source of whatever recent adjustments may be required by the changing economic, social, and intellectual setting of the Gospel. The subject of sanctification as the means to glorification is the supreme theme of Holy Scripture and the point and purpose of our religion as an agent of God's Kingdom and the tool of this pattern and product. The whole programme is summed up in the two commandments to love God totally, and the neighbour as the self, neither of which can be fully understood unless seen in the light of Christ both ways, nor be adequately and perpetually performed without the work of Christ and the Holy Spirit. 'Beloved, now are we the children of God; it doth not yet appear what we shall be, but we know that when we see him we shall be like him for we shall see him as he is' (I John 3:2). There used to be a party game called Guess Who? at which photographs of baby days were exhibited, and the adults present had to guess who was which. To link the one with each seemed beyond the reach of phantasy. Some were bearded like the pard or dewlapped like the Thessalian bull, paunchy, scrawny, and bore little resemblance to Curlylocks or Tousled-hair in party frock or sailor suit. The change which had in fact taken place seemed inconceivable. In fact there is always a going up or a going down, as the lift girls call. Samson realized how his self-confident, self-indulgent, self-willed course had brought him to the depths when he cried, 'I will go out as at other times and shake myself, but he wist not that the Spirit of the Lord had departed from him' (Judges 16:20).

No by-pass round the cross

The essence of the operation is realizing the original nature of man before he was spoiled, releasing the divine spirit, removing the evil spirit, so that there is no fifth column within. Jesus alone could say, 'The prince of this world cometh and findeth nothing in me' (John 14:30). Nevertheless Jesus knew what it was to be tested in every particular as the rest of mankind, and more so, because the jealous spoiling spirit

sought to corrupt his divine mission by appealing to his saving
motive with methods which by-passed the pattern of atoning
death and resurrection. 'Truth nailed upon a cross compels
nobody; its appeal is addressed to free spirits,' said Nicholas
Berdyaev. 'If thou be the Son of God' is the devil's attempt
to sap the divine self-confidence and sow dissension in the
inner councils and relationships of the Godhead. Every suggestion of eliminating the cross is satanic temptation and a
hindrance to resurrection.

Christ fits all together

The saving deeds of Jesus Christ focus what has always been
there to see, and bring to light the structure of the universe
and the processes of history and community. It is rather like
the puzzle-pictures in children's comics, where we see
mountains, seas, castles, trees, and all the clutter of ordinary
life, and are told that the outline of a man, the true overlord
of the place, is hidden camouflaged in some part, to be spotted
if the right perspective and focus are achieved. We turn this
way and that, furrow the brow, exclaim in exasperation, are
tempted to abandon effort, when suddenly we see him, marvel
that we were ever so blind and foolish as to miss him, and
thereafter can hardly see anything else. He dominates the scene,
reveals it under control, sets the seething, heaving mass of
detail in manageable proportions, whatever kaleidoscopic
pattern is produced by the shudders of nature or of man. In
him the pattern is seen as fitting together. The jig-saw appears
as proleptically complete, even though we 'have a heritage of
joy which yet we may not see', tending towards its perfect
end. We have the completed picture to work to, so that confusing pieces can be fitted in. There is a preview of the end,
a blueprint, a ground-plan with elevation, and cross-sections
on all floors. The programme is in our hand, with explanatory
notes. We know what is going on, and who is up to what! We
can share the vision, the approach, the spirit, the means and
methods, the motives and mission. This *is* sanctification, and
to be totally devoted to this *is* entire sanctification. The cross
of Christ in this sense is the set-square; the ground-plan of the
universe is cruciform. The end has appeared, and the principles

of God's prevailing will are known in the person and passion of Christ. 'The prophets who prophesied of the grace that was to be yours searched and enquired about this salvation; they enquired what person or time was indicated by the Spirit of Christ within them when predicting the sufferings of Christ and the subsequent glory. It was revealed to them that they were not serving themselves but you, in the things which have now been announced to you by those who have preached the good news to you through the Holy Spirit sent from heaven, things into which angels long to look' (1 Peter 1:10–12).

Chance for all to share in programme

The reception of this offer is by the same response of trust— mental, emotional, voluntary—as brought mankind into filial restored relationship with God in the first place. There is no difference, and no specified time-schedule or temperature-chart for application to every person. The work is happening all the time but first becomes definite when we make conscious response in the various picture-settings. It may well be that the full implications of total commitment do not appear at once or for a considerable time. There may well build up a profounder inner struggle than existed before conversion precisely because the Spirit of Christ is refining and searching the heart and higher standards of requirements are forcing their way into consciousness. There is no doubt that such a second crisis does appear for many people, and maybe for more than is commonly realized. Dr T. R. Glover remarked that most people need reconverting at forty however Christian they had been before. Maturity is not only a gradual process but also may well include a short-term crisis of abandonment which to evade would fixate a man below the level of either his innate possibilities or God's infinite promise. Such a second time of blessing could rightly be distinguished from the innumerable blessings and crises of experience which characterize every truly Christian life. In this sense those are right who say that to have a thousand blessings excepting the second is to have missed what would have made all the difference to the other nine hundred and ninety-nine. The error comes when what is for many an indubitable fact is elevated into doctrine which is applied to all in a mechanical and doctrinaire manner. The essential business of the programme-promoter is to ensure that all know about the promise and possibility and intention, and also make definite offers with opportunity for specific response.

5   Watching the snags

'Be not righteous overmuch.' (Ecclesiastes 7:16)

'ONCE bitten, twice shy', is an ancient proverb distilled out of the long history of the human race. Anyone with experience of life, faced with a proposition, automatically peers under the surface, behind the scenes, and examines the situation all round and through and through to discover any possible snags. Life is a practical business, which necessitates working under limitations; wisdom therefore includes visualizing a situation beforehand, as far as possible, so as not to be caught unawares. There will be enough unexpected hindrances later which will test all our resources without wasting effort in coping with foreseeable difficulties.

Like hinds' feet

Heights are notoriously dangerous; the greater the height the bigger the drop. One false step may be disastrous. Christian summitry and top level talks require a cool head and an exquisite sense of balance. Perfection is a perilous term. We can sympathize with Charles Haddon Spurgeon when he remarked that he had only met one perfect man, and he was a perfect nuisance. Yet risk is no argument for evasion, but rather a challenge to man's spirit. The conclusion to draw is not to play safe, toddling in the lowlands, but to take the steps of faith with the help of God's promise that he will make our feet 'like hinds' feet to walk upon mine high places' (Psalm 18:33; Habakkuk 3:19). He assists us to keep our footing on the mountain peaks like the chamois, who can leap on the sharpest point of pinnacle and stand firm. Nevertheless, the most skilful mountaineer can never afford to relax his watchfulness. His eyes are skinned; his whole frame, to the tips of his toes and fingers, is alert, and beginners would be very foolish not to heed his instruction, warning, and example. There are

90

snags and hazards all around, and the heights of holiness are
no exception. Our souls have more to fear from the religious
world than the wicked world. The worst is the corruption of
the best.

Humbug of holiness

A too exclusive preoccupation with holiness by itself distorts,
and may even pervert, this precious teaching. Sanctification
is not meant to be isolated from the rest of the Christian theme.
It is both an end and a means to an end, and is not only
the climax of God's purpose with man but also the essential
commencement of His work through man thereby fitted to
further the best interests of mankind. Even then it is part of a
completer purpose, namely the glory of God. In any case it
demands people of great insight and strength of character to
enter frequently any holy place. Familiarity soon breeds contempt, or a concealed cynicism, or a stylized complacency, each
of which is a defensive evasion of candid assessment. It is
reported that a conversation once took place between Thomas
Cook (the then Principal of Cliff College) and Samuel Chadwick
(at the time a tutor, and later Principal) in which one remarked
to the other, 'Have you found it more difficult to be a Christian
at Cliff than anywhere else?' The other agreed. Some people
would be puzzled by this, but there is really no mystery about
it; anything else would have been the subject of puzzlement.
Where any movement or group forms a self-enclosed community, abstracted from life as it ordinarily has to be lived,
an element of artificiality inevitably seeps in. In the confined
limits every whisper echoes like the shouts of boys in the
public indoor baths. The wide-ranging human mind has its
attention riveted on far too narrow a range of interests. Where
there is also a very lofty ideal (especially when it is isolated
from the antiseptic of rational investigation and is unrealistically
interpreted, unrelated to the Scriptural attitudes hitherto outlined) there is a more obvious inclination to odious comparisons
and unreasonable disappointments. The very concern with
holiness assumes and develops a sensitiveness of spirit which
therefore feels deeply and is easily pained. In the Jewish
Temple Holy of Holies, entered once a year by the High Priest,

there was nothing beyond the cubic content of the place, except possibly a spider or two and some dust. It required a person of exceptional spiritual insight and maturity of understanding to undertake such a role successfully. The same types of reaction can be predicted in any group or institution in the world devoted to the specialized cultivation of spiritual excellence, whether within Christianity or any other religion. Hugh Burnett's amusing series of cartoons about the monastic life, *Top Sacred, Nothing Sacred,* and *Sacred and Confidential* could be paralleled at Cliff College in every respect except the monkish dress. Indeed they might be considered a detailed commentary on the theme of this chapter! Holiness movements are inevitably prone to such temptations. So easily there gathers round them a kind of hot-house atmosphere which requires superbly sane handling to achieve the same limited purpose as a greenhouse, which at best is meant only to supplement and assist, rather than supplant, nature. Some day, perhaps, a wise, kindly, constructive person will write an illuminating book on *The Humbug of Holiness,* with the sole purpose of releasing the subject for wider appreciation.

Too holy by half

The answer to the problem is not a contemptuous or ignorant dismissal of holiness movements, denominations, or teaching, but an attempt to understand the Scriptural base and the human need which propels them into existence, a refusal to allow them to monopolize the field by default of our cultivation, and the provision of a more coherent, balanced, and practicable alternative. Meanwhile we must deal as honestly and faithfully as possible with the deviations which can occur, listing and examining them both to recognize their symptoms and to appreciate their causes. In a famous series of letters to his son on preparation for life Lord Chesterfield wrote, 'I believe there is more judgement required for the proper conduct of our virtues than for the avoiding their opposite vices. Vice, in its true light, is so deformed that it shocks us at first sight, and it would hardly ever seduce us if it did not first wear the mask of some virtue. But virtue in itself is so beautiful that it charms us at first sight; and as with other beauties, we think excess impossible; it is here that judgement is necessary to moderate and direct the effects of an excellent cause' (Letter 30). It is true that the noble Lord is recommending the typical eighteenth-century version of the classical Greek counsel of moderation in all things, rather than the balanced outworking of the enthusiasm of holy love as Jesus embodied it, but there is no valid reason why we should not spoil the Egyptians and baptize worldly wisdom into Christ, so long as it is transformed in the process! It is as possible to be too holy by half, as to be too clever by half. Perhaps this explains why a certain clergyman's wife commented that her husband was never so difficult to live with as when he returned from a spiritual convention. Partly no doubt it was attributable to the fact that under such intensive battery conditions the nervous system of the one partner had been tuned up to a shriller pitch than the one left to free-range development.

Lynx-eyed scrutiny

The most obvious temptation, once the area of holiness teaching has been seriously entered, is a lynx-eyed scrutiny of comparative attainments, in oneself and others. Any hint of superiority is an affront to natural pride. Immediately there is a hypercritical microscopic search for inconsistencies. It is almost impossible to avoid comparisons between oneself and others, upwards or downwards, either way. Questions of sincerity and hypocrisy arise. The upshot is a jungle of useless, harmful accusations and counter-accusations (more often thought than spoken), together with a futile mixture of self-despisings and self-justifications. Inevitably sooner or later there is injected into the discussion the phrase 'holier than thou' (Isaiah 65:5), with its equally obnoxious counter-attitude of 'unholier than thou', which is only an inverted Pharisaism. From the point of view of the claimant of holiness there easily develops a patronizing attitude of assessing other people's spiritual attainments, sometimes going to the lengths of ostentatiously shaking the head in the presence of the one under judgement, or nodding significantly to the self-appointed jury-clique, with lips pursed critically, eyebrows raised a little wearily, and grimacing along the pew with the pious smirk of the initiated. When the subject of scrutiny is absent the conspirators huddle together with pained and furtive expressions to bemoan his downfall. The whole attitude is basically a destructive corruption of holiness.

Touchiness

The sensitiveness referred to produces a variety of defensive reactions. Perhaps the first on the list is a certain touchiness, which helps to explain the personal relationship disorders which tend to afflict holiness and faith and prayer movements, after the first flush of enthusiasm has inevitably—and providentially —passed away. There is an exposed mucous-membrane surface to the personality which is denied the ordinary defences of unregenerate human nature. The slightest unpleasant stimulus makes it quiver. The inevitable rubs and limitations of creaturely life assume a seriousness out of all proportion to their importance. Further, any suggestion that one is less than perfect, than claimed or self-expected, becomes a personal affront, an assault on the citadel of spiritual integrity. Sheer necessity for spiritual self-preservation demands an almost violent reaction against what must seem the sapping of the foundations of character and morale. Personal relationships therefore become strained, and, as with the love-hate links of kinship, blown up in proportion to the proximity and intensity of the original involvement. Since violence and explosions are ruled out by the self-picture of unruffled calmness, there is either a recurring pattern of sudden loss of temper, followed by abject humiliation and apology, or, more likely, a rigid control is exercized which results in a permanently grieved expression.

Stylized attitudes

Another reaction is to develop artificial, stylized attitudes, which become a kind of second nature so that we maintain them even in the privacy of the bathroom. In all circumstances there appears a bland smile, an exaggerated jocularity, a warehouse full of smooth phrases for oiling through embarrassing situations, perpetually putting other people at a disadvantage if they find it necessary to resist us. Temperament plays a large part in the form this kind of defence-mechanism assumes. Some exuberant natures bounce around exuding a great draught of pseudo-goodwill, while the more phlegmatic quietly bulldoze their way through with a smug immunity to criticism. Apprentices to holiness in such a setting tend to adopt the current fashions of phrase and pose, unaware of the rationalizing capacities of the human heart, whereby the unregenerate, not to say unsanctified, residue of self-will, squeezed into inaccessible cavities of the personality, assumes sanctimonious vestments for the purpose of resuming its interrupted reign. Genuine sanctity is not produced by such stereotyped means. Leonardo da Vinci, a uniquely versatile artist, was an energetic genius who nevertheless could not produce his masterpieces without much groaning of spirit. A much slicker and more rapid sculptor, Perugino, churned out statues by the barrel-load. Leonardo once made a caustic reference to Perugino when the former was commissioned to produce casts for a large series of figures of saints for a particular ecclesiastical establishment. Once when his wife called him to dinner he shouted down, 'Serve the soup while I pop another saint in!' If there is one truth above another about sanctity it is the presence of originality and naturalness, straightforward and fully engaged in bending all powers to achieve the purposes of God, not producing a standardized type.

Sophistication of conscience

An allied temptation is to the sophistication of conscience, whereby we find good reasons for doing what we want or need to do, and persuade ourselves that everything we do is right. Daily we are involved with people and circumstances which circumscribe our freedom of Christian action. Somehow we must pacify our conscience, and the covenient mechanism known as rationalization is soon in full production. It is so uncomfortable to live with an uneasy conscience. Before we know where we are, moral schizophrenia (split personality in terms of character) has enabled us to combine dubious business ethics with unctuous piety. When we move in the exalted realms of entire sanctification we learn even more profoundly than in our pre-conversion state that 'the heart is deceitful above all things, and desperately wicked. Who can know his secret faults?' (Jeremiah 17:9). The prophet knew from experience how crooked and slippery was the subconscious mind long before Freud introduced such phrases to the language. 'Satan himself is transformed into an angel of light' (2 Corinthians 11:14), and can wear his wings and halo with a naturalness born of his heavenly origin. It is harder for the keen Christian to admit the subterranean manoeuvres which are taking place within him than for the worldly man who candidly admits that he is governed by self-interest and the advantage of the in-group to which he belongs. The sanctified become as familiar as any Jesuit with the craft of casuistry. One of Charles Wesley's hymns, with its unusually ambiguous phrase for so clear a stylist, hints at the narrow margin between the objective and the subjective dominance in interpretation:

> *I want the witness, Lord,*
> *That all I do is right.*

Finicky censoriousness

By another slight deflection from the plumbline of genuine holiness we arrive at a finicky censoriousness, pedantic niggling at other people's conduct. Jesus had little use for those who tithe 'mint and anise and cummin, and have neglected the weightier matters of the law, justice and mercy and faith' (Matthew 23:23). He proceeds with one of his blisteringly ironical pictures of blind guides straining out a minute gnat from their food and swallowing a camel—hump, hairy hide, and hoofs and all! Holiness does not mean tut-tutting all over the place, and holding up hands in shocked horror. To be shocked is to be put out of useful circulation. Much of the peccadilloes which roll the eyeballs of the unco' guid are attributable to inherited social patterns of behaviour, adapted to particular circumstances of history. It is notorious that evangelicals in one country can be extremely censorious about personal adornment which is perfectly acceptable to evangelicals in another, and vice versa. Something has slipped far out of proportion when the use of cosmetics becomes a major factor of exclusion while hurtful gossip remains unchecked. (At heart there is a continuing preoccupation with the putrefying carcase of supposedly dead sin, with the carrion-instinct reasserting itself under the guise of sanctification: 'where the carcase is, there will the vultures be gathered together' (Matthew 24:28). What matters most is the fundamental slant and attitude of people and society towards the purposes of God in their fulness. God is particular, but not fussy. Small points matter, like clean sparking plugs, but they must be kept in their place under the bonnet, and any attention should be concentrated on our own needy state in these matters, except in so far as another requests help for a similar purpose.

Oblique murder

When this particular finickiness in relation to other people becomes chronic the result is a kind of oblique murder. Indeed it might be suggested that one of the main dangers of superficial holiness is the substitution of obliquity for iniquity. Nothing is quite straightforward. The ball bounces back at an unexpected and unnatural angle. The normal phrases of open conversation become suffused with suspicion, till 'My dear brother, speaking as a friend . . .' becomes a warning prelude to a singularly nasty piece of sabotage. The fraternal arm curls round the shoulder and the warm cotton-wool clutched in the palm of the hand conceals the point of the knife neatly stuck between the shoulder-blades. The constant query is whispered from mouth to ear, 'Is he sound?', which means 'Does he toe our party-line? Does he dare to show any independence of judgement?' If he is suspect by the measure of these man-made manifestos, smear his reputation; kill his good name. Put him on the black list, or at best the grey list. This twisted rage is expressed in art form possibly with the starkest outline in Robert Browning's lyric, 'Soliloquy in a Spanish Cloister'. One old monk is watching another who is expert with flowers.

> *Grrrrrrr! Water your damn'd flower-pots, do!*
> *God's blood, Brother Lawrence, if hate killed men,*
> *Would not mine kill you! . . .*
> *He-he, his lily snaps . . .*

97

And so it goes on, as the unhealthy mixture of perfectionism and a secluded community produces its destined morbid end like the scum on a stagnant pond. Hence the bias to belittlement in the sanctimonious jargon of brotherhood, and the perpetual drip of discouragement. Sir Thomas Browne's comment might be written in indelible ink on the tongue of us all: 'He who discommendeth others obliquely commendeth himself.'

Morbid introspectiveness

When the perils are realized, and the inward source of such perverse reactions recognized, the next obvious trap is morbid introspection, always suspiciously lying in wait to catch oneself out in unworthy motives. There follows a perpetual taking of the spiritual temperature with the bedside chart zig-zagging melodramatically up and down, a source of absorbed interest to ourselves, an infallible but wearing method of ensuring attention from other people. Since all feeling exists in the nervous system, and is related intimately to physical states, a hypochondriac absorption in our own aches and pains, physical as well as spiritual, lures us into an appalling inner dungeon. Perhaps this explains the phenomenal number of advertisements in religious papers for remedying every disorder from toe-ache to heart-ache. Never was there such a catalogue of pills, ointments, and treatments. Concentration on the sensation of blessing is likely to arouse such self-centred concern because the same nervous system is the only medium of transmission. As in all walks of life the secret is to keep the eye away from the self and on the object. Seek to be a blessing for God to your fellows rather than to obtain and retain a blessing for yourself! Of course it is necessary to exercise the self unto godliness (1 Timothy 4:7) in the gymnasium of the spirit, and to have plenty of net-practice to see the ball cleanly before the match, but even there the object of the exercise is to get the eye off one's own movements and reactions to a spontaneous encounter with the object in view. At one period the mystic initials reverberated round the college, B.T.; they stood for Blessing-Tester, the type of person whose self-absorption and general lack of common sense tried the patience of the very elect! Incidentally some kinds of prayer create rather than cure illness. Whenever the main aim is to create a sensation of excitement destructive tension is introduced into the community, and less resilient nervous systems cannot absorb it without damage. The resultant invalidism is strengthened in its apparently saintly martyrdom and pallid patience through the attention vouchsafed by the assurances of prayer which keep the patient in the centre of attention. False sympathy is one of the killers, as much as is unloving antipathy: both are the enemy of zestful living.

Artificial stimulus: tranquillizer

Two spurious medicines are self-generated by this morbid state whereby some evade the more obvious wasting disease described above. Artificial aids are sought either to calm down or stir up. Religion becomes a kind of spiritual tranquillizer in the first case, striving after an unnatural calm and unruffled surface of the emotional life. Sanctity becomes a study in still life, like the pictures of piled-up fruit in a bowl. A bogus passivity substitutes for spiritual peace. There is a kind of spiritual narcissism which loves to contemplate its own undisturbed state, its *ataraxia,* while others are in fact carrying the can. The distinction is missed between responsible forethought and useless fretting. The peace of God is likened by Paul to the ordered strength and disciplined fighting force of a Roman legion. There is a place for drugs in certain unbearable emergencies, and there is a legitimate place in religious therapy for the anaesthetics of God, the providential coma, the clutching to the warm, soft, and comforting bosom, but health seeks the reduction of such assistance to a minimum.

Artificial stimulus: conventionitis

The other abuse is to use religion as a stimulus to sensation, however refined and clothed in sanctity. It is the equivalent of dram-drinking, a kind of spiritual alcoholism, or living it up, with a feverish concern to arouse a state of exaltation, even if only for the momentary ingurgitating gasp of air in the throat, which is the split-second satisfaction of the gluttonous seeker after orgiastic sensation. Beware when you find yourself developing an addiction to that sudden sharp intake of breath

99

which may well be a necessary compensation in the early days after conversion for those who have previously led a vicious life. Their nervous system has suffered a violent torsion, and cannot immediately find the new equilibrium. Great patience is needed with such people, and also great wisdom in the process of weaning. We ought every time to ask what will best tend towards God's ends for this person taking fully into account the actual condition in which they find themselves. Mature Christians should beware of too much visiting of conventions for deepening the spiritual life. It is rather like the lamentable phrase about the devotional side of religion. Conventionitis can foster spiritual sclerosis, a hardening of the arteries, which has a law of diminishing returns like the roué's, with his ever-increasing thirst for an ever-decreasing satisfaction. Eventually the personality is like a squeezed orange, or a hollow-eyed turnip-lantern with the wick run dry, which lights up only when the familiar stimuli are applied and the conditioned reflexes go through the motions. Ecstasy is indeed one of the blessings which satisfy the god-given need for the vivid, spectacular hour, the loss of the guarded self in self-transcending abandon; but, as always in God's wisdom, it is the unpredictable bonus thrown in over and above the ordinary interest on instinctive capital honourably worked in normal obedience. The childish demand for excitement for its own sake, even in exalted states of religious sensations, receives the same treatment as all spoiled grown-up children: 'He gave them their desires, and sent leanness to their souls' (Psalm 106:15).

Doctrinal fastidiousness

The same mistaken attitudes reveal themselves mentally also in doctrinal fastidiousness. Some are so insistent on hairsplitting points of doctrine that they can have no fellowship with other Christians who cannot sign on the dotted line of the manifesto, so carefully drawn up as almost to guarantee exclusion, because of genuine difficulties and hesitations. There either develops a rigid dogmatism which excludes all but the party-liners, or a degenerating system of mental reservations, double-think, and double-talk. It is, of course, possible to suffer from this disease in reverse, and be morbidly scrupulous over

individual items of faith like particular miracles and raw
metaphors like 'the blood of Christ'. The mark of this attitude
is a disproportionate emphasis on rarefied issues which give
the self a sense of undue importance, separateness, and
superiority. Some try to be more refined than God! Holiness
movements seem to have a special tendency to separation over
such remote points, often almost beyond settling. Thus there are
those who prefer the teaching that sin is eradicated by the full
work of the Spirit, while others contend that it is suppressed.
One might hazard a guess that both have a contribution to
make. It is difficult to suppose that God would intend to do
half a work if He came to remove the sinful state which is
the root cause of man's sinful deeds; in this sense He removes
the root so that the fruit may not appear. But the picture of
root and fruit does not exhaust the subject; it is limited to the
relationship of cause and effect, but does not describe the
actual nature of the state of sin, which in fact is a wrong
relationship with God. Such a wrong relationship must be
radically removed, but plainly it is possible for relationships
to deteriorate again if the proper attitude of trust and obedience
is not maintained. In this sense sin may return, and from one
point of view it would appear that if it returned it had in
fact been present unobserved all the time and merely held
down. Theologically, in terms of the actual state of sanctification, the eradicationists would appear to be correct, but
psychologically, sociologically, and historically the suppres-
sionists would seem to supply a corrective. Another conclusion
might be that both are reacting against each other over an
unreal issue precipitated by an inadequate setting-out of the
terms of the problem in the first place. What is manifestly a
contradiction to the claim to have received the blessing of
entire sanctification is the patronizing, almost venomous,
manner in which one has heard one type refer to the other.
There must be something wrong with any teaching on the
subject which leads to clearly unchristian tones and facial
expressions.

Theological confusion about grace
The doctrinal shortcomings reveal themselves most fatally

in the theological confusion which sometimes results. Thus it has been stated that the completely eradicating work of sanctification removes men from the necessity of grace. People have even been known to refuse to sing the hymn lines

Oh to grace how great a debtor
Daily I'm constrained to be!

because sin had been uprooted from the heart and therefore grace was superfluous now, however essential in the past. The logic of this view is that the supreme end of growth in grace is to grow out of grace, which practically amounts to falling from grace. It is overlooked that were God to withdraw His initial grace in pardon, justification, regeneration, the sinner would revert to his guilty status and sinful state, because such right personal relationships depend not only initially but also continuously on the free gift of God's favour. Equally, the sanctifying work is totally a work of grace, requiring the continuous response of faith. The metaphor of root and fruit, it should be recalled, is valid only for the relationship of sins to sin, in the same way as faith to works, and goodness to virtues. The root itself turns out to be a relationship, right or wrong, to God Himself, who imparts His nature and the requisite relationship to the full; therefore it is more and not less true that, when man accepts the gift of entire sanctification he is daily a debtor to grace. Theological accuracy matters, but doctrinal finickiness is disastrous.

Theological confusion about a second work of grace

A further perversion of the teaching, especially when bound up with the idea of a second work of grace distinct from conversion and its concomitants, is the suggestion that a person can have a saved soul but a lost or wasted life. In so far as it is true that people can be converted without progressing any further, and thus fail to produce the fruit which should have been forthcoming, the fault must surely lie in inadequate teaching about conversion and salvation, whereby the believer does not realize that continuous growth is expected of him by the power of the same Spirit which commenced the work. Doubtless many believers opt, consciously or otherwise, for a mediocre level of Christian attainment, while it cannot be said that they have ceased to be converted. Nevertheless, in so far as they are real Christians theirs cannot be said to be a lost life, except in such a roundabout sense as to be completely misleading. The intention of such assertions is to highlight the necessity for a profound crisis of complete surrender even after conversion, but the phraseology is calculated to produce disastrous results in thought and practice. That such a second unique and revolutionary experience may well happen cannot be denied, but much harm can be done, both to the recipient and to other Christians, by such distorted teaching. It belittles the initial work of salvation and divides Christians illegitimately.

Fear of reason and beauty

The inadequacy of much teaching on this subject of sanctification is revealed in its failure to come to terms with the real world as God has made it. Sin can indeed corrupt God's natural gifts so that they divert man from concentration on the main business of the Kingdom of God, but this is neither automatic nor intended. This unreality expresses itself in several ways, but primarily by narrowing the range of interests and concerns of the believer, so that while he has the centre of the Gospel he lamentably restricts its circumference, which is as wide as God's creation, else why did He make it? Internally there arises a fear of using confidently the powers God has placed within His creatures to investigate, understand, and enjoy—both the intricate details and the total integration of the cosmos. The curtains are drawn to exclude the antiseptic light of reason and the healing light of beauty. As a consequence the soul is stunted, and whole areas of the personality which were meant to be developed in the all-round life of the Spirit either atrophy or emerge in freak forms. At the root lies a certain fear, springing either from unhappy earlier experiences, childhood training, conversion indoctrination, or reaction against aspects of experience which are outside the previous range of those affected. Since the experience of entire sanctification at the heart builds up confidence it is not altogether unnatural that any area of life in which the believer is not confident should seem to be a sapper of the very assurance which gives him his strength.

The story of the man born blind (John 9) has much to teach Christians about the limits of assurance both in conversion and sanctification. The central change in himself he could only deny by refusing the plain evidence of immediate experience. He knew he had been blind; he knew he now saw; and he knew that Jesus was the agent of cure. All these were aspects of one experimental fact, and nothing could shake his confidence on this point. Beyond this point he would not confidently step at the time, though he did not claim that his knowledge was the limit of knowledge. He was prepared to listen to trained minds of any kind respectfully when it came to assessing the implications of the wonderful work for the status of Jesus. He was even ready to express tentative opinions on his own behalf that Jesus was at least a prophet. Further he was prepared to rebut plainly inadequate estimates of Jesus' relationship to God which failed to do justice to the facts. All in all he withstood the temptations which assail the man of strong and legitimate convictions to restrict thought and appreciation to the area where he feels secure. Belittlement of reason, beauty, and natural goodness is no mark of a healthy experience of entire sanctification. Full salvation brings us 'forth into a large place' (Psalm 18 : 19; 2 Samuel 22 : 20) of endless and abounding interest.

Hindering development

The narrowing of range of interest has other unfortunate results. At one time there were those who regarded the many trees in the grounds of a certain College as if they were sacred like the Asherah, the pagan groves, which were the scenes of such goings-on as stung the Hebrew prophets to incessant denunciation. Nothing must be cut or changed. The day of reckoning came when an un-English type hurricane uprooted or smashed down some fifty trees, and damaged irreparably another fifty. The sin against the trees was revealed in the spindly, whispy, misshapen appearance of those remaining. On the steep hillside, painfully overcrushed, each had been fighting upwards for light and air. Growth and change are of the essence of God's creation. Nemesis awaits all attempts to restrict growth, except in accordance with the divine scheme for regulating it in the interests of the harvest God requires.

Distortion of sex

Two other distorting effects may be noticed, one on the personality, the other on society. The failure to do justice to God's first creation vitiates man's experience of the second. The new or second birth is so absorbing that the truth can be forgotten or suppressed that there could have been no second birth without the first. Since the survival of the race is an essential prerequisite for anything else that man may attempt, it follows that the reproductive drive is likely to be heavily loaded. Since it is located within the human organism inescapably man has to come to terms with it perpetually. One way or another it will exercise one of the most powerful influences on man's life for good or ill. It is therefore not surprising that Satan focuses a great deal of attention on this area. Equally, therefore, it is not surprising that sanctification may well find this to be one of the first and last, if not absolutely the most important, area of difficulty. The fact that the experience of sanctification includes the element of ecstasy, which has to use the same nervous system as any other feeling to which human beings are prone, means that measurable sensations will be stimulated, and the excitement may easily slither from one category to another by sympathetic transfer.

The subject of sex is sadly mishandled when the reverence which is its due becomes a subtle evasion of honest acceptance. Coy references to 'the ladies' take the place of straightforward acknowledgement of both basic human oneness in personal relationships and differences of physical and temperamental reaction based on biological function. The moral schizophrenia previously referred to appears now in its emotional equivalent. The two parts of life are separated, and either there is no real reconciliation in the mind (merely an ungainly lurch through a divisive partition), or reconciliation is achieved by dressing up the basic facts of sexual relationship in euphemistic language. The result is a kind of evasive sensuality or emasculated lechery which leads either to hypocrisy, breakdown, or a morally enervating sentimentality. Knowledge and reverence must go hand in hand; the absence of either can spoil the possibilities. A frequent phrase about 'the material side of life' reveals the slightly off-centre comprehension of the relationship between the material and the spiritual in human experience. There is no material or spiritual side to life. The spiritual is expressed through the material, or it is not expressed at all. The material and the spiritual are like two steps in the same block of material. The first step in time and space is the material, but it is meant to be so used to reveal its purpose in the spiritual, (the second step which interprets the first step, and for which the first exists). 'But it is not the spiritual which is first but the physical, and then the spiritual,' as the Apostle Paul sanely exclaimed in his supreme exposition of the resurrection (1 Corinthians 15:46). These two are not being separated in this statement, but apportioned to the correct relationship of time on the one hand and importance on the other. They are as indivisible in relationship, and as unalterable in order, as our Lord's summary of the ten commandments—to love God with all abilities and the neighbour as the self.

Social outworking

The other deficiency relates to the social outworking of the Gospel. Sanctification is for the service of God, whose purpose relates to the whole wide world of men. It is quite untrue to suppose that no social outworking resulted from the doctrine of entire sanctification. The reverse is the case. Most of the great humanitarian reform movements of the nineteenth century in Great Britain can be traced (as one main source) to the evangelical revival as concentrated primarily, though not exclusively, in original Methodism and its various out-fanning movements. These were by no means merely ameliorative, but led to Parliamentary statutes and to much that is best in the Welfare State. One of the outstanding instances of the effect of the experience of the doctrine among a particular group of folk was the revolutionary impact of the Lincolnshire farm-boy, John Hunt, and some fellow-students at Richmond Theological College in the nineteenth century. Before he was forty years of age he had died, but had also converted Fiji from a cannibal island, established churches all over the islands, both as living fellowships and as buildings, translated the Scriptures into the native tongue, begun educational and medical work, and all in all laid the foundations of a social order which can stand comparison with any. Amidst these phenomenally apostolic labours he wrote his *Letters on Entire Sanctification* which are possibly the classic exposition of the subject.

Limited to personal salvation

At the same time it must be admitted that holiness movements as such rarely seem to produce like results, and it is a common charge even against the Wesleyan movement that it failed to realize anything like the full implications of its teaching. With the growth of material success following its inculcation of thrift and industry, and its releasing of able lower-class citizens from their disabilities so that they rose into a higher social and financial class in a generation or two, came the temptation to adapt their standards to philanthropic amelioration rather than fundamental political and social change. Thus Communism has been called by Dr Hans Lilje 'a God-given scourge to a degenerate Christianity'. Dr R. W. Dale, the famous Congregationalist preacher of Carr's Lane, Birmingham, commented, 'The solution of the immense practical problems which this doctrine suggests have not been courageously faced.' Wesley himself stated that 'the Bible knows no holiness but social holiness.' The standard model of holiness-reception is the Day of Pentecost, and the whole point of the experience is that it was shared. It was not so much that individual believers were filled with the Spirit and then conjoined with others in like case, but that the conjoining was an essential and simultaneous element in the total work, which was individually realized, so that each and all 'possessed their possessions' (Obadiah 17).

Intransigent individualism

At this point comment may be made about the frequent charge of intransigent individualism against the teaching of entire sanctification, expressed in terms which appear to undervalue Church order, recognized ministry, and the sense of the ecclesia, the continuous people called by God in terms of their historic destiny as a community with a consequent undue emphasis on the outcrop Church as koinonia or intimate fellowship, interpreted as a gathering of like-minded souls for mutual edification rather than as an intimate group-expression,

107

localized at a particular time, of the long-term and universally extended ecclesia. The New Testament never refers to an individual saint but to the saints as a community set apart for God's use. 'They without us cannot be made perfect' (Hebrews 11:40), and neither can we be made perfect without them, both spiritual ancestors and spiritual descendants. Beware the bias to contrast the holy huddle of the perfectly like-minded with the mass of lesser Christians and the necessary element of routine in an ordered community which has to function through centuries. True sanctification is corporate, and accepts gladly the necessity of an ordered historic Church (however monopolistic views of that order may be resisted) as part of the inheritance of the Gospel for the work of sanctification, both in its membership and for the world.

Eternal juveniles: useless sacrifices

Before reaching the fontal origin of the deviations two more points may be noticed. The first is the unreality of the expectations engendered by the promises if divorced from a truly Scriptural context. At one extreme are the eternal juveniles, bobbing up irrepressibly despite repeated failure, without any consistent achievements, and with the spurious ideals excusing the lack of any available results. At the other extreme are those who in their passionate desire to lay all on the altar for the Lord damage themselves and other folk with useless sacrifices. While it is necessary to cut off hands and feet, and pluck out eyes, and cut loose from the natural ties of kinship and even friendship if these genuinely hinder the work of the Kingdom, there is no virtue either in making such sacrifices for their own sake or in the circumstances which may make them necessary. A particular instance affects young folk in training for a career. Should they pack it up, and go to some Bible College instead? While acknowledging the possible exception one is bound to say if the opportunity is immediately present, 'Get trained; you will be more useful to God, yourself, and everybody else. If thereafter opportunity serves to pick up the basic Biblical and evangelistic training, by all means do so. If you are not qualified to receive the training you would need for effective service in some particular field, and you are otherwise free, get the basic training in Bible and evangelism first, and pick up the preliminary qualifications on the way. What you must not do is to break into a training-course if you can possibly help it.' More and more does Paul's example in missionary service speak to our generation, both in his tent-making and ministry, his college training, and his pioneer yen to seek the regions beyond the present confines of the Church.

Not righteous overmuch

Many years ago a Wesleyan minister, W. L. Watkinson, wrote a sermon on the text from Ecclesiastes, which heads this chapter, 'Be not righteous overmuch', and it must by now be painfully evident that such a text and sermon is necessary. Throughout there is an attempt to improve on the perfection required in Scripture. One is reminded of the Russian Lyeskov's story about a steel flea presented by English craftsmen to the Cossack Ataman Platov when he visited this country in 1815. The flea was a mechanical model which jumped when wound up by a key so small that it was visible only through a magnifying glass. When the Ataman showed it to his Tula craftsmen one of them rose to the foreign challenge, and boasted that he would improve on the English effort. His answer was to shoe the flea. The shoes were as perfect as the flea, but, alas, when the flea was shoed it could no longer jump!

Degeneration of koinonia

Incidentally, the very koinonia, or intimate spiritual fellowship beloved naturally of holiness, and kindred movements itself degenerates if kept to itself. The separatist attitude prevents fresh air from circulating, and the atmosphere becomes rancid. The impact on the outside world becomes practically nil. Inwardly the intertwining of lives and mutual concern in caring so easily becomes nosy-parkerism, failing to mind one's own business, being far too interested in every up and down and roundabout of personal relation, feeling, and fortune. Soon the whispered gossip echoes through the corridors, and reverberates up and down like the yodelled messages in the Tyrolean valley. Family life suffers terribly under such circumstances. The whole community exercises a restrictive influence on its members, and usually some dominant figure or family emerges who becomes a self-appointed pope or Curia, insisting on authority to interpret the Spirit's leading to each individual. With the friendliest intentions and gestures the personality is enfolded, manoeuvred, and even bludgeoned out of its rightful and God-given independence of judgement. Other people's lives are fully taken charge of, and any resistance appears as blasphemous refusal to do God's will.

Self-reference in apparent self-obliteration

When we delve to the heart of these deviations it gradually becomes clear that all are in some sense variations on a common theme, which has to do with the very nature of the operation itself, namely, the transformation of the self. At every point there is self-reference at the occasion of apparent self-obliteration. The more we examine the problem the more it is seen to be what to do with ourselves. There is an apparent contradiction and paradox at the centre of it all, which may help to explain the odd contrast between the claims of the sanctified and the sheer obstinacy and sweetly overbearing manner in which they bend life and other people to their well-being. Everything is judged as it fits convenience, and the right to exemption is assumed from normal procedures and disciplines. There is also the narcissism which contemplates its own reflection of the beauty of Jesus, and draws its own fan-worship, feeding on the self-parading personal blurbs, with photographs of jovial dynamic personalities on the publicity hand-out. Such methods may be properly used to awaken the attention of an advertisement-sodden mass public, but it should be recognized as the children of light trying to be as wise as the children of this world. It is worldliness baptized into Christ, but the temptations are still there, and more dangerous because more concealed. The slogan might be coined, 'None of self, but look at me!' How different from the Unitas Fratrum and the Friends of God, those medieval movements which eschewed personal publicity and maintained a rule of anonymity lest any kudos should accrue to themselves. From these groups came books like *Theologia Germanica,* which outside the Bible influenced the young Luther most in his reforming career.

Preoccupation with self

Perhaps Theodore Monod's hymn, from which the original phrase above caricatured is taken, illustrates the point adequately. The writer carries the singer by clear stages from one extreme—'all of self, and none of Thee'—to the other—'none of self, and all of Thee'. Within its limits the hymn is an excellent exercise for increasing the screw on the resistant ego. With an adequate footnote on the meaning of the term *self* the hymn could hardly be bettered, but as it stands it is capable of misinterpretation. In the very act of elimination there is preoccupation with the self, which still utters the final words, and asserts itself even in the assertion of self-abnegation. At the end the self is as self-evident as at the beginning, and if care is not taken the self is more aware of itself and its own virtue in self-annihilation than at the beginning. The personality becomes self-centred in spite of itself.

Superficial humility

The fact is that God did not create the self that it might be annihilated, but that it might be perpetuated in right relationship with Himself. Without the self there would be nothing to save, and God would be cheated of His original creative intention. What must disappear is self-will, the acceptance in any form of the individual or the group as the centre of the universe, whose will and interests must prevail at all costs or be modified only by a compromise of mutual self-interest, so long as that requirement lasts. From this fundamentally askew attitude all else distorts at increasing ratio as it develops, and reappears in disguise in the supposedly sanctified, unless there is a realistic and Scriptural assessment of the truth about man in relation to God and the world He has made. The difficulty is pin-pointed in such a virtue as humility, the opposite of the pride by which man fell. It is difficult to speak of humility humbly, for it makes a good shirt but a bad overcoat. One student in the college of holiness is reported to have given himself a hundred marks out of a hundred for humility. The profession is soon exposed when taken at its face value. One woman in a class meeting wearied the members with reiteration of her unworthiness. Eventually the class-leader was driven to deal with the

111

matter, and one evening when she was wallowing in the mire, saying that she was no good at all to anybody, he observed, 'Yes, Sister So-and-so, we all know you're no good.' 'I'm as good as you are any day!' she immediately snapped back.

Need objective standard

It may be concluded that the errors turn on a failure to evaluate the true relationship of the self to God and the world. Since experience happens within the experiencing self the material, the feelings, the opinions, the decisions, are all made there inescapably. The important point is to realize that the object of experience does not originate within the self, which is meeting another mind, heart, and will, made known in the Scriptures and in the world which exists apart from the self. The art is to recognize the objective pattern, purpose, and power, and by constant contact therewith, within and without, to be conformed thereto by all legitimate external pressures, freely accepted, and by all internal momentum, freely exercised. In short, the secret is to keep looking unto Jesus, the originator and completer of our faith (Hebrews 12:2), in the total setting of Bible, Church, and the world of nature and men. Cardinal Newman, in his Parochial Sermons, describes the situation in sharp outline. 'If we take our eyes off him (Christ) for a moment, and look towards ourselves, at once those excellent tempers fall into some extreme. Charity becomes over-easiness. Holiness becomes tainted with spiritual pride. Zeal degenerates into fierceness. Activity eats up the spirit of prayer. Hope is heightened into presumption.' W. L. Watkinson shows how men gain a reputation for some excellence, warm-heartedness, outspokenness, gentleness, merriment, and before they know where they are the whole virtue flowers conspicuously out of all proportion. Another notable nineteenth-century preacher, F. W. Robertson of Brighton, wrote, 'Most of us in this world are monsters with some part of our being bearing the proportions of a dwarf: a feeble dwarfish will—mighty, full-blown passions.' Or, as Shakespeare's jester Touchstone commented long ago, we are 'damn'd, like an ill-roasted egg, all on one side'. The heights of holiness demand an increased self-scrutiny kept in its place by an even greater concentration on exposure to God-scrutiny.

True self-denial

Before concluding this chapter two related themes deserve a paragraph. The clue may well be found in the true understanding of self-denial. One of the most quoted sayings of our Lord reads, 'He called unto him the multitudes with his disciples and said unto them, If any man would come after me, let him deny himself, and take up his cross, and follow me' (Mark 8:34). Is there not a connexion here with Peter's denial of association with our Lord in the High Priest's courtyard, and the threefold question and answer after the resurrection between Jesus and Peter about the devotion of the latter? 'Peter was grieved because he said unto him the third time, Lovest thou me? . . . Thou shalt stretch forth thy hand, and another shall gird thee . . . Now this he spake, signifying by what death he should glorify God . . . Follow me' (John 21:15–19). The margin refers back to the prediction of Peter's behaviour under pressure: 'Thou canst not follow me now . . . Thou shalt follow afterwards . . . The cock shall not crow, till thou hast denied me thrice' (John 13:36–38). Love of the Lord, denying, crucifixion, following are all linked together in both passages. To deny the self is to do what Peter did to Jesus, and say, 'This person is not my Master; I am under no obligation to follow him, or to share his fate.' It is the extremest form of asserting that we are not our own master. Of course Peter knew who Jesus was, as did all present. It was not knowledge of Jesus in itself which was the damning thing, but being one of His followers, accepting Him as leader and controller, and following Him. The self still exists, is recognized, but not accepted as leader and controller. If Christ is to live in me, there must be a self for Him to occupy. Paul expressed the paradoxical truth when he said, 'I have been crucified with Christ; it is no longer I that live, but Christ who lives in me; and the life I now live . . . I live by faith in the Son of God, who loved me and gave himself for me' (Galatians 2:20). Sanctified man must be faithful to his true self as the God within him is to Himself. Jesus made it plain that man must love himself, in the way that God knows and loves him, else he cannot love his neighbour as he should. To die to self is to abandon self-centredness as the pattern reaction, the natural

113

centre of reference for decision. 'Except a grain of wheat fall into the ground and die, it abideth alone' (John 12:24). Self-denial, or dying to self, is the obverse of Christian-affirmation, as Christ-affirmation is the obverse of self-denial, and the positive is more important than the negative, though the former cannot exist without the latter.

Devious self-love

Unselfishness is not listed in Cruden's Concordance to the Bible; nor is *selfishness*. The Bible prefers the affirmative word *love,* which is contrasted either with *hate* or *self-will* (Genesis 49:6; Titus 1:7; 2 Peter 2:10). The whole concept of unselfishness is almost guaranteed to lead folk astray, as it concentrates attention on the doer of the unselfish deed. It can occasion much ill-will, as C. S. Lewis's acidly humorous epitaph suggests:

> *Erected by her sorrowing brothers*
> *In memory of Martha Clay.*
> *Here lies one who lived for others;*
> *Now she has peace. And so have they.*

The atmosphere becomes laden with martyrdom and the emotional blackmail which reminds beneficiaries how much has been sacrificed on their behalf, thus riveting the sense of obligation upon them. My father once remarked that he wished he did not live in so unselfish a household. Everybody says to each other, 'You have the salt', until no one takes the plunge and the whole meal is held up with useless unselfishness. Everything would move more efficiently given a little sanctified selfishness and restraint on the debauch of self-offering. The iniquitous state is self-love (2 Timothy 3:2), self-centredness, self-will, self-indulgence, the idolatry of our own way, and above all self-righteousness. There is no true release, even in sanctification, until it is fully realized that the self has a natural tendency to see itself like Joseph's sun and moon and stars and sheaf which stood upright, while the others bowed down (Genesis 37) to the godlike, even sanctified, figure in the centre of the picture. Things take a turn for the better when the citadel of self-importance and self-will has been overcome, and brought under the control of the rightful master; circumstances are more likely then to turn out favourably for the advancement of the Kingdom of God, as illustrated in the careers of Gideon (Judges 7:9–25), Nehemiah (1:3–11), and Esther (4:8 ff.; 5:1–13).

Fixation

The remaining snare is the attempt to fix or maintain the blessing of entire sanctification, as with Peter on the Transfiguration Mountain. If Mark wrote under Peter's direction then here is a confession of apostolic stupidity by one who could have expunged it from the record. With three boxes he thought he could imprison the high and passing hour. The intenser the experience the profounder the temptation to pin the hour down like a butterfly exhibition. 'Remember Lot's wife', warned Jesus (Luke 17:32), the one who looked back from behind her husband with a last long lingering glance at the place where her heart was really engaged. She became a pillar of salt, a fitting symbol of fixation, petrification. Hoarded manna always rots and stinks. Wisdom therefore is not too concerned about retaining the blessing as a sensation. It is more blessed to give than to receive, take, or grasp (cf. Acts 20:35). The blessing is in order to bless, and as we bless and share the blessing we retain as well as receive. Even if so saintly a soul as Fletcher of Madeley insisted that he lost the blessing on several occasions because he failed to testify to the blessing, it must still be said that the view, though sincere and effective so far as it went, fell short of full insight into the Bible message. The blessing undoubtedly includes the maintenance of a happy fellowship with the Heavenly Father, and is not merely a high level of moral attainment, but the consciousness is the more effective when the self forgets the self to find itself in fulfilment of purpose.

Maturity and awareness

In conclusion it must be said that where such a relationship exists it is the mark of maturity and sanity to be aware of it. There is nothing inconsistent with proper humility in receiving the assurance that perfect love has cast out fear, and that love of the brethren is evidence of the passage from death to life.

115

Not to know when such a profound change had taken place would be the mark of spiritual loss of identity, a prelude to lunacy. Equally, should any enquirer wish to know whether Christianity worked and self-centred attitudes could be removed, it would be the plain duty of a responsible man to share the evidence of his heart. The safeguard is that other folk in the fellowship can check the outward evidence, the enquirer can set any claims alongside the Lord in the Scriptures, and the believer's own conscience has to live with itself in the presence of the One whose eyes are purer than to behold iniquity without some jab on the sensitive parts.

Insidious degeneration

Finally it must be emphatically stated that this analysis of snags is not meant to be used destructively to provide an escape-hatch from the challenge of the teaching about entire sanctification, nor to make anyone feel either superior or inferior, but simply to do what it says to watch the snags, and ensure as far as humanly possible that the work of Father, Son, and Holy Spirit is not spoiled for lack of practical forethought. There is no limit to the promise and power of God in righteousness and holiness, but there are human attempts to improve on God's standards and methods which may look promising but whose net effect is to complicate and distort what should be direct and simple in its essence. Hosea gently reminded his people of the insidious degeneration which awaits the unwatchful: 'Grey hairs are here and there upon him, and he knoweth it not' (7:4).

6   Generating the energy

> '*I am not ashamed of the gospel: for it is the power of God unto salvation*' (Romans 1:16).
> '*For Christ also hath once suffered for sins, the just for the unjust, that he might bring us to God, being put to death in the flesh, but quickened by the Spirit.*' (1 Peter 3:18.)
> '*By his great mercy we have been begotten again unto a lively hope by the resurrection of Jesus Christ from the dead.*' (1 Peter 1:3.)
> '*And they were all filled with the Holy Spirit.*' (Acts 2:4.)

WHEN all the thinking, planning, cautious foresight are completed the whole affair remains inert on the drawing board or the desk unless and until energy is generated, distributed, and expended. Mankind is all too familiar with glossy prospectuses and grandiose promises, and his experience far too often justifies the weary sigh of Haggai, 'You have sown much and harvested little; you eat, but you never have enough; you drink, but you never have your fill; you clothe yourselves, but no one is warm; and he who earns wages earns wages to put them into a bag with holes' (1:6). Nothing happens without cost and effort for somebody. If anything is free to one, another has paid. Since mankind obviously has not adequate resources for the business of total salvation (however much he may and ought to contribute within the total scheme) God alone must generate the required energy and carry the responsibility of cost, if anything adequate and positive is to be achieved.

Source of energy

Where then does the energy originate to operate the programme outlined? There must be such a source because in fact the scheme has been put into operation, and a measurable output can be recognized. The simple answer is that the agent of supply is the same source which conceived the energetic idea, devised the agenda, outlined the programme, thought through the snags, shaped the necessary forms, and has already imparted some practical and effective understanding of what it is all about. The pressure descends from 'above, where Christ is, seated on the right hand of God' (Colossians 3:1), which means the Father and the Son together are in complete agreement of mind, heart, and will, and the full development of the original Plan B scheme has been carried through in terms of objective, historic action in this world, and is in full-scale production. From such unanimity, both as bond and expression, the power is released, as the Holy Spirit, proceeding from the Father and the Son. Just such personal energy is responsible for the creation and order of the measurable world known to science, and the immeasurable world known to personality. It is the same world understood in differing though related dimensions, and so constructed as to make possible development, divergent direction, and divine concentration into the human situation at a precise and particular point of time and space.

Location of power station

The site of such specific concentration is geographically and historically identifiable in the area known as Palestine some two thousand years ago. The concentration was so intense that it is seen most clearly within the narrow confines of a virgin's womb, a cattle-stall, a carpenter's workshop, a below sea-level river, a fisherman's boat, an upstairs room, an olive garden, a midnight miscarriage of justice in a law-court, a narrow cruciform gibbet, a rock-hewn tomb, and a garden at dawn. Even this potted summary of the point of impact can be reduced. The simplest single symbol, both of the power, the pattern, and the purpose is the cross stuck into a few square feet of Skull Hill just outside the Holy City of Jerusalem. There was the place of spontaneous combustion at the point of irrepressible bursting into flame. It was some weeks before this fact was fully realized and effective; at the time it seemed to those most concerned, whether for or against the figure strung up there, as the final running down of whatever had been hitherto wound up. 'We trusted that it was he who should have redeemed Israel' (Luke 24:21). When the Cross in this sense is referred to, the symbolism includes the resurrection as the completion of one integrated action. Jesus came 'to cast fire on the earth' (Luke 12:49); he was the incarnation of energy and its accompanying heat, the constructive friction of disciplined and directed resistance. The cruciform pattern of generation was indigenous to his being, and by conscious intention he directed what was also indigenous to the created world. He is the radioactive concentration of what is diffused throughout the universe, but in him raised to the level of self-awareness without fault, leak, or short-circuit. The power was always being generated; the cosmos originated and is maintained in this way; it was and is and always will be active on the same principle and pattern. Before Jesus was individualized as in the Gospel story the power-station was present, but either invisible or only partially visible with developing increase of visibility. It was as if God's people needed to be prepared and trained before they could be let loose in the generating-centre. Inexpert or hostile hands can do immense damage proportionate to the power available. In due time, however, there was an opening and an unveiling ceremony, when 'the veil of the temple was rent in two' (Luke 23:44) and the hitherto concealed Holy of Holies was made available for the public.

Capital investment

The capital for the operation, both as price and energy, is the basic holiness of God as previously described. 'To the theologian the changeless holiness of God stands for the like capital to that which the physicist finds in the uniformity of nature' (P. T. Forsyth, *The Cruciality of the Cross*, p. 144), i.e. the absolutely necessary assumption without which neither theology nor physics can begin to operate. In each case man is bankrupt and unable to do business without accepting as axiomatic the unified rational, dependable, energetic idea. Holiness, as described in Scripture and realized in the Lord Jesus Christ *is* the power, pays the price, and exerts the energy, and the first step thereafter is to establish effectively and

I

unmistakably God's holiness, authority, Kingdom, will, on earth as in heaven. Thus the model prayer begins, 'Our Father, which art in heaven, hallowed be thy name, thy Kingdom come . . .'. In other words God does things in His own way.

Generating plant

Once man has disobeyed, misused his delegated powers, like the tenants of the vineyard (Mark 2 : 1ff), judgement and mercy become necessary to rectify the situation, and both must be seen to reflect energetically and effectively the holiness of God. He must be seen to be in control in His own way, otherwise chaos follows. Yet such holiness must be exercised so as to make rather than break those who cooperate by humble faith and patient obedience. The significance of the Cross of Christ for the Christian first of all is that there the authority of God is vindicated in the way He chooses as best to achieve His purpose of reconciled relationships, having regard both to the gravity of the rupture and to the helplessness of the patient. He pays the penalty, foots the bill, exerts the life, and interfuses the whole fabric of raw material with qualities required to transform and perfect it. Since He is dealing with the foundations of integrity, character, destiny, and community there can hardly be a more fundamental work. 'The moral substratum of all sound states is the Kingdom of God, and the Kingdom of God is established at the Cross' (P. T. Forsyth). God imparts His energy in its fulness, creative and recreative, at the Cross; He sets up His generating-plant on Calvary.

Already existent

It is important to establish the fact that the energy in question has already been generated. The energetic idea is already in motion. The creative process exists as a going concern. Nobody can deny the rhythmic surge of the cosmos, intricately interacting continuously. 'Turn but a stone, and start a wing.' The engine is throbbing; the whole creation groans, travails, heaves with vitality, and 'Our hearts beat time to music of the skies'. The systole and diastole of the heart, the inhalation and exhalation of the lungs, are type-patterns of life.

To what purpose?

Nobody can deny that civilizations have risen and fallen, expressing this life in conscious patterns of society. They are marked by struggle, challenge, experiment, discipline, response, and, in some form, trust and obedience or their opposite. Humanity 'rolls round with the year, and never stands still . . .', but to what purpose? The most fitting symbol is the Buddhist wheel of existence, just round and round the treadmill ever returning to the same point, like the seasons, birth and death, with ultimate sense of emptiness like Ecclesiastes' vanity of vanities, with possibly the addition of the concept of the spiral staircase, though even this would be an act of faith in some kind of achievable purpose. Indeed, it is almost impossible to exclude the idea at least of temporary purpose and a sense of the need for right adjustment to whatever is considered the final power in the universe; in other words, there is a basic idea of the holy, the powerful purpose to be served, however inadequate, perverse, or even diabolic.

Bible contribution

Nobody can deny the contribution of the Jewish-Christian world-view as represented by the Bible to Western civilization, which has cradled modern science, pure and applied. Early intermixed with Greek philosophy and Roman jurisprudence and administration, and preserving both when the original matrix decayed, this organic force has kept alive the conviction of dynamic universal purpose with standards of fair dealing, integrity, compassion, and the human values generally, together with constructive dedication. The mysterious movement is seen under the control and guidance of a living, loving, lifting God, who shares the effort, comes inside the situation, with ability to overcome and renew.

Place of the cross

Nobody can deny the central place of the Cross at the heart of this purposeful momentum. The thought of the Cross has achieved far more for humanity than all the exhortations of the Sermon on the Mount, essential as those are to full understanding of the outworking of the Cross. Here it is that the upper and nether fires burn and glow in concern, conflict, commitment, with the flame of love and the flash of contact, incinerating the dross of base desire, and reviving all valid life.

Continuing dynamism

Nobody can deny the continuing dynamic effect of the Cross to this very day. It has power to pardon and purify, thus putting into useful circulation again those who would otherwise be either a nuisance to themselves and others, or certainly less than the best they were meant to be. We recall that falling short of the mark or aim is still sin, a lack of sufficient trust and obedience. Justification, regeneration, sanctification, all flow from this source. The whole redemptive cost and effort is focused, though not exhausted, here. The power of God unto salvation in all its forms is generated at this spot marked X. Whether it is the Roman Mass, the Salvation Army blood and fire meeting, or a wandering evangelist in a tent preaching about the One who died in our place, the final power is the same. Countless are the stories of those converted in the first place and sanctified in the second by this old, old story of Jesus and his love on the green hill far away. Countless also are the stories of one man laying down his life that another might live, so that the pattern of the Cross is seen below and above. The uniqueness of Jesus lay in His person, His character, His work. Human, obedient, and trustful sacrifice is a genuine but hazy representation of what is seen in its purity and clarity in the Cross of Christ. Total commitment is the natural response to such a self-offering. We have a debt we can never repay. Christian ethics is moved by gratitude. Evangelism, witness, service, spring from this heart transplanted into the believer's heart. The diseased feelings and corrupted attitudes are drained away, and a new healthy bloodstream pumped by the supreme blood-transfusion system of the world. 'The blood of Jesus, God's son, cleanses us from all sin' (1 John 1:7), so that men can walk in the light without fear of exposure, and have genuine partnership in the Gospel with one another. The emergence of the Church itself was a signal act of divine forgiveness. It became the Church of pardoned sinners, pilgrims on the heights of holiness.

Transforming energy

These facts constitute an extraordinary phenomenon when the original function of a cross is recalled. Crosses were ten a penny in the Roman Empire. Slaves and vermin were strung up thereon. The aim was to destroy not only life but reputation and influence, to smear the name with contempt for ever. To the Jews, the good people, it was a scandal, shocking like the little trigger on the mouse-trap which, when released, allows the spring to snap back with immense immediacy, thus inducing a shock like stepping in darkness on a broom-head whose long handle without warning smites between the eyes. To the Greeks, the clever and aesthetic people, it was a repulsive absurdity, a despicable offence against reason and beauty. The positioning of the body and the nailing through hands and feet guaranteed that the power to retain any dignity by muscular effort was impossible, and the total dead weight of the physical frame dragged on the palms of the hands to prevent any grip. Nothing could be more humiliated or helpless, and the whole shameful exhibition ensured maximum publicity like an advertisement hoarding. The intention was to reveal the opposite of what the world recognizes as power. Yet within a weekend the most intimately broken associates had been restored to hope, faith, and love. Within a couple of months a much larger group of impotent nobodies became dynamic somebodies, such a force to be reckoned with as led to clashes with the secular authorities. Within a few years the movement had reached the capital city of the most impressive empire, in terms of organization, that the world had ever known, and in about three hundred years, for good or ill, had become the established religion of the empire whose reluctant representative pronounced the judgement which hammered its Founder to the Cross. After two thousand years the same sign stands inescapably for compassion and the indomitably persistent encouragement of all that builds men up rather than destroys them. It still stirs reaction, favourable or unfavourable, but cannot be ignored.

Present realism

This meteoric career, which lasted as an official ministry for possibly a couple of years (a little more or less), and which apparently ended as a burnt-out squib, is still glowing, not to say blazing, and affecting human life at every level from the highest to the lowest. It affects education, medicine, farming, social welfare, compassion, human values, art in all its forms. Where is there such a two-way power, drawing and scattering, holding and losing, fetching and carrying, transforming lives, situations, institutions, societies, laws, customs? The surprising thing is not the smallness of its impact on history and the present, but the fact that it has made a dent at all in such a tough world of change and decay. The late Archbishop William Temple used to say that it was true that only one-tenth of the social work that needed to be done was being done, but that nine-tenths of that one-tenth was being done by Christian people. Maybe the proportion has altered since then so far as consciously motivated Christian service is concerned, but it is hard to avoid the observation that much of the humanist and conscientiously non-Christian service rendered has a Christian momentum from the past, but by a sad failure at some point the presentation of the Gospel in word and life has become divorced from its relevant form of appeal. Dedication is still recognizable in the world, though mainly seen either in relation to technical responsibilities or voluntary service apart from the deepest needs of the human spirit for eternal destiny and supernormal assistance. What is hard to deny is that primitive Christianity was vibrant with a triumphant sense of conquest over the sappers of man's confidence, sin and death, without parallel in the history of the world. Furthermore, through all the vagaries of history and the resistant earthiness of the human containers, the message of the Cross has retained its ancient power as a present reality. Only a supernatural institution could have survived such insane mismanagement, as G. K. Chesterton once put it. 'We have this treasure in earthen vessels, that the excellency of the power may be of God, and not of us' (2 Corinthians 4:7).

Energy of Jesus

It is permitted not only to establish the fact, but also to examine the works. High in the Tyrolean mountains is a dam fed by glaciers, and then pipelines take the water down the mountainsides with all the alpine pressure from above, down to the turbines in the generating-station, on which the growing economy of Austria largely depends. The plant itself is strangely silent, presumably because under such perfect control, but one enters the powerhouse almost with bated breath and a sense of the holy. The actual mechanics are enclosed in scrupulously clean and neat metal covers, but one is left off so that visitors can see the works, whereby one kind of energy is transformed into another to serve the wellbeing of the populace. The whole process has to be stirred into action and geared to produce results. One of the great themes of the Bible is that God is a worker, not a contemplated aristocrat, an idealist philosopher, a theoretical moralist, but One with His sleeves rolled up, engaged in production. Jesus' first recorded words, when he was twelve, apart from asking questions of the authorities, were, 'Do you not understand that I am compulsively in the same business-house with my Father?' (Luke 2:49). 'My Father worketh hitherto, and I work' (John 5:17). One of the most outstanding characteristics of Jesus is His energy; wherever he moves things happen; there is heat of some kind, opposition, devotion, gratitude, complaint. He strides ahead of the disciples, or into the midst of the Temple traders, or among the various groups who loathed each other's guts but combined to liquidate the One who challenged their interests and cosy hide-outs. Nothing deflected him from the Father's will of salvation. The same energy runs through His life as broke through the frustration of the closed inn door and transformed the stable-manger, and remained with Him to the end. The holy love of God in a tiny trembling solitary seed fertilized the womb of the Virgin Mary, and nothing could stop that incarnate eternal life developing and breaking through the tangled mass of man's accumulated taffles till daylight dawned and fresh air blew, and man's latent, crushed capacities for fellowship with the Father in the universal family were restored.

The mechanics of the job

As the Gospel story is studied, and especially the heart of the works in the last week of our Lord's life, and on the Cross, the constitution of the mechanics is laid bare for man's inspection. The original energetic idea, holiness, righteousness, love, which pulses measurably in creation and immeasurably in personality with a simultaneous double-beat of outflow and inflow, meets in objective historic encounter a specific resistance which is obedient and trustful, and swings round at the impulse of holy love, itself both driven and driving, transforming the energy received into a form of energy which itself can be transformed into every other conceivable kind of energy which is required for man's total salvation. In such a mechanism there is usually an arm or surface of some kind which receives the pressure of the original form of power, and by absolute obedience both to its own best nature and to the nature and form of the power impelling it, is moved so as to be able to cause movement. It is in a sense both assaulted and assaulting, though in proportion to its complete adjustment and fitness to the purpose in view, the chastisement or stripes are constructive; they bring health.

The shape of the Cross

Essential to the success of the job is the right material, devoid of fault, seasoned to the pitch of perfection, shaped to the task both on the receiving and the giving side in the right place at the right time, connected to the power and the distributing apparatus, together with skilled and dedicated management and technicians. Jesus has and is all these factors in Himself, the A to Z, the omnicompetent one, who shapes and wears the yoke which harnesses Him both to the power and the situation. Herein may be seen the mechanism of the Cross, in so far as personality and its relationships can be described in mechanical terms. The pressure of this pattern of personal and purposive energy is continually at work, though it reveals itself more at some times than others, but is always consistently itself, whatever alien powers may intrude. Occasionally in the Gospels the shadow of the shape falls on a scene. At the circumcision of Jesus, the aged Simeon who completely identified himself with the historic people of God as they had developed by his time, prepared the Mother of Jesus for the shape of things to come. 'Yea, a sword shall pierce through thine own soul also' (Luke

2:35). A famous picture shows the boy Jesus in His father's woodshed toward sunset, stretching His weary arms, and the shadow of the Cross falls on the wall. At the onset of His public life the commander of the alien troops assaulted His inner assurance about Himself and His method of work in the Temptations. The demon-ridden were the first to recognize the one whose very presence threatened their instinct of self-preservation. His key pupil echoed the diabolic diversionary tactics as the Cross was screwed a little nearer at Caesarea Philippi. On the Cross itself, at the crunch of the lever of power, the same undermining suggestion sought to deflect the movement of heart, hands, and feet, which were the connecting surface to receive and impart the power of holy love. 'He saved others,' they jeered, 'himself he cannot save' (Matthew 27:42), little realizing that this was precisely the method required.

Foreseen pattern

As he grew in wisdom Jesus saw more and more clearly the likely pattern of events, and steadfastly set His face to go to the place appointed, at the centre of government, power, turmoil, danger, and death. He felt the constriction of destiny and the stifling stench of man's complex self-will. The pipeline narrowed and the force of the jet increased. The essential current is within the frame and consciousness of this solitary individual. 'He trod the winepress alone', apart from the machinations of Satan, who threw in everything regardless. 'Hell from beneath was moved to meet him at his coming', and the accumulated conflicts were externalized in Gethsamane Garden, where he wrestled with all that went wrong in Eden Garden, with blood, and sweat, and tears, but also with prayer, obedience, and faith. It is no accident that when Sir Winston Churchill, whose picture of summit meetings and top level talks provides this extended exposition of entire sanctification, spoke to the British people at the absolute nadir of their fortunes, he challenged their spirit of resistance to apparently invincible evil by offering these very ingredients from the final preparation of our Lord for the moment of supreme encounter and the establishment of the generating-station which brought the top level talks at the Christian Summit into practical action. When the prayer ended there was nothing more anybody else could do; 'arise, let us be going,' Jesus said; the tap was turned, the lever pulled, and the vast creative theme shuddered into gear. Throughout the occasion He was in control; betrayal, denial, flagrant injustice, flogging, mocking—nothing could deflect the mechanics of salvation. Hence to the sympathizers He announced that they should not weep for Him, but for themselves; His life was not taken from Him; He laid it down Himself.

Using momentum of attack

Thus all the stages of the theme, scene, agenda, language, programme, snags, are all present in the one person who moves to that place where celestial top-level talks are made irreversibly actual on the Christian summit, known as Golgotha or Calvary. All the dimensions of height, depth, length, breadth are concentrated here. Willingly He opens His hands for the nails which fix Him in the position where He can be used to transmit the energy which has driven Him all the way. His outstretched arms act like paddles, sails, flails, wings, propellers, turbine-plates, any suitably shaped surfaces to catch power and transmit energy. The heart of the universe throbs and shudders as the mighty turbine accepts the pressure from above at full stretch, but another element enters the scene at the same time from below. The thud of the lead-weighted leather thong on quivering flesh, the stab of wreathed thorns pressed on the head, the laceration of spear in the side, the raucous hubbub of the morbid crowd, the tough indifference of soldiers on a routine execution job, callously throwing dice for His clothes, the pathetic helplessness of His mother and the one attendant disciple, the blasphemous railing of a criminal strung up by His side, all served to remind Him of the pressures seeking to destroy Him. All the momentum of Hell was let loose to crush His effectiveness in life or in death. His morale, His feelings, His ideas, His body, all were assaulted. The Songs of the Suffering Servant in Isaiah, especially the fifty-third chapter, possibly illuminated more than any other Scripture passage understanding of the mode by which Christ demonstrated with superb irony how this very destructive energy could be used to further the purpose of love. He uses the momentum of the attack to throw the attacker, by a kind of agapean judo (*agape* is the Greek word for distinctively Christian love). Satan's strategy backfires when faced with the Cross, and is utilized as a form of jet-propulsion for celestial activity. As the great flails assail and the great weals appear He remains immovable except to exude constructive love, praying for His assailants, absorbing the shock, the poison, the abuse, with the confidence that He can bear it in His nervous system, and cause it to rebound to the glory of His Father, and the wellbeing of all who will accept what He has to offer. Not even here will He exercise any compulsion but that of reality, truth, and love. No wonder the poet Francis Thompson can say of him as of the setting sun, 'Thou dost thy dying so triumphally.'

Successful issue

Indeed the dying was so triumphant, so perfectly in accord with the Father's will and the nature of creation and personality, that the forces of decay, corrupted by sin, could not hold Him down. Despite the extreme precautions of the authorities, the despair of His followers, (most usefully expressed by the women who went to embalm a dead body and guarantee decent treatment at the last for the only relic of their love and hope) the huge stone was rolled away, the body had disappeared, so that the embarrassed authorities were driven to the lame explanation that the friends of Jesus were body-snatchers: the exhibition of the embalmed corpse of Jesus would have cut the nerve of any historic movement except for a pathetic handful of incurable phantasy-thinkers. He appeared to a number of people with such vividness and actuality that the majority could not doubt His conquest of death and the whole scene was transformed out of all recognition. New possibilities, opened up, and, after some lurching, equilibrium was struck, and the destined transmitters of the energy were ready to be linked up to the main transmitter, and become sub-stations themselves, where the same power was available by the same means of which they themselves become a part. Wonderful works of constructive compassion appeared among them, and the fellowship of the Holy Spirit brought communication, community, communion, and a contagious capacity which has spread ever since. One of the simplest sentences to express the reality of what happened is in the New English Bible translation of Peter's words when he was miraculously released from prison and found himself in the cold night air in a familiar street: one can almost see him pinching himself as he says, like one waking out of what he thought was a dream, 'Now I know that it is true!'

Unsuspected possibilities

This attitude is the experimental attitude of faith which refuses to allow the limitations of logic, (which is a useful machine to serve the process of thinking, but is utterly dependent on the material fed into it, however expertly it may be handled) to bully it into restricting the possibilities latent in a world of dynamic energy and personal will and mind. Unsuspected potentialities lie everywhere around mankind. Man knows a temporary transcendence over nature in fact, quite apart from the Biblical injunction. The units of energy composing the human body are dynamically renewing tissue all the time to maintain vitality and integrity under adverse pressure. The student of the human mind and emotions, especially under the conditions of the test-bench of the psychiatric parlour, knows that intangible attitudes like faith, hope, and love can enlarge the possibilities in a situation and a group of persons beyond measurement or prediction. Time and space may well become man's servant rather than his master. In one sense what happened on Easter Day was to bring into the open what was always true, which was why Christ could go and preach to the spirits in prison (1 Peter 3:19), and as the Creed says, descend into Hades, the apparently shadowy abode of the dead. He brought life and immortality to light through the Gospel (cf. 2 Timothy 1:10) because they were there to be brought into full view. The possibilities always inherent and active, received their fullest demonstration in the resurrection of Christ, the new Adam, the firstborn of many brethren (including those born before His birth), the inaugurator of a new race and a new régime. Paul concludes his concentrated exposition of the resurrection as it affects mankind with words which echo in challenge and reverse the sad refrain of Ecclesiastes of old; 'Wherefore, my beloved brethren, be ye steadfast, immovable, always abounding in the work of the Lord inasmuch as ye know that your labour is *not in vain* in the Lord' (1 Corinthians 15:58). The next sentence lands the whole operation plumb in the middle of economics, the shop, the business, the budget, the exchequer, refugee and famine relief, practical caring generally, and politics: 'now concerning the collection' (16:1), which refers to the contributions made to help those in need. The remainder of that chapter is worth reading to see the matter of fact way this fabulously busy pioneer exemplified the pattern outlined in relation to a higgledy-piggledy mass of detail. Indeed, the whole of this letter is a classic instance of one working out and applying the whole project with no textbook to help him beyond the Old Testament, and no precedents, because last year's minutes did not exist. Two words emerged by degrees through a kind of survival by spiritual aptness—love and edification. The latter word literally comes from the world of building-construction. Eventually he puts the two words together in one sentence; they click, so to speak, into place: 'love edifies' (1 Corinthians 8:1). A Christian is one who links with this energy, and endeavours to the best of his opportunities to build people up into the community of constructive purpose. Circumstances may defeat the ideal forms in which he would prefer to exercise that energy, but there is no doubt where his bias lies, and the bent and spring of his total self. 'He may be dead, but he won't lie down.'

Handing over the works

On the Day of Pentecost the works, so to speak, were handed over to the workers. The same divine control, unalterable pattern, purpose, and power were available, but for the full efficiency of the job it was wise for Jesus to retire from the immediate scene as a palpable presence, even though His return for final accountancy was made very clear, with the added precaution of keeping the date a secret to save men from presumptive calculations. It was now possible for the followers to do greater works than the Master, and to be led into truths not yet revealed, though none of these would contradict the consistency of the necessary vital truths already given. Every generation, even decade, or year or two, has its fashions in clichés, (which spread like an epidemic of measles spots from conference to conference) and ours has heard much about involvement, contact, caring, communication. Every one of them is clearly set forth in the Gospel. What perhaps is not so well known is that the other cliché about man becoming fully independent and mature, able to take responsibility for his own life and the controlled exploitation of the world and its resources, is also clearly in Scripture. It was there in the beginning when man was told to subdue the earth, but it is also in the New Testament, closely allied with the very theme of sanctification. 'Now in putting everything in subjection to man, he left *nothing outside his control*. As it is, we do not see everything in subjection to him. But we see Jesus, who for a little while was made lower than the angels, crowned with glory and honour because of the suffering of death, so that by the grace of God he might taste death for every man. For it was fitting that he, for whom and by whom all things exist, in bringing many sons into glory, should make the *pioneer* of their salvation perfect through suffering. For he who sanctifies and those who are sanctified have all one origin' (Hebrews 2:8–10). Unless mankind learns the truth that his maturity and independence, which truly Christ gave to believers during His earthly life, is still set in a context of reverence for the holy, the righteous, and the loving nature and purpose of the one centre of rationality, beauty, and goodness in the ultimate personal mind and will, the very maturity will prove but disillusion, and the technical triumphs add up to triviality. The dimension of immeasurable values and powers remains a constant, transfusing the measurable, and true maturity includes the ability to cope with both at the same time. Herein lies the contribution of Christ to reconciling the supposed dichotomy between the two or more cultures, one based on literacy and the other on numeracy, values, and figures. From the beginning this theme has recurred as a dominant note in this series, and it is believed that only within some suitable form of the doctrine of entire sanctification is the truly reconciling idea and activity to be found. Calvary is the clue to

Parnassus (the mount of beauty), to Areopagus (the mount of philosophy and argument), to Mount Mathematica, as well as to Mount Sinai (the moral law), and to the mutual relationship of them all. Here all summits meet.

Side-effects

The awakening of conscious powers, both one's own latent possibilities and the infusion of new abilities, such as happened to the nth degree in the upstairs room at Pentecost, as also in the fear-closed room shortly after Easter Day, could not fail to produce excitement, and it is likely that in the initial stages of any new apprehension of the divine power there will be exuberance, sometimes expressing itself in uncritical and criticizable ways, and yet a necessary part of the proceedings, with a providential, if limited, importance in the total event. Christianity has a bias to overflowing; it is happier with the plus than the minus sign. If love divides, it does so only to multiply, as when Jesus broke the bread and fishes to feed the hungry multitude (John 6). Thus the tongues of flame, of divine fire, rested on each of those present, and also the ability to communicate with those usually divided by incapacity to understand each other's speech, together with the addition of glossolalia, an ecstatic (some would say, psychic) state. Paul, a trained and logical mind, knew the experience from the inside, and obviously found it of value as a private edification, though its public manifestations gave him considerable anxiety, as we learn from his first letter to the Christian Church in Corinth (chapter 14). It is not without significance that his concentration of teaching on the subject surrounds the summary of his teaching on Christian love, which was almost squeezed out of him by the very lack of balanced appreciation evinced by these immature Corinthian Christians on the relative value of love and tongue-speaking. Since the subject is frequently raised, indeed inevitably so when the Holy Spirit and the total work of grace is under consideration, it is necessary to comment on it. Neither the exclusive elevation of it to a compulsory mark of full Spirit-possession nor the scornful or timid banishment of it to the periphery, or further, of the Christian Church, does justice either to facts of history or experience.

Nowhere is it taught or urged in the apostolic preaching, though it is recognized on occasion as a valid sign of the presence of the Holy Spirit (Acts 10:46; 19:6). Where it is urged as an essential the doctrine and experience becomes divisive at a point where Christ does not divide, and such teaching must therefore be judged inadequate. In fact in such hands it tends to develop techniques for ensuring artificially the production of the desired symptom of excitement, with a premium on a routine which becomes as monotonous and stunting to the critical faculties as any mechanical ritual. Equally, where conventional religion reigns, there is a stunting of the emotional nature which is at least as harmful as its opposite, if not more so. Lack of feeling is a sure sign of death. The main point to grasp is that the total work in the revelatory deeds of the Gospel became totally available to believers, in, through, and by the Holy Spirit, as insight, power, and guidance, with the generated energy pulsating through their fellowship into the world beyond.

The method exposed

To profit fully by the energy generated it is not enough to examine the works from the outside; it is necessary and possible to get inside and see the process from within. Only so can the mind and method of the designer and operator be truly understood so that effective cooperation may ensue. The design of the Cross stands out at first like a jagged tooth or a sore thumb. Christian theology owes a great deal of its initial impulse to the need to rationalize the apparent absurdity, scandal, and embarrassment of so shockingly impossible a means of publicity and propoganda according to established associations. Beware of all belittlers of theology, the attempt to understand the workings of God's methodical mind. He has deliberately exposed His method to those with eyes to see, though each generation has to interpret it in terms which release its energy as and when required. The one caveat is that in the enthusiasm to be relevant the Church must distinguish between relating its message to contemporary thought and practice, and adapting it thereto. Certainly the message and the power must be related to the situation, but the Gospel and not the situation

134

is the permanent and dominating factor, so any adjustment is primarily of the situation to the Gospel, not the Gospel to the situation. In other words the final environment to which adjustment is made satisfactorily, if damage is not to follow, is the Gospel, and not the situation, which inevitably changes. Trying to keep up with the fashions of this world, in thought as well as adornment, must surely be one of the most exhausting pastimes. One grimly amusing irony is to see the Church throw overboard some doctrine to which contemporary allergy is allegedly prone, only to find it fished out and served up with fresh parsley in reduced and secular form. The deceitful heart reappeared with Freud, and predestination with George Bernard Shaw and the determinists generally. Entire sanctification means that the given Christian message is treated with supreme reverence, subjected to the ablest and most sincere examination, and demonstrated as capable of exerting itself in relation to whatever changing circumstances may arise.

Mechanism of transference

The mechanism, so far as such analogies are adequate to personal and communal processes, of salvation in its practical fullness of effect is set forth in the Suffering Servant strands of the Second Isaiah. The extraordinary similarity between that behaviour and the personal relations involved in psychotherapeutic treatment is dealt with in another work entitled *How the Cross Saves*. It is important to note the limits of that theme, which deals largely with the subjective processes involved in both doctor and patient, and the curative relationship between them. There is no suggestion that such a description is a psychological substitute for the theology of the Cross, or an explaining away of the mystery of God's saving action. The purpose is practical—to see *how* the theology works out so that man may fully profit by the work. The question still remains, and indeed is raised by the very practical consideration itself, as to why God did what He did in the way He did. The theology is primarily the why, and secondarily the how, of the operation. Psychology is primarily the how, and only secondarily raises the question of why, though neither can be totally divorced from the other. The centre of the work, and

K

the most tricky part of the process fraught with the greatest possibilities of success or failure, is the transference of the patient to the doctor, and the consequent retransference from the doctor to whatever worthy purpose is most adequate to maintain health. This transference psychologically is the equivalent of substitution theologically. The longsuffering healer in both cases bears the penal consequences of the sufferer's state.

The distinction should be recalled between penalty and punishment. True punishment contains the element of deserving, but the whole significance of this pivotal moment is that the one bearing the shame and 'scoffing rude' is utterly undeserving of such treatment; indeed the reverse is true; he should be receiving grateful reward. The hope of such suffering, creative love, in its trustful obedience to a higher will, conceived as absolute, is to outweary all wrath and contention, as James Nayler the Quaker put it in his last will and testament, and to create a rebound of positive health. Love ousts hate and substitutes itself, begets faith and the confidence which replaces fear, and makes voluntary obedience to the correct will feasible. The process includes not only unresentful acceptance of undeserved buffetting, but also the positive response of intercession for the transgressors, in word and deed (1 Peter 2:19–25; Isaiah 53). Such intermediary prayer is the heart of the matter, for there the healer makes and maintains contact with the source of energy and direction, the Father's good pleasure or beneficial sovereign will. Bruising is intricately bound up with the process. The pentecostal power and pattern is revealed in passion, pain, and prayer. The Holy Spirit is released in fulness in this central moment, and continuously acts as the mode of Christ's presence in the Church, illuminating and applying Christ's finished work. The Spirit is the Paraclete, the one called alongside to help as the strong standby in interpretation, encouragement, and in competently thoroughgoing friendship to the uttermost limit. If human parents, with all their shortcomings, give good gifts to the children, 'how much more shall your heavenly father give the Holy Spirit to them that ask him?' (Luke 11:13).

The place of passion

One essential element in this energy-producing work is passion. It is not accidental that the death of Jesus and its attendant circumstances are commonly known as His passion. A particularly helpful comment appeared from the pen of Roger Lloyd in the *Guardian* of 30 March, 1961. 'Passion is made up of personal intensities, woven into a single-minded and exclusive concentration of potent desire upon one person or one cause . . . What is essential is the sense of being driven, the concentration of every resource of personality, and the numinous element of the ultimately mysterious . . . Jesus is wholly concentrated on the flawless doing of the whole of God's terrible will, and is driven by His compulsive sense of the inexorable determinism of "the Scriptures". Mystery is woven into the heart of every incident, the theological mystery of the atonement and its universal need, the human mystery of His own quailing body which cries "Take this cup away", protests "My God, why hast thou forsaken me?" and adds, "Nevertheless, not my will but thine". There is indeed no actor in that dark scene who is entirely his own master. All are gripped by forces stronger than themselves; and this in itself is the indelible mark of authentic passion in whatever field of life it appears, and over which it is always dominant. Passion of any genuine kind is the most intense of all human experiences. Because it is something which happens to human persons, and is inconceivable apart from them, the underlining of personality is one of its invariable achievements . . . The four reasons for His death which He gave himself were that the Scripture should be fulfilled, that human sin might be remedied by forgiveness, that men should be raised to eternal life, and that He might "enter His glory". Authentic passion is always crammed with achievement since it is its condition. But as a matter of verifiable history no passion has ever been as potent as this one, and all its values are there to refresh us.'

The place of pain

Such passion must issue in pain as well as pleasure. 'Behold and see if there be any sorrow like unto my sorrow' (Lamentations 1:12), 'He was a man of sorrows (or pain) and acquainted with grief (or sickness)' (Isaiah 53:3), but this experience was not accidental: 'Surely he hath borne our griefs, and carried our sorrows' (v. 4), and He knew the reason: He was making himself an offering for sin; 'he bore the sin of many . . .' (vv. 10-12). Does anyone know a saint who has not suffered? In some sense the painful experiences of life are an essential ingredient in the experience of sanctity. Robert Browning wrote a few years after the death of his wife Elisabeth Barrett that 'the general impression of the past is as if it had been pain. I would not live it over again, not one day of it. Yet all that seems my real life—and before and after, nothing at all: I look back on all my life when I look there and life is painful. I always think of this when I read the Odyssey—Homer makes the surviving Greeks, whenever they refer to Troy, just say of it, "at Troy, where the Greeks suffered so". *Yet all their life was in that ten years at Troy.*' A slightly different angle on the same theme is shown by Mrs Josephine Butler, whose name is linked with her pioneer work among women who had been driven to the lengths of selling their bodies. Few know the origin of her concern to seek out human need. Her little daughter Eva leaned out too far over a balustrade to welcome her parents returning from a party, and fell to her death at their feet. This never-to-be-forgotten scene never left her. 'Would to God I had died that death for her!' was the almost Scriptural cry wrung from her heart. The family moved from Cheltenham to Liverpool, and there her life's work began. 'Who can write the rationale of sorrow? And who can explain its mysteries, its apparent inconsistencies and unreasonableness? I suffered much during the first months in our new home. Music, art, reading, all failed as resources to alleviate or to interest. I became possessed with an irresistible desire to go forth and find some pain keener than my own—to meet with people more unhappy than myself . . . I had no clear idea beyond that, no plan for helping others; my sole wish was to plunge into the heart of some human misery, and say to the afflicted people, "I understand. I too have suffered." It was not difficult to find misery in Liverpool.'

Place of identification

Jesus is able to help because He has been where mankind is. Ezekiel was more effective when he could say, 'in the evening my wife died, . . . and I sat where they sat' (Ezekiel 24:18, et al.). How often the comment is heard, 'You know; you've been through it.' There is what has been called a residence requirement. Tohoyiko Kagawa and Albert Schweitzer are outstanding examples. Frank Crossley of the Manchester engineering firm, sold his house in Altrincham and came to live in Ancoats, Manchester, amidst his work-people. On another occasion he came off the magistrate's bench to stand in the dock with a Salvation Army lassie. The artist constantly seeks to identify himself with those for whom he is doing his work. He must live intensively, imaginatively within the material medium of expression to master its properties and possibilities. This involves restrictions and anguish in some measure, and certainly when spoiled human nature is the medium to be shaped in beauty.

Reciprocal interchange

The agony includes receiving as well as giving. Such communication is never a one-way process. The identification includes for Jesus taking to heaven a human brow. The superior must be willing to receive from the inferior. Beneficiaries must be allowed the dignity of bestowal. God rejects none of the varying gifts His children bring Him, including the myrrh of grief, the wormwood and the gall. There is thus a reciprocal interchange, whereby Paul can make the apparently blasphemous claim to 'make up that which is lacking in the afflictions of Christ' (Colossians 1:24). In one sense there can be no deficiency in the finished work of Christ on the Cross, but part of the energy He uses is mankind's contribution of already existing suffering. Thus Philip J. Fisher prayed, 'O Thou who didst gather up into Thyself on Calvary the sorrow of all the world, and whose heart was pierced with many deadly spears, to Thee I offer my little gift of pain, that united to Thy redemptive suffering, it may be sanctified for the healing of the wounds of men.'

Place of prayer

Such prayer reminds that priestly prayer, mediating meditation, which is a primal link from man's side, begins on God's side. The prayer life of Jesus is largely private. His frequent practice was noted in the Gospels, but only a handful of glimpses are granted of the inner converse where the Father and the Son transacted business together. The pulsing heart of the Father was in the Son and vice versa. The innermost dynamo and transformer was the dialogue of conversation. 'The prayer that reached heaven began there, when Christ went forth. It began when God turned to beseech us in Christ —in the appealing Lamb slain before the foundation of the world. The Spirit went out with power and function in it to return with our soul . . . Herein is prayer, not that we prayed Him, but that he first prayed us, in giving us His Son to be a propitiation for us. The heart of the atonement is prayer— Christ's great self-offering to God in the Eternal Spirit. The whole rhythm of Christ's soul, so to say, was the Godhead going out and returning on itself.' (P. T. Forsyth, *The Soul of Prayer*, p. 15). Here is the systole and diastole of the heartbeat of the universe at its personal summit. The top level talks continued in the heart of Jesus, which stopped only to identify Himself with death itself, and recurred by the sheer power of incorruptible holiness.

Key to the process

Our Lord took the lid off hell and opened the door in heaven, which none but He can open or shut. The Cross is the key by which the mystery of heaven and earth, in the book sealed with seven seals, is opened. Each seal broken increases the thunderous approval of the souls in the eternal presence, but when the final seal was slit 'there was silence in heaven for the space of half an hour' (Revelation 8 : 1), unforgettable and indelible, as the secrets of God's engineering were laid bare for Tom, Dick, and Harry to profit withal. The unaided human reaction of abhorrence and contempt in relation to the Cross was turned into compassionate concern by a radical reversal of estimate, and 'the stone which the builders rejected became the head of the corner', (one of the favourite quotations from the Old Testament in the New). All the leverage of God was exercised on the Cross of Christ, the fulcrum, lever, tool, machine and engine where the energy is generated, and still flows.

Pattern of saving act from within

To conclude, there is offered a suggested method of understanding the pattern of the saving act from within, so that the believer may both grasp and be grasped by that pattern. Each of the sentences spoken by Jesus on the Cross might be considered as the words of a man actually engaged in the critical and decisive moments of his life's work, and therefore a kind of running commentary on the most significant points as he saw them at the time. The first is 'Father, forgive them for they know not what they do' (Luke 23:34). Here is a positive outgoing prayer of wholehearted forgiveness from the perspective of God, understood as Father in the Biblical sense, perceiving the inward ignorance even of the crudest and the most sophisticated would-be murderers of God, thereby turning a destructive deed into a potentially constructive force.

Reconstruction

The second saying runs, 'Truly, I say to you, today you shall be with me in Paradise' (Luke 23:43). Here is a specific offer and promise of reconstruction to a disintegrating personality. Paradise is the immediate presence of the King, accessible only to His Son, and therefore a coveted and morale-boosting privilege. The negative forces have been held and repelled on the one hand, and on the other the positive forces have been consciously engaged for particular need.

Relationship possibilities

The third saying falls into two related parts: 'Woman, behold, your son! . . . Behold your mother!' (John 19:26–27). Mutual responsibilities of relationship, both by nature and friendship have their claims, and must be attended to, uniting those who, though intimately entwined with the saving person, cannot fully share the totality of surrender and effort. The claim for priority over natural ties Jesus makes in general, but such

141

extreme statements must not be treated as an excuse for evading such responsibilities.

Price of expenditure

The fourth saying is, 'I thirst!' The yearning of physical nature still remains, and there is no high-falutin' pretence of superiority to claims and pains of the human organism. Such sacrificial expenditure of suffering energy exacts its toll. Is it fanciful to catch overtones epitomizing the yearning to 'see the fruit of the travail of his soul and be satisfied' (Isaiah 53:11), in the words 'I thirst!'? (John 19:28.)

Abandonment

The fifth saying plumbs the depths. Here is the acrid taste of death as a spiritual as well as a physical phenomenon. The identification with need exhausts all resources and produces a sharing in the terrifying abyss of emptiness. It is true that the words come from the early part of Psalm 22, which ends on a note of triumph, and had strength remained with our Lord he may have reached those words, but the fact remains that he didn't, and the sharing of such an experience by the Son of God is one of the most powerful illustrations of identification and involvement, with an immense appeal to poor doubting humanity. Had it been the only or last word the effect would have been different, but there are two more.

Completion

The sixth word with triumph and relief cries, 'It is finished!' (John 19:30). The work is complete and the connexion made; the communicating line between heaven and earth, God and man, is satisfactorily through whatever divided. The cable is laid and the messages are passing freely from end to end. The two separating factors are sin and death, and of these sin is the worse. The work which breaks the hold of sin and establishes clearly the divine holiness is the power that rules the world, because it deals the death-blow at man's supreme, sapper of confidence, guilt, and because it opens the life-gate that all may go in. Here is the description and demonstration of the perfect work as God does it. The sense of accomplishment fortifies the soul, and the imminent cessation of effort summons the final gasp of all energy thrown in to cross the line to fulfilment.

Final commitment

The seventh and last word leaves nothing more to be said. 'Father, into thy hands I commit my spirit' (Luke 23:46). When all struggle at every level of existence has spent itself the fundamental conviction which has sustained all the way along reasserts itself. The final movement is abandonment to the upholding of the everlasting arms and hands. Trust and obedience have triumphed; holiness is established; love has outlasted all its enemies and remained true to itself; the leverage of hope and new life begins to move into action; the generating-plant exercises its power; energy flows forth; and 'faith works by love' (Galatians 5:6).

Imaginative sharing

By imaginative sharing in the energetic work from within, through the explanations of the One in the course of doing the work, mortals can both understand what is happening, how it is happening, and participate in the work, thereby taking up the Cross, partaking of the afflictions of Christ, being crucified with Christ, dying daily to self-will, denying themselves as their own master, and becoming workers together with God, filled with the Holy Spirit, agents of blessing, creation, and the furtherance of God's will, kingdom, power, and glory.

7 Conducting the operation

'I beseech you, therefore, brethren, by the mercies of God that ye present your bodies a living sacrifice, holy, acceptable unto the Lord, which is your reasonable service.' (Romans 12:1–2.)

'Come to him, to that living stone, rejected by men but in God's sight chosen and precious; and like living stones be yourselves built into a spiritual house, to be a holy priesthood, to offer spiritual sacrifices acceptable to God through Christ Jesus . . . But you are a chosen race, a royal priesthood, a holy nation, God's own people. . . .' (1 Peter 2:4, 5, 9.)

'Finally brethren, we beseech and exhort you in the Lord Jesus, that as you learned from us how you ought to live and to please God, just as you are doing, you do so more and more. For you know what instructions we gave you through the Lord Jesus. For this is the will of God, your sanctification . . . Rejoice always, pray constantly, give thanks in all circumstances; for this is the will of God for you. Do not quench the Spirit, do not despise prophesying, but test everything; hold fast to what is good, abstain from every form of evil.' (1 Thessalonians 4:1–3, 5:16–22.)

MOST of the main background points have been mentioned, though not by any means every conceivable item. Each deserves much fuller treatment, but there is need for an overall picture with a succinct survey of the principles, patterns and processes involved, always keeping an eye well fixed on the pioneer and completer of the work, the Lord Jesus Christ. Now arrives the constant question of the actual operation in progress. After the energy generated at the Cross, with the opening ceremony past, the initial excitement over, there remains the problem of maintenance, the day to day continuous production in the salvation business.

Continuing process

It is important to remember that the mechanical simile has its limitations. Men are not saved by the barrel-load acquired by a cleverly organized sweeping of the trawl-net. The process is more organic than mechanical, rather like an unfolding bud. A film of the unfolding process can be shown in slow or quick motion, and either way we are staggered by the perfection of each stage, adapted for achieving its main purpose. Whatever place is left for suddenness and drastic intervention there is always a process, usually before and certainly afterwards. Some of the greatest Christians have noted this fact. Samuel Rutherford, the Scottish saint, remarked, 'Alas, I think I shall die but minting and aiming to be a Christian . . . We go in at heaven's gate with our book in our hand, still learning.'

Patience with chores

Patience can hardly be stressed too much. 'Ye have need of patience' (Hebrews 10:36) or endurance, with ourselves and with God, as well as with other people. Oats in Lapland mature in a few weeks, but they do not yield the same nourishment as the wheat which takes six months to achieve fruition. Sown in a moment, cereals grow over months. All productive machinery requires endless patience to keep clean and oiled. Dirt, dark, ignorance and antiquity, cockiness and complacency alike hinder proper development. The familiar hymn, 'Take time to be holy; speak oft with Thy Lord,' is never irrelevant. One thing is certain: the patient endurance will be maintained by the same means with which it was begun. The operation is conducted to the same pattern and by the same power as has already been manifested in the energetic idea which found shape in the creation, the incarnation, the cross, and the resurrection, and came to full conscious life and effectiveness in the experience of the Holy Spirit. The text-book is in our hands, and the shop-floor of the Church exists for training and production. Whatever is done needs to be deliberate, regular, and frequent, not to say continuous. Central to our Lord's teaching are words like watch, pray, endure to the end. The largest proportion of any worthwhile job is hackwork, slogging along a rough road, staggering under a cross, ploughing through a sodden clay, going over much the same ground. An eminent doctor remarked, 'I get tired poking into people's ears, and looking down their throats and having them say "Ah".' As Edna St. Vincent Millay put it, 'Life goes on forever like the gnawing of a mouse.' Catholic masters of the life of prayer are very familiar with 'the dark night of the soul', and have learned to declare that aridity, or dryness, is fervour, precisely because God is loved under trying spiritual conditions and without thought of reward in ecstatic feelings. Since God's model on earth was a carpenter perhaps the simplest picture of the continuous patient process comes from the workplace where he learned his trade of dovetailing and construction in more senses than one. Phyllis Hartnoll has a poem entitled 'The Carpenter' which catches the necessary spirit of humble, obedient, trustful, meticulous persistence.

Silent at Joseph's side He stood,
And smoothed and trimmed the shapeless wood,
And with firm hand, assured and slow,
Drove in each nail with measured blow.

Absorbed, He planned a wooden cask,
Nor asked for any greater task,
Content to make, with humble tools,
Tables, and little children's stools.

Lord, give me careful hands to make
Such simple things as for Thy sake,
Happy within Thy house to dwell
If I may make one table well.

Linking mechanism

In order to ensure this maintenance work a sure connexion to the source of pattern and power is essential. So far as our theme is concerned the internal means of such connexion are faith, prayer, and discipline. Faith is the gripping link-word. The description given earlier in terms of an equation may usefully be repeated: faith equals evidence plus reason plus imagination plus fascination plus courage plus persistent experimentation. Faith is not contrasted with evidence, or reason or knowledge in Scripture, but only with sight. Faith incorporates evidence, reason and all the other elements mentioned, and transcends all. Faith is an indispensible organ of knowledge; no kind of knowledge can exist without trust in man's powers of observation, measurement, investigation, analysis, reasoning by deduction or induction as seems most appropriate to any given situation. There is no such phenomenon as an unbeliever. Men are distinguished by the object of their faith, which represents finally their assessment of the ruling power when the whole sum of existence and creation is totted up.

One of the precisest illustrations of the basic faith described in the eleventh chapter of the letter to the Hebrews is the Kon-tiki expedition, undertaken and recorded by the Norwegian Thor Heyerdahl. He was an archaeologist puzzling over the similarity of culture between the South Sea Islands and ancient South America. One evening he was semi-consciously relaxing, listening to the roar of the breakers and the crooning of ancient legends by an old native. Suddenly his wife asked why the breakers came only on the east side of the island. With equal suddenness he connected the ancient legends of the godlike figures who came over the sea on rafts with the prevailing winds and currents. In a flash he saw how it was possible for men to come across these vast oceanic miles; the vision inspired years of tedious and oft-frustrated search for every conceivable type of evidence. At long last, after much derision or apathy from the experts, he decided to make the balsa-wood raft to the documentary specifications he had discovered. A whole saga covers the attempt to obtain the materials and assemble the craft, but he trusted and obeyed even down to details he

147

could not understand. After many adventures on the surface of the sea, he and his few devoted companions arrived at journey's end. Even then, when his little radio tapped out the message of arrival he was not believed. Many of the finer points of faith are in the details of the story, but it was this practical kind of faith by which the mighty men and women of early days in the history of God's people achieved their glorious contribution to the furtherance of God's kingdom. 'This is the victory which overcometh the world, even our faith' (1 John 5:4).

Source of faith

This attitude, when addressed to persons, is better summed up as trust or confidence. As people are subtler material than things or processes, the form of faith must also be subtler, more flexible and elusive, yet the same ingredients are present. In essence faith in a person and his purposes, patterns, and powers, means that he is considered genuine, dependable, loyal, able, trained, reliable, jannock. Faith in Jesus Christ means that He is considered to be as genuine as God is genuine, dependable, able, and willing to effect the will and rule of His heavenly Father. In particular it means aligning the self with His purposes, shaping life to His pattern, accepting His promised power. In so far as self-knowledge, illuminated and measured by the personality, teaching, example of Jesus, arouses a sense of insufficiency and resistance, there is a sense of sin and guilt, which is the greatest hindrance to whole-hearted cooperation and effective relationship. The work of Christ is directed to the total salvation of mankind, but this particular condition of guilt cannot be by-passed or belittled. Therefore Christ's most immediate and basic work is salvation from sin and guilt, as well as their concomitant perversions of character, emotion, mind, will, personality, and physique, both individual and corporate. On the Cross the testing-point of this work is revealed to its fullest extent.

O love of God! O sin of man!
In this dread act your strength is tried;
And victory remains with love:
For He, our Lord, is crucified.

In contemporary vernacular the Cross is the crunch, where and when all the destructive weight strikes with maximum impact. Could the faintest speck of hate, resentment, distrust, disobedience, have been present in Christ at that moment the coldly malign fury of Satan would have scalpeled it out, and all the pressure of hell would have frayed it through and split it open. So much of one piece was our Lord, with Himself and His Father, like the seamless robe woven throughout, that none of His accusers could find any fault in Him beyond some apparent breach of their own misconceived standards. Here was holiness supreme, and even the undermining disillusion of death likewise proved powerless. Guilt is harder to cure than disease and death. He who masters guilt masters mankind's worst tyrant. The reversion of the world is his. And Christ did it without deviation from the strict path of justice or the vindication of holiness in all legitimate forms. Therefore He is to be trusted; He bears the weight of human sin, despair, grief, guilt, hope, faith, anxiety, and love. Salvation and redemption are therefore by faith in Jesus, both as justification, regeneration, and as sanctification, full, free, and entire.

Union with Christ

The mere imagined impossibility of such a consummation amidst the tangled jungle of human motives, relationships, situations, the massive historical movements and tumultuous heavings of nature, does not settle the matter. Grace and faith together operate a dimension of possibility in, through, and beyond the measurable world of prediction and the corrupt fatigue of cynicism. Such doctrine does not deny the frequency of failure or inadequacy, or the statistical probability of sin abounding, but it does give elbow-room for manoeuvre, and a penumbra of possibility which would never be revealed apart from grace and faith; to that extent the world would be infinitely poorer without it, and hope and love, frail windflowers, would lead an infinitely more precarious existence. When Harold Abrahams, one-time world champion sprinter, was asked whether his secret was not keeping his eye on the winning-tape, he replied, 'No; ten yards beyond!' Men are meant to be more than conquerors, over-overcoming (Romans

8:37). One of Paul's favourite prefixes is hyper-, i.e. above, over, transcending. Holiness in its entirety, therefore, entire sanctification is by faith in Jesus, as is perfect love, maturity, wholeness, completeness, fulness of the Spirit, blessing, and any other term in the whole dictionary of the subject. The life, the spirit, the person, the work of Jesus Christ, who is the life, spirit, person, and work of God made flesh, is transferred to believers, and exists and operates therein by and as the Holy Spirit. The words of a Ranter hymn express the thought in a fresh and direct manner.

My soul is now united to Christ the living vine;
His grace I once had slighted, but now I feel Him mine:
I was to God a stranger till Jesus took me in;
He freed my soul from danger, and pardon'd all my sin.

Soon as my all I ventured on the atoning blood,
The Holy Spirit entered, and I was born of God;
My sins are all forgiven, I feel His blood applied,
And I shall go to heaven, if I in Christ abide.

By floods and flames surrounded, I still my way pursue,
Nor shall I be confounded, with glory in my view;
Still Christ is my salvation—what can I covet more?
I fear no condemnation, my Father's wrath is o'er.

Faith, grace, and history

To conduct the operation successfully the attitude and relationship of faith in Jesus Christ, crucified and risen, applied continuously by the power of the Holy Spirit, is an essential prerequisite. All the way through it is imperative to recall that such faith is itself a response to what has already been done by grace in and through the historic work of Christ, 'whom, not having seen ye love; on whom, though now ye see him not, yet believing, ye rejoice with joy unspeakable and full of glory' (1 Peter 1:8). For such a relationship to be adequate, satisfying, perpetual, it is essential to keep reading the Scriptures, and especially to meditate on the Gospels where we see Jesus with sufficient fulness and detail to 'know whom we have believed' (2 Timothy 1:12). It is quite unnecessary to

150

be much moved by alarmists who assert that subsequent generations cannot know the Jesus of history. Either our faith is built on sand (and therefore doomed to be revealed as fantasy in the day of reckoning) or the dynamically dramatic pictures of Jesus, seen through four pairs of diverse but skilled eyes, are substantially accurate. He was either historically the sort of person we read about there, or there is no criterion to reassemble the flotsam and jetsam of the wreckage left over, apart from human whims and estimates, which in the nature of the case are biassed, conditioned by time and place, and woefully capricious and unreliable. To have faith in Jesus is to put confidence in His picture, pattern, purpose, power, as revealed in Scripture, and to act thereon, using all available resources he suggests. Throughout there is reciprocity, conversation, even argument, trial and error, pardon, power, and the full range of personal and corporate relationship.

Love and controversial social situations

The exact expression of this relationship in the ever-changing circumstances of human life will face us with many head-aching, heart-searching, and will-challenging decisions, and faith in Christ does not exempt man from doing his homework. Especially in an increasingly complex and unified mass mobile society, individual responsibility seems enormously circum-scribed and traditional approaches to situations often irrelevant. One urgent aspect of holiness is therefore the sober investigation by trained minds in close conjunction with many not so highly trained (though not by any means deficient in common sense and experience, at the greatest possible variety of levels of responsibility) of the actual facts, influences, processes at work in the world seen in the light of Christ's revelation. Especially is this required where Christians are involved in controversial social situations. How does love work out where direct personal relationship with everybody concerned becomes literally impossible? The simplest answer in principle is that true justice is the public form of holy love, but the specific expression still remains to be discovered in many cases. Thus every legitimate expertise is required to be laid on the altar in cooperative study, teaching, and service.

L

Coping with the impossible

The Gospels themselves provide an illustration of the principles of approach to the apparently impossible situation in the one miracle story (apart from the Resurrection, which is always treated in a class by itself) to be found in all four Gospels, the feeding of the five thousand. Before our Lord called for supernatural resources He took five steps which anyone could have taken had the thought occurred. The situation underlined the unwieldy structure of the problem, far from shops, late in the day, short of money. The disciples react in the obvious way by suggesting dispersal. Our Lord first demands facing the problem: 'Feed them; assume the responsibility.' Second He requires examination of resources: 'How many loaves have you? Go and see.' With a mixture of cool science seeking numerical accuracy, and of civil-service precise recording of statistical accuracy, He issues a form with a dotted line for reply. Thirdly He controls the problem by splitting the people into groups with aisles between, and making them sit down: a sitting crowd cannot crush. Fourthly He utilizes the available personnel, and restores morale by giving each a portion of responsibility and resource. Fifthly He divides the pitifully inadequate resources in such a way as to multiply them. Only then does He give thanks and pray for the unpredictable and immeasurable supplies beyond calculation.

Such an analysis does not belittle the worship-inspiring deed of supernatural power, but outlines starkly the conditional steps open to all who desire to exercise faith in apparently impossible circumstances. When dealing with the depths of the personality and its outworking in complex social circumstances the matter is not so clear-cut in handling, but the principles are the same. First, face the responsibility in terms of God's will, even your sanctification. Second, examine the resources, including natural goodness and every human aid to the improvement of human nature and society. Third, break down the problem, the self, the social milieu; separate into sections for accessibility; bring the surging mass to a sitting posture under control. Fourth, give the disillusioned and responsibility-evading self into the command of the Lord, even where there seem to be several selves. Let the Lord divide the resources, breaking up their present inadequate and grotesquely misshapen adherence to each other (cf. Legion), resorting, and reassembling under a unified command. There is still a miracle of divine grace required, but the factors involved in the situation are organized and in position and condition to be used. When, as often though not invariably happens, there are twelve basketsful left over, the Lord expects us to gather and use the spares. Divine bounty does not excuse waste. Faith, in this practical, personal, persistent sense, is the primary necessity for conducting the operation so far as human beings are concerned.

Power of prayer

The next great connecting link is prayer. Indeed it is inseparable from faith. Faith is the doing aspect of the activity, prayer the speaking aspect. In any essentially personal relationship, which includes moulding and directing, there is bound to be a deal of talk. Co-workers discuss the job in hand, and keep in repair their friendship for each other. Recall the description offered earlier of prayer as a mutually trustful conversation, focusing the total relationship in verbally framed form, which includes all potential items of personal response. Prayer is one essential means by which we get to know our colleague's mind. In so far as he is a very senior colleague he has to pray for us and within us with unutterable groanings to enable us to ask and converse effectively. His Spirit intercedes not only with us and for us, but also within us and through us. The partners get to know each other better this way. In the nature of the case specific answers cannot and ought not to be predicted or mechanically determined. Prayer enlarges the orbit of operations, and maintains that decompression chamber of the personality which ensures the possibility of communication between two pressure systems, heaven and earth, whereby the resources of each are available for the other. As a practical suggestion F. B. Meyer's accidentally discovered emergency prayer-formula is worth consideration. When once in danger of losing his temper before a noisy group of children, Meyer spontaneously prayed, 'Thy patience, Lord'. The effect was marvellous. Thereafter in emergency he used the formula, 'Thy . . . , Lord', inserting the appropriate characteristic

required. During my Mother's last illness my Father typed out
and sent to her the following verse, which he found in her diary
after she died:

> *There is an eye that never sleeps when fade the beams of*
> *   light;*
> *There is an ear that never shuts when fall the shades of night;*
> *There is an arm that never tires when earthly aids give way;*
> *There is a love which never dies when earthly loves decay.*

When this verse was published once in *Joyful News* some years
ago, a veteran Cliff College tutor, universally recognized as
incarnating the spirit of sanctification in its most natural and
human form, George Allen, wrote to give the name of the
author, J. A. Wallace, and its source in the *Methodist Sunday
School Hymn Book* with which he grew up in the 1870s. He
added two more verses which had been a standby to him
many times since, which fit in aptly at this point.

> *But there's a power which man can wield, when mortal aid*
> *   is vain,*
> *That eye, that arm, that love to reach, that listening ear to*
> *   gain.*
> *That power is prayer; which soars on high, through Jesus to*
> *   the throne,*
> *And moves the hand which moves the world, to bring salva-*
> *   tion down.*

Prayer, faith, holiness and the kingdom

Prayer is the vocal and articulate exercise of faith, as faith
is the practical expression of our prayer at grips with life.
Holiness is God's creating, judging, saving power at work,
and its manifestation is His kingdom. Faith and prayer are
essential constituents of man's free response, without which a
fully conscious, cooperative, and effective citizenship is not
possible. 'God's Kingdom . . . cannot come without our praying
. . . because its coming is the prayerful frame of soul. So . . .
with God's freedom. It is absolute. But it reckons on ours. Our
prayer does not force His hand; it answers His freedom in
kind' (P. T. Forsyth, *The Soul of Prayer*, p. 96). 'It is not a

spiritual exercise merely, but in its maturity it is a cause acting on the course of God's world . . . Nothing can alter God's . . . large will and final purpose—our racial blessing . . . But for that will He is an infinite opportunist . . . His *intentions* are amenable to us if His *will* is changeless . . . The effect of prayer which admits God into the recesses of the soul is to destroy that spiritual density, not to say stupidity, which made our religion cheery and vigorous because it knew no better, and which was the condition of getting many obvious things done, and producing palpable effect on the order of the day. There are fervent prayers which, by making people feel good, may do no more than foster the delusion that natural vigour or robust religion, when flushed enough, can do the work of the Kingdom of God' (ibid. pp. 125, 127, 24). 'The worst sin is prayerlessness. Overt sin, or crime, or the glaring inconsistencies which often surprise us in Christian people are the effect of this, or its punishment . . . The history of the saints shows how often their lapses were the fruit and nemesis of slackness or neglect in prayer . . . Not to want to pray then is the sin behind sin . . . Prayer is the assimilation of a holy God's moral strength . . . The prayerless spirit saps a people's moral strength because it blunts their thought and conviction of the Holy . . . The root of all deadly heresy is prayerlessness' (ibid. pp. 9–11, 35).

Elementary prayer advice

In order to avoid mere general exhortation there follow relevant portions of the basic guidance in the use of private prayer-time given to Cliff College students.

Over the centuries a variety of schemes for prayer have been worked out, and it is useful to examine as many as possible, but without a sense of rush. Hurry is the death of prayer. People differ in circumstance and temperament, and it is not God's purpose to mass-produce standardized models of sanctity. At the same time it is far too easy for us to make our own temperamental tastes the standard. We have to work out our own salvation, because God is working in us. We shall therefore be willing to experiment. At different stages of life we shall probably be compelled to use different approaches, thus preventing staleness and over-familiarity, two great enemies of effective Christian living. These suggestions now made are intended as preliminary guidance to use most profitably the time of prayer and to avoid needless floundering. There will be certainly a good deal of feeling the way by trial and error, but this is part of life; we cannot live entirely on anyone else's direction, just as we cannot live entirely on our own.

Conversation

In any activity the first point to establish is what we are trying to achieve. In relation to God, our aim is to know, love, and serve Him to the best of our ability. The knowledge of the Christian God is personal, and involves direct relation-ships which require intelligible and two-way conversation. The conversation can take at least two forms. There is the kind of dialogue which may break out at any time when we are engaged together in work with somebody else, though always governed by a proper respect on our part for the rank and responsibility of the person we are working for. Ejaculatory prayer is a familiar example of this kind of conversation.

Advantage of routine

There is also more formal consultation. A meeting or interview is set for a particular time and place, and there is an agenda to work through with decisions to be made which must be carried into effect. The Quiet Time is an essential element in the second of these forms. It will therefore have an element of order about it which experience shows to be usually the most effective method of doing what is necessary. It is not necessarily appropriate to have all the items every day. Some may be better dealt with weekly or monthly. Life is full of emergencies which disturb the set order, but we are more likely to be able to cope with the sudden demand if all our other affairs are under control, and we shall also recover more quickly if we have a set pattern which requires attention when the emergency has passed.

Otherwise we lurch from crisis to crisis—a nerve-wracking experience—and never really achieve anything positive. Religion becomes a series of emergency measures.

Getting to know God

How do we set about achieving our object? We must obviously believe in God as made known in Jesus Christ. 'He that cometh to God must believe that He is, and that He is a rewarder of them that diligently seek Him' (Hebrews 11:6). The shape of prayer will be determined by the One with whom we are conversing. The Bible tells us what He is like. God is the Supreme Ruler of the Universe in all its aspects, physical and spiritual. He is Creator, Judge, King, Father. Those are the main characteristics of God, though the picture can and must be seen in much more detail.

Posture in prayer

We must adopt a proper attitude of reverence, whatever else. 'The fear (or awe) of the Lord is the beginning of wisdom' (Psalm 111:10; Proverbs 9:10). Reverence is shown outwardly by a physical posture. Kneeling represents humility and obeisance. Standing represents respect and readiness for service. Lying flat on the face represents complete surrender of any kind of resistance, and complete abandon (but this is not to be recommended for reasonably self-controlled persons. Do not be alarmed or contemptuous if such physical prostration is manifested during times of religious excitement). Lying or sitting (except at a desk or for purposes of concentration, recording, or work) are the least fitting postures.

Names of God

We meditate on (i.e. consider attentively) the nature and authority of the One we are approaching, and concentrate on what He has done to give us this opportunity. For this purpose we gather descriptions of God from Scripture, and ascriptions of praise to Him. It is useful to build up one's own collection of prayers from Scripture. Use a notebook, preferably strong loose-leaf of good quality paper, and not too large to carry around if necessary.

Agenda of prayer

We must face God directly. Adoration is the right beginning, and the next two obvious responses are thanksgiving
and penitence, including confession. If anything needs
putting right, and can reasonably be done without harming
anybody else, restitution should be made. The centre of
prayer then becomes intercession and petition, the first
praying for others, the second for oneself and immediate
concerns. These prayers will include the search for guidance.
Thereafter acts of trust and dedication are required, preparing for acts of obedience. A period of mental silence is
helpful. All the way through God is talking with us, but it
is wise to still the clamour of our own noisy spirits to
concentrate on listening.

Material of prayer

A framework or agenda has been suggested. Now we
must look more carefully at material to use, which is
inexhaustible. To survey the whole warehouse is impossible,
and in any case would be overwhelming. Only a com-
paratively few sections can be opened up.

Praying from the Bible

The foremost source is the Bible. The best praying takes
wing from the base of Holy Scripture. Begin with the mighty
assertions and promises of God. Deal first-hand with God in
Christ through His Word. Prayer is intelligible and verbally
formulated response to what God has already done. The
Bible is grist for the mill, the raw material of the devotional
life.

Spiritual classics

There is the treasury of Christian devotional writing.
Christians for nearly twenty centuries have written prayers
and diaries of their spiritual pilgrimage. It is immensely
helpful to familiarize oneself with what others have
experienced. One of the most valuable uses of private
prayer-time is to read great spiritual classics, and to include
some belonging to other traditions than one's own.

158

List of books

St Augustine's *Confessions*, Brother Lawrence's *Practice of the Presence of God*, Samuel Rutherford's *Letters*, Bunyan's *Pilgrim's Progress*, William Law's *Serious Call to a Devout and Holy Life*, George Fox's *Journal*, Philip Doddridge's *Rise and Progress of Religion in the Soul* ought to be compulsory reading. The great Christian mystics could also be used—Tauler, St John of the Cross, Madame Guyon, Richard Rolle of Hampole are a few.

Daily readings

Books of daily readings and prayers can be used from time to time to maintain freshness and to keep us out of a rut. One of the masters here is Harry Emerson Fosdick with *The Manhood of the Master, The Meaning of Prayer, The Meaning of Faith, The Meaning of Service*. These latter have the subject divided up into weekly sections, each subdivided into days, with comment and suggested prayer. Each week there is an extended summary and amplification of the previous day's reading. Dr E. Stanley Jones has a series of books for daily meditation of which *The Way* is useful to begin with. Oswald Chambers's *My Utmost for His Highest* is a well-tried series of daily readings. Other helps are *Daily Light, A Devotional Diary,* (J. H. Oldham), *A Diary of Private Prayer* (J. Baillie).

Hymns as prayers

The hymnbook is an obvious source. Most hymns lend themselves to use as prayers. The very size of the *Methodist Hymnbook* guarantees a wide range of subject. *Divine Worship* suggests a form for adapting hymns as prayers.

Poetry and drama

Literature provides another contribution, particularly poetry. Great Britain has a great store of devotional poetry on a high level. John Donne, George Herbert, Henry Vaughan, and Thomas Traherne are four to begin with. The religious drama of our own day has much valuable material.

Daily press

The daily paper reminds us constantly of subjects for prayer. We are surrounded by news which moves the heart and mind towards divine resource for human need.

Get to the point

Avoid the sentimental, the trivial, the mush of popular religious devotion. Keep prayer strong, lithe, and clean. Avoid florid language or elaborate metaphors. Get to the point.

Daily discipline

The third link-word to connect the teaching and the power to people and situations in the day-to-day routine is discipline, sometimes known as the daily walk. The Christian is not kept going merely by an initial momentum which becomes a kind of perpetual motion. The Christian life, like any other kind of life in this world, partakes of the characteristics of space and time, which means variability and wear and tear. There is a law of undulation operating throughout the total range of human experience. Part of the hygiene of holiness is to learn how to handle the high and low hours, both in their temptations and their opportunities. Without spending space on these matters in detail it may be noted that a careful study of the Mount of Transfiguration and of Elijah under the juniper tree provides the necessary guidance. At whatever extreme of emotion or circumstance, however, and at all conceivable stages in between, there is a common secret of effectiveness: our Lord exhorted his followers to take up their cross daily and follow him. In other words the believer is to be crucified with Christ and die daily, which is not meant to be some hysterical self-flagellation or morbid preoccupation with death, but accustoming the total self to the Christian pattern-reaction. The instinctive attitudes which revolve around self-interest, our own or our own group's, must be taught and conditioned all the time to lay down their lives in the interests of the Kingdom of God, and rise again to a different kind of life, still the same instincts but redirected and Christ-controlled. A continuous adaptation of the nervous system to the correct response is required, as with battle-trained troops, enduring hardness like a good soldier of Jesus Christ, so that the whole personality automatically slips into the most effective stance and posture to master the situation presented.

Purity of heart

The divine purpose, pattern, power, and person, together with the necessary skills and abilities, are meant to become second nature. At the centre, in the heart, which is the spring of motive, in the inner workings, where the Father sees in secret, the prayer, the faith, the self-discipline, the compassionate plans are at work as we are born again, Christ is formed in us, and we are filled with the Spirit. The energetic idea and final power, modelled and manifest in Christ on the Cross and at the Resurrection, are by the indwelling power of the Spirit at work inside man in the same way as in Him, imparting His straightforwardness and creative approach. The same texture of material is built up within the believer, able to stand pressure and suffer wear and tear without damage, and without ceiling of cost or demand for payment, with the maximum momentum of constructive love, thereby keeping the spirit of the law. Concentration is the heart and basis of the matter. Purity of heart really means concentration of attention and resources on the supreme object of concern and commitment. Men see what they are interested in. The senses become attuned by desire, by training, by practice, to whatever dominates the life. An eliminating filter process develops which excludes clutter and maximises every faculty. Simone Weil, the French worker-philosopher who increasingly devoted herself to the Christian life, despite scruples which prevented her accepting baptism, describes how her life of prayer was based on saying the Lord's Prayer with absolute concentration, going over and over again the individual items. Further she confessed to envying Christ His sufferings on the Cross, and especially the split second of death when the veil of sense is torn asunder to reveal the truth and glory beyond. Whatever emotional need prompted such a statement (which many might think extreme), at least she had penetrated very close to the heart of the matter. She knew where the clue was and how to use it. The prayerful trust and obedience of the Son of God in relation to the Heavenly Father is the power behind and beyond the sacrifice which reaches at once its nadir and its zenith in the split second of the death of Christ, understood in the total moment of the Resurrection and Ascension. The end hove in view; the clouds a moment unfurled; the holy city was visible; heaven came down the souls of men to greet, and glory crowned the mercy-seat. The motive and the method of sanctification are here revealed in the daily discipline.

Finished product

The relation of eschatology (the teaching about the end and purpose of the whole creative process) to sanctification, blessing, and purity of heart may be illustrated from road-works. Over a period of eight years a mile or so of road outside this College was in process of widening and straightening. A great deal of the work was straightforward navvying, like John the Baptist, bulldozing the heights and using the material to fill up the hollows till all was level, and straightening out the crooked, smoothing the surface. The work seemed interminable quite apart from the inevitable hazards of weather, shortages, and breakages. Mud was everywhere, and a litter of machines, tools, materials, equipment, and more mud. In reply to a muttered imprecation one of the roadmen remarked, 'But it will look lovely when it's finished!' There spoke one who had worked on similar jobs and seen them through to the end, when traffic could flow unimpeded, and the purpose of the road was functioning effectively. The present state of affairs is intended to be related directly to the purpose in view, and all effort is subdued to achievement of the end. Meanwhile much of the apparent chaos and discomfort is attributable to the need for a vast amount of underneath work.

A total work

Quite apart from laying proper foundations, trenches have to be dug to carry a variety of pipes and cables, for sewage, water, gas, electricity, telephone, and the like. If this work is scamped, and a delightfully finished surface imposed prematurely, nemesis is sure. Sooner or later cracks and discolouration will appear, and the work will have to be done over again, the whole thing ripped up, and time and money wasted. So it is with God's work of sanctification. The work has to be done thoroughly from inside outward and from underneath upward, even though there are outward and downward pressures to help in the process. 'Man looketh on the outward appearance, but the Lord looketh on the heart' (1 Samuel 16:7). It is important to remember that the work needs to be done as a whole, with an overall plan and a proper order of procedure. Primarily the work of sanctification is a total work, not a tinkering around with small points. Nevertheless, faults appear in the best laid schemes and processes, so particular points of repair and obvious wear and tear need to be watched without becoming pettifogging. With the Psalmist the believer must be prepared to say, 'This is my infirmity' (Psalm 77:10), and take appropriate steps to keep guard, strengthen, protect, at such points. The sanctified man does not thereby cease to be an ordinary human being with a particular physique, temperament, background, environment, a limited creature, with specific strong and weak points. It is also true that the assumption of outward attitudes can help the total process and work inwards, like the clippie who whistled not because she was cheerful but to get cheerful, rather like John Wesley's 'Preach faith until you have it and then you will preach faith because you have it.' The power of suggestion stemming from an assumed attitude can reinforce good intentions, though if it is understood solely as a subjective mechanism it loses more than half its effectiveness. 'A Christian is meant to be as outward as a Pharisee, and as inward as a Quaker', as John Wesley put it. As between the two, however, there is no doubt where the priority lies. Even the outward habit is the result of a conscious inward choice to reinforce an inwardly chosen attitude.

Overall tendency

So far as the actual realization of sinful thoughts, words, and deeds are concerned in the regenerate and sanctified person (and since this state is essentially a relationship, deviations and fluctuations are possible, even probable, in view of human frailty and constant pressures on every hand) perhaps the best comment is in the form of a poem in which an aged negro is being twitted by a smart youngster who has come across the Scripture words 'The just man falls seven times a day' (Proverbs 24:16):

> *'Unc' Si, de Holy Bible say,*
> *In speaking ob de jus',*
> *Dat he do fall sebbun times a day;*
> *Now, how's de sinner wuss?'*

> *'Well, chile, de slip may come to all;*
> *But den de diffe'ence foller—*
> *For, ef you watch him when he fall,*
> *De jus' man do not waller!'*

The built-in discipline restores equilibrium; trust and obedience reasserts itself. When I was a little boy a dear old childless couple, with a most healthy-minded devotion to children, gave me a little Dutch lady who stood up on a rounded-weight base, and however far or long she was held down, once the interfering factor was removed she shot up straight again. She could not be kept down interminably except by interminably applied force. Like Peter and John in prison for their faith, 'when they were let go they returned to their own company' (Acts 4:23). The personality bounces back to its true position, the prevailing bent and tendency of its being.

Three reasons for backsliding

Before leaving this section Hugh Redwood's acute observation (made after a genuine, thorough, lasting conversion experience) on the reasons for his backsliding after an initial inadequate conversion is worth pondering. He adduces three reasons for the miserable interlude of defection. First, too much publicity attached to his conversion and witness. He was prematurely exposed as a trophy of grace. Paul immersed himself for three years in obscurity before emerging as a public figure, and even then had a longer period maturing in the rough and tumble of life and trade in his own city. The second failure was absence of teaching on prayer, its method and ups and downs. While those who have been brought up amidst prayer at home and meetings for the purpose may well have picked up a deal of know-how almost in spite of themselves, many have had no such privilege, and can flounder despondently, or even soar disastrously, unless some wise counsel is provided. The prayer of the Danish existentialist Sören Kierkegaard might prove a useful starting-point. 'Teach me to rule my flesh and blood so that I can say with the apostle, I die daily.'

The third factor undoing conversion is failure to relate holiness to daily work (Hugh Redwood, *Bristol Fashion*). Perhaps a description at once more comprehensive and more exact, would be failure to relate holiness to daily living, because that life begins at home (like charity, of which it is the supreme exemplar) as well as permeating the whole of existence. Beyond the basic virtues and attitudes of a Christian as such, wherever he is, it is also necessary to show the young (and not so young) believer how to relate sanctification to the specific conditions under which he or she has to work with other people. Here a tremendous responsibility rests on more experienced Christians who know the particular setting to guide and encourage those taking the first tottering steps. Equally such mature Christians would know that each needed to encourage the other constantly. How is it possible to maintain such standards as are required unless Christians seek to build each other up in the fellowship of Christ and His Spirit? The problem of relating the attitude of sanctification to daily life remains constant throughout life. It is a pipedream, without foundation in reason, Scripture, or experience to suppose that there is ever any time, place or stage of life in which it is easy to be a Christian, or where we can dispense with any atom of grace and resource available. 'I see grace groweth best in winter,' exclaimed Samuel Rutherford from the midst of his trials. Discipline, training, 'a technique of mutual provocation to love and good works', as a Student Christian Movement Secretary phrased it many years ago, are never out of commission. Therefore watch, pray, endure to the end, rejoice always, in every circumstance give thanks, take up the cross daily, let self-control in the Spirit be seen by all, and let the searchlight of the Holy One have

165

unhindered access, for 'men perish with whispering sins, nay, silent sins, sins that never tell the conscience they are sins, as often as with crying sins: and in hell there shall meet as many men that never thought what was sin, as that spent all their effort in the compassing of sin' (John Donne, Sermons).

Place of the Church

Once the connexion has been made it becomes clear that a combination is also required whereby the individual believer is incorporated into the life of the Church both to receive and to give. Part of the Gospel is the Church as a going concern. The Love of God, received through the grace of the Lord Jesus Christ, is exemplified and applied by the fellowship of the Holy Spirit, which is also the fellowship of the apostles. In its large sense as the Great Church extending over space and time, the Church is the People of God, belonging to Him, because bought by Him, preserved by Him, and bearing His peculiar branding-mark. From the divine point of view this People is the ecclesia, the elect and chosen, who have responded to God's gracious offer in Christ, and thereby are separated to His will and purpose, marked off for His own use. In relation to itself amid its inner life this ecclesia is manifested as a series of intimate fellowships or koinonia, a word that means partnership, laying resources alongside each other in mutual trust for an agreed purpose, like James and John in business with their father! Whatever blessings are bestowed are primarily for all who will hear, accept, and adjust accordingly. Sharing is of the essence of the operation from the beginning. Both aspects of the Church are needed, the majestic, continuous, almost impersonal manifestation common to technical Catholicism, and the warm, intimate, gathered, personal manifestation commoner among what are inaccurately called sects, with their more immediate and spontaneous responses to the Gospel and the means of grace.

Holiness of the Church

It is vital to recall that one essential mark of the Church is holiness. The Church is meant to be one, holy, catholic (or universal), and apostolic, i.e. founded on and living by the apostolic message, which is the only available source of authoritative information about the mind of our Lord on the function and nature of His Church. Plainly there ought not to be any contradiction between these characteristics which merely bring out differing facets of one organism. The greatest cause of division historically has been over the relation of catholicity to holiness. How far should the Church be a society of saints or a community of the baptized in the correct legal continuity? In practice neither conforms to New Testament experience or to the facts of history. Some form of unity there ought obviously to be. A disunited Church contradicts the Gospel of reconciliation, and makes nonsense of the Church's claims. The problem is to find the form of unity which does justice both to the requirement of a true Gospel, a clearly marked qualitative difference between the Church and other institutions, and a recognition of the strangely mixed-up character of human life and society as man has to live it, whereby actual individuals and congregations are in such diverse and strangely assorted stages of spiritual understanding and relationship. This was always so, and no one should be misled by unhistoric fantasies about some Church which was composed one hundred per cent of one hundred per cent sanctified people, even if Charles Wesley did sing about 'meek, simple followers of the Lamb'.

A great deal of the New Testament is taken up with tackling a far from ideal Church. Nevertheless, there is no warrant for accepting as satisfactory an average standard of respectability, or assuming that the Church's business is to be chaplain to the natural man. There is no escape from the challenge to conversion, regeneration, and sanctification for the Church as well as, or even more than, the individual. The Church is intended to be God's instrument for the service of His Kingdom, and an instrument should be as perfect as can be achieved. Therefore it must not accommodate itself to the spirit of the world, which has little to do with superficial matters of personal adornment and recreation, and much to do with pride, aggressiveness, slander, scheming, mental reservations, status-seeking, censoriousness, sanctimoniousness, meanness, exclusiveness and the like, all of which can co-exist with a great show of separa-

M

167

tion from the world. The great test is whether or not the slant of the Church is towards the constructive reaction of Christ to the destructive situation without ceiling of cost or insistence on a statistically equivalent return, however spiritually interpreted. Essential to the conduct of the operation of sanctification is membership in the Church and whole-hearted and sacrificial love for her, building her up in every way to fulfil the various functions outlined in Scripture. The Eastern Orthodox have much to teach us along this line. A great Russian prophet, Khomiakov, expressed the intimate relationship of the believer to the Church in words which might seem extreme to those of us who are so familiar with the fractured churches of the western world: 'the Church is truth and life. She is the inner life of a Christian, more intimate than the blood in his veins.' Our Methodist forefathers lived the Church in this way and were not unique in this.

Priestliness of the Church

Perhaps the most important theme to stress in our day is the priestliness of the Church. The function of the priest is to be the liaison-officer between the divine and the human. In the strictest sense of the word there can be only one such priest, the mediator Jesus Christ himself. God is His own interpreter and man's interpreter as well. The Church is intended to be the vehicle for the continuance by Christ of His priestly work on earth. 'It is God's corporate priest in the world . . . In the communion and power of His intercession it intercedes for the world. By Christ's grace it believes for the world, it confesses vicariously the sins of the world, it offers itself as a sacrifice for the world, it praises God for the world, it stands and acts between sinful man and holy God' (P. T. Forsyth, *Congregationalism and Reunion,* p. 73). For the sake of Christ who bought her with a signal act of pardon and free grace the Church is committed to sanctify herself for the sake of the world. She is the link-community.

Baptism and holiness

How is the believer incorporated into this link-community? Peter gave the answer on the Day of Pentecost: '. . . be

baptised, every one of you, in the name of Jesus Christ . . .'
(Acts 2:38). The main significance of baptism is integration
into a community, not a private blessing. It is the outward and
corporate exhibition of the mechanics of incorporation. In
simple elemental symbolism of water for cleansing and immersion for dying and rising, baptism sets forth the Gospel which
creates and maintains the Church and brings believers into the
community by regeneration. 'Therefore we are buried with him
by baptism unto death; that like as Christ was raised from the
dead by the glory of the Father, even we also should walk in
newness of life' (Romans 6:4). Again, 'our old self was crucified
with him so that the sinful body might be destroyed, and we
might no longer be enslaved to sin. For he who has died is
freed from sin. But if we have died with Christ, we believe that
we shall also live with him . . . So you also must consider
yourselves dead to sin and alive to God in Christ Jesus'
(Romans 6:6–11). In a missionary situation—a totally new
area for business, so to speak—believers' baptism will be the
norm, though even here, apart from the individualistic society
of the West, families may well be included with the head of
the household.

Where Christianity has become established, whether officially
or unofficially by the sheer breadth and continuance of its
influence, the question of the relation of the children brought
into the world to the accepted beliefs and standards becomes
urgent. If they are not born saved are they born damned?
If the latter, ought parents as Christians to bring them into
the world at all? If they accept the responsibility of begetting
offspring presumably they believe that they are born to be
born again and that they should be claimed for God by all
available means. 'While we were yet sinners Christ died for
us' (Romans 5:8), and indeed before we were born. His
prevenient grace is available and at work apart from our
consciousness or our existence, and the outward, visible, and
corporate sign of that grace in relation to claim for God and
initiation into the Gospel community is baptism. As applied
to those not able to understand and offer conscious response
it remains an incomplete service, and requires some form of
confirmation when the candidate makes his own response.

There is no objection to this in principle; indeed it acknowledges the strangely mixed-up business of human life and the curious involvement of the Gospel community therein, as also the odd and inscrutable relationship between sovereign grace, human freedom, and the influence of heredity and environment in all their intricacy. Within the ever-changing relationship of the Church and the world both geographically, historically, psychologically and sociologically room must be found for flexible variety of usage both in relation to custom and to conscience. What ought to be avoided is deliberate repetition of baptism, which is a once-for-all sacrament by its very nature. Where there is legitimate doubt as to whether all righteousness in this matter has been attended to, conditional baptism may well be observed, not because individuals cannot be saved without baptism (experience is clear that they can so far as spirit, character, fruit and influence is concerned, else the Quakers and the Salvation Army were outside the fold) but because appropriate outward form matters in relation to the Church in its existence in this world, and represents the objectivity of the Gospel, the Church, and the grace of God (apart from man's response which itself is conditioned by these factors and their incarnational embodiment). The conscientious protest against their use as fully efficacious apart from personal relationship has historically been required, but such protest, like nonconformity, is not a church, but a principle reforming churches, which should acknowledge the rebuke and share full fellowship with those who have taken the sacrificial stand for conscience' sake without any stipulations of rebaptism, reconfirmation, or reordination.

The Lord's Supper and holiness

The Churchly form which most clearly exhibits the principles of maintenance is the Lord's Supper, or Sacrament of Holy Communion. The simple elements of bread and wine, food and drink, nourishment and vitality, with profound associations both natural and supernatural, represent the very stuff of renewal without which repair and resilience do not take place. Again the primary significance of the service is not its effect upon individual participants, but its propriety for the corporate life of the People of God. Its full effectiveness does not depend upon itself or some prescribed canonical ritual, though there is not unlimited liberty of usage (for all essential Christian rituals the shape of the redemptive drama prescribes the structure and the substance, though as with all living things enormous variety of adaptation in detailed features is both possible and desirable, not to say essential). However scholars may argue about the precise relation of the Last Supper to the Jewish Passover it is extremely difficult to dissociate the two entirely, especially as our Lord expressly related His death and resurrection to the Exodus, or deliverance from Egyptian slavery. The heart of this event was a rescue and renewal of opportunity for freedom, dignity, and destiny in the service of the divine purpose. It was an act of salvation and redemption at great cost, without which the rest of the providential and saving work would have been impossible. The purpose, pattern and power of God are revealed in such concentrated acts at particular moments of history; they are always the same and at work, but often hidden or obscure. Those who profit thereby live by the faith aroused and created by such events, but they need constant reminder of the model event, not as a fixation on the past, nor as merely a postponement of responsible action to an imagined future repetition, but as a present aid to faith in the immediate operation of the same factors. The heart of the matter is the effective drama, which both expresses and aids the gracious saving purpose, pattern and power. When Jeremiah acted his parable through the streets with a yoke upon his shoulders he was not merely expressing an idea, but introducing a potent factor into the situation. Thus our Lord associated the compelling power of the uniquely memorable event of His death and final words with a simple ceremony of deed and explanatory word as the most lasting form of ensuring the correct recording and effecting of His will and covenant with its attendant benefits. The service of Holy Communion incorporates the drama of Gospel redemption, and thereby helps to impress the pattern, impart the power, and further the purpose of the Triune God. The supreme note therefore is thanksgiving, for which the Greek word in English form is eucharist; hence the prevalent fashion in ecumenical circles for the use of the term Eucharist for the description more familiar to Free Churchmen as the Lord's Supper. So far as accuracy is concerned in bringing out one essential aspect of this means of grace the term is valuable, though the other term is more truly descriptive. In so far as it is an attempt to keep up with the Joneses it becomes just another instance of sycophantic snobbery adopted by the ecclesiastical *nouveau riche*. The rediscovery of the inner Biblical meaning of the rite, and its place in the process of sanctification (requiring revision by all churches of their previous approaches) is one of the encouraging features of the present day.

Preaching and holiness

In many ways the service of Holy Communion is the pattern for Christian worship, but one distinctive feature of Christianity is its public, missionary, and social nature. Its mystery is an open mystery, and while it has its proper reserves it is not a secret society, unless forced into such an unnatural position by the hostility of the secular authorities. One of its means of grace is public worship which centres around preaching, or the proclamation of the saving message 'in the demonstration of the Spirit and of power' (1 Corinthians 2:4). The object of the exercise is to restate, illustrate, expound, and apply the creative message so that believers will be reinforced in life and service, that those in various stages of belief and unbelief may be brought into full adherence to the saving work, and that those who either disbelieve, or have never really heard at all in any significant sense, may hear, understand, and accept. Rightly handled, with a due appreciation of its purpose, worship centred round preaching is one of the great aids to sanctification, but it requires an adequate proportion of instructed believers at the core of the congregation. The full diet of worship includes hymns, prayers, reading of Scripture, and offertory: and these elements are not meant to be set in contrast to preaching or in subordination to it, but are essential parts of a total unit which has preaching as the supreme offering of the Gospel in intelligible, powerful form both to God and man, together with the total response in faith and service of the congregation. In so far as such response is not forthcoming, the power of God is still manifest because such rejection or ignoring still has its effect, however minute and apparently unobservable. Preaching is the continual telling, explaining, commending, releasing of the purpose, pattern, and power as laid down in the programme. Preaching is action to impress, impart and impel. It is holy action to a holy end.

Public worship and holiness

The setting of public worship has its value also for sanctification. Many who do not as yet appreciate to the full what is happening are exposed to the pattern, the pressure, the power, the purpose, the programme, not illegitimately but voluntarily while still not completely aware of the value of the experience. The family life of the Church is seen on parade, so to speak. The narrow limits of the family are broadened though still within the scope of the holy. There is a hint of the large-scale activity of God, though still at a size which is not too overwhelming to grasp. The public assembly of God's people in one place lifts holiness out of the private huddle of the like-minded, and teaches the valuable lesson of a wider tolerance of different types of Christian. The whole range of artistic and practical gifts should be at the disposal of worship despite all the proneness of human nature to worship the work of its hands, and to substitute the creature for the Creator. From time to time the Puritan recall to the heart of the matter is necessary, but it is a reflection on human nature in the Church when such radical scything is the only alternative. There is no question that the Father is to be worshipped 'in spirit and in truth' (John 4:23), and He is not confined to any human construction. At the same time nothing but the best is good enough for God, with due regard to the resources of the worshippers. There is more beauty in the simply proportioned and unadorned walls of many a village Bethel than in the tawdry clutter and ornate embellishments of some more wealthy and pretentious edifices. When strictly functional a church building has an atmosphere all its own of the holy and the awesome, though its aim should be to use space to serve grace.

Intimate fellowship and holiness

It remains true that the most intensive cultivation of fruit and flower is in the smaller plot. The number twelve has a more than arbitrary significance: it appears to be the numerical unit for a group engaged in frequent practical fellowship. John Wesley's Class Meeting and the Communist cell in a factory use the same social mechanism; here is the cell of constructive energy between the family and the assembly. Jesus 'ordained twelve that they might be with him' (Mark 3:14). Possibly the most fruitful work is done by either minister or layman in the small informal group he gathers to instruct, guide, and share in the Christian life. One of its temptations will be a certain preference for its own company and its own preservation; this is the way to death; it contradicts the nature of its existence, which is to be a saving unit. The aim should not be spiritual self-preservation, but training for fitness in service. Otherwise it will become deformed, or rot and drop off like an emotional ingrowing toe-nail. Let the Bible be its programme and local need its agenda. Here is the secret of koinonia, fellowship in the Gospel, the warmth and intimacy of the Church, which was so marked a feature of its earliest manifestations. Within such a group the most effective discipline and encouragement to love and good works has scope to operate. Dr Samuel Johnson's words may be baptized into Christ, 'The greatest benefit which one friend can confer upon another is to guard, and excite, and elevate his virtues.'

Holiness, witness, evangelism, and service

Such fellowship and means of grace prepare us to take our full share in the three-pronged outreach of the Gospel through the Church—witness, evangelism, service. These are not three separate activities but the normal outworking of a truly Christian life. The English form of the Greek word for witness is martyr, one who reveals to the utmost the integrity of his evidence. A witness is one who imparts what he has seen and heard so that an accurate story, both as to fact and interpretation, is made available to all those entitled to the information for the purposes of responsible decision and action. His function is to supply undistorted evidence. He must produce the goods, fit the bill, be an adequate sample of whatever he advertises. One good witness is worth ten thousand clever advocates. If our witness is deficient our story will not be believed, even if it is true. In the sphere of the Gospel the witness must be a recognizable cut off the genuine original, up to standard 'according to the measure of the stature of the fulness of Christ' (Ephesians 4:13). Evangelism and service alike fail to function efficiently unless the witness is valid. The life must accord with the claim, but equally there must be readiness to explain the motive and purpose of the witness, as and when opportunity naturally occurs. Attempts to engineer artificially opportunities for witness ultimately produce their own antidote. The warning symptoms are soon noticed by the potential victim, and protective gambits prepared. William Wilberforce used to work out what he called 'launchers' to direct conversation into channels for witness, but while the purpose is praiseworthy the means are fundamentally a form of unbelief. The devious approach thwarts the directness of relationship essential to Christian love. When Paul says, 'being crafty I caught you with guile' (2 Corinthians 12:16) he is quoting a charge against him of using his trade to make himself independent of the Corinthian stipend and thereby putting himself in a strong position in relation to their discipline. He repudiates the suggestion: 'Did I take advantage of you through any of those whom I sent to you?' (v. 17). Beware of the self-conscious smirk of the keen evangelicals who think they have scored a smart one for the Lord, or somehow are fulfilling the injunction to be as wise as the children of light. This does not mean doing the same kind of thing, even for sanctified purposes, but showing the same astuteness to size up situations, and the same practical and efficient vigour in appropriate action for the purposes of the Kingdom.

Principles of evangelism

Evangelism is the natural life of the Christian. It has only a secondary association with the paraphernalia of evangelistic campaigns, which are but specific manifestations of a temporary and local nature of the native life of the Church. Evangelism is sharing the love of God as effected in Christ and imparted by the Spirit. Such love exists only as shared. The full nature was revealed only in Christ in the pattern of the saving act, and fully realized as available only with the gift of the Spirit. The love of God appeared in the world both by creation and salvation, and the latter appeared in perfection only through the incarnation, atonement, resurrection, ascension and Pentecost. There are three Biblical principles of evangelism, incarnational, atoning, and pentecostal, and they work only in this order; none can be omitted, by-passed or reordered. The operation is not in full working order till stage three is reached. Men see the love of God shared in practical action in actual people and groups or they do not see it at all. The message has to be human and mix in with them. The upshot of such identification is bearing unmerited burdens in the course of effecting reconciliation. The consequent breaking of separating barriers makes actual community possible. The experience of community, with its accompanying communion and communication, releases the true homing instinct of the human personality. The Father and the family are realized in actuality, and freedom, with its accompanying fulness of experience and development, operates. When these things happen the Kingdom of God is manifest and vindicated. By this means the operation is conducted at the level of new business and colonial development. The travellers are out and the sales-department stretched to utmost capacity. Three words of our Lord are now seen in true perspective: 'come; abide; go'. From whatever centre believers start locally their interest moves in ever-widening circles, beginning at Jerusalem, via Samaria (the half-way fringe), to the farthest circumference of human need.

Caring love

The emphasis on evangelism stresses the necessity for imparting the message articulately, so that men may reflect and respond consciously, but obviously it is more likely to impress if the witness corresponds, and both evangelism and witness issue in practical service along the lines so clearly marked out both by our Lord and by James. The service required is inclusive salvation at the point of need. Adjustment is limitless; no one need ever be bored! 'Christianity taught us to care. Caring is the greatest thing. Caring matters most!' exclaimed Baron von Hügel. One sentiment impossible to the Christian is embodied in the slogan 'I couldn't care less!' The love required is superhuman, but such a description includes human love, and does not negate it. Our Lord shows the way, as Mrs Josephine Butler remarks: 'Now look at Jesus. He never talked about love of souls, and never judged people as a class. He always took the man, the woman, or the child as a *person;* and He loved the whole being of that person; so that He won the lost woman by His *manhood as well as His Godhead.* Jesus respected the sacred thing called personality . . . We must emphasize the human side of caring, the acting of love, the kindness in action which goes farther than words. *I don't believe you know what a poor unspiritual creature I was when I first began rescue work.* The spiritual lessons came—were given to me while I worked. Indeed, *the humaneness was much stronger than the deep love of Christ in me at first. But God used that fierce human love and human pity and human anger against injustice among men towards the human sinner'* (Letter to Miss Foraith). Let us always study closely the example of our Lord in His approach to people at whatever level. His subject was life, His method freedom, and His atmosphere fellowship. Exploitation, patronage, humbug, inhumanity and rigidity were the objects of His attack. He was truly human and divine, and according to the limits of our situation we are to be totally committed to His attitude, spirit, and approach.

Place of the minister

For the conduct of the operation and the application of the available means people are required. Diversity of operations and gifts are required and supplied, but a twofold division of labour appears as part of the Gospel gift—ministers and members. Both share in the priestly, linking work. The ministers continually exercise the official range of the Church's activity. They exercise a representative priesthood; it does not differ in kind from the priesthood of the laity, but it is different and more specialized in function. The word translated *laymen* simply means the people who belong to the community whatever it is, quite apart from whether they have any special function and training therein. Where occasion requires the layman, technically so called, may exercise any or all of the functions of the minister, but with due authorization for particular times and places. The principle of lay administration of the sacraments, for instance, is vital to a true conception of the Church, even though it will not be the normal practice. Indispensable to the Church of God's grace is open-endedness. The corollary of the priesthood of all believers is the responsibility, as much as the privilege, of both minister and member. Each is meant to be moulded by the purpose, the pattern, and the power to which reference has constantly been made. The same trinity appears at every point. Meanwhile it may be said that respect for the ministry is the self-respect of the Church. A Church with a mean doctrine of the ministry and a patronizing or hostile attitude to the ministry hinders sanctification. So also does a patronizing, exclusive doctrine of the ministry and attitude by the ministers. Let each help the other to perform the appointed functions to the full. Sanctification should end any unnatural division between the ministry and the membership. Ministers are members with the same responsibilities, but with a specialized function which should appear when required. They are not meant to be a third sex, with their humanity suffering from a strangulated hernia. There ought not to be any gap to overcome between ministers and members: only a proper respect as well as love for each other in mutual edification. Usually the context of service differs, apart from a common overlap of human responsibilities.

The Bible and holiness

All the way through there must be constant reference to the Bible. Some years ago a money-in-the-slot machine for a great variety of ice-creams was devized. In the middle was a list of instructions, but the public generally was either too lazy or too fearful to study what was provided. There were many complaints about the difficulties people experienced in extracting the desired dainties. Eventually the makers had a huge notice affixed to the machine: WHEN ALL ELSE FAILS, TRY READING THE DIRECTIONS! The same advice might be sent round to every believer. Whatever new truth God has designed to break forth from His holy Word, as John Robinson, the Pilgrim Father par excellence, wrote, it will not contradict His already-revealed truth. The Holy Spirit does not add to the written record, but unfolds, interprets, and applies to new situations the mind He has already in principle made known. The treasure is in earthen vessels, and needs extraction, but the specific vessel of history and geography within which God has chosen to convey His message is not to be jettisoned, but retained as the appointed means of conveyance with its own contribution to make to the treasure, which needs to be seen both in its original and in its continuously present context. Both matter for the safeguarding and effecting of the truth.

The authority of the Bible resides in its capacity to effect its purpose as the pulsing, communicating record of the special revelation of God. Its claim to historicity is not exempt from the ordinary canons of investigation and in fact stands up well to such examination. Where human tests can legitimately be applied they must be undertaken without fear or favour, though an equally radical scrutiny of the investigators is required, lest some particular philosophical or personal bias distorts the results and smuggles in a canon of interpretation which guarantees misunderstanding. When all is said and done the Bible stands or falls in human estimation by the powerful effect of its dominant message of salvation. In the chapter on outlining the programme the basic pattern and sequence of events to produce creative results even in the most unpromising conditions is outlined. There are many ways to read the Bible, each with its appropriate blessing, but the most important is to live inside its coherent structure of approach to events, discover the grain of God's universe and then work down and up, in and out, and back and forth throughout it. Take any unit of sense, either sentence, story, slab of teaching, and write out the inner shape, till it becomes second nature. Note the taut and sinewy language, the sequence of events, the type and clash of personality and environment, the weight of history, the atmosphere of expectation. This way grace comes, and illumination, and a hunger and thirst for the Word of God develops which makes it like manna and ambrosia to the soul.

The entirety of sanctification

In practice is has proved impossible to confine these reflections on entire sanctification to the doctrine itself. The whole Christian message and life is integrally involved. While many profound themes have been touched upon it is hoped that none has been treated superficially or irrelevantly. The great aim has been to see the subject in its proper context from the beginning, and summarize, concentrate, and focus the essential pattern, purpose and power, so that—at whatever point the subject is picked up—its simple essence may be clear, its immediate application visible to a particular aspect of Christianity and life, and the most hopeful attitude lucid in which to approach any other desired application. Major matters of controversy in the fields of large-scale power conflicts remain largely untouched, but it is doubtful whether any one mind could properly pontificate on such themes. It is a matter for thankfulness that so many trained and experienced Christian minds, and others with sufficient sympathy to share the travail, are studying such subjects with ardent concern. From the very beginning it is clear that the Bible is not only concerned with small-scale business; sanctification must be entire in aspiration and expectation even if not always completed in achievement.

Tests of sanctity

Before leaving the subject, in the hope that others may take up the discussion and think the approach worthy of serious comment, some general guidance on the kind of attitudes which might be expected from any true Christian might be expected. The Roman Catholics have accepted officially a two-standard Christian life, which Wesley saw from another point of view, and which has much in actual experience to justify it, even though the New Testament does not encourage such a division. Consequently it has had to work out a system of assessment for sanctity. Baron von Hügel, writing to the Quaker Stanley Jones, reminded him of the four requisites laid down for such a purpose. First the candidate must have been loyal to the Faith. Second, he must have been heroic under trial. Third, he must be able to do the impossible, humanly speaking. Fourth, he must be radiant in the stress of life. Von Hügel concludes, 'The Church may conceivably be wrong in insisting on the first three of those conditions, but it is gloriously right about the fourth.' No other religion makes joy a virtue, and its absence a sin! Equally we must beware of synthetic joy, the pathological inability to suffer grief as Jesus suffered. At every point genuineness is the test. 'Buy the truth, and sell it not' (Proverbs 23 : 23), 'Test everything; hold fast to what is good, abstain from every appearance of evil' (1 Thessalonians 4 : 22). Beware substitutes, larded unction, conspicuous humility, the greasy alternative to real tact whereby the religious get their own way at the expense of declaring their hand. Nevertheless the advertisement on the rear of buses poses a proper question: Is your oil up to standard? The smooth working depends on and produces the oil of joy.

Detailed guidance

In the section on outlining the programme reference was made to the catechisms and elementary codes of Christian conduct discernible in the New Testament. Without covering the same ground again it may be noted that there was both a negative and a positive aspect. John Wesley himself wrote guidance in great detail for his followers relative to the circumstances prevailing at the time, and gave a list of Christian do's and don'ts. In terms of fundamental attitudes St Augustine's famous dictum, 'love God, and do as you like' is correct, but human nature is far too prone to give itself the benefit of the doubt under the pressures of everyday life. Something more precise is called for. Too much of Protestant teaching assumes a very high level of maturity on the part of its adherents. Equally, of course, the Catholic attitude tends to prevent ethical maturity on the part of the general mass of the faithful, flourishing best where the people are acquiescent in priestly direction.

Rough and ready test

Dr Norman Snaith, in broadcast talks on problems of behaviour facing a Christian, devised a useful rule-of-thumb approach. He divided ethical problems into three main groups. The first contains things obviously right and required. The third contains things obviously wrong and to be shunned. The middle category contained things which are neither right nor wrong in themselves, ethically neuter, but this group could be subdivided into two sections: (a) containing things which on the whole, though they could be spoiled, had a tendency more easily to promote good ends, and (b) things which on the whole, though they could be rightly used, had a tendency more easily to be associated with deleterious effects. On the margins throughout there will be doubtful decisions, and both people and stages and circumstances may alter cases. The general standard to apply is building up the welfare of the Kingdom of God.

Negative holiness

Negatives are important. Insulation against shock, fences against disaster, warning notices are part of love and caring. To avoid the by-path meadow saves time and energy. It is possible to be too hoity-toity about one's moral safety. 'Let him that thinketh he standeth take heed lest he fall' (1 Corinthians 10:12). In particular the Christian must resist the conformist patterns of a self-centred community. Awkwardness is relative to a situation, and if the general drift is downward the Christian has no alternative to awkwardness. He bears the mark of his owner, and is by average standards a peculiar person. Nevertheless he must not exaggerate his awkwardness or rejoice in it as such. He must learn the art of Jesus to be the friend of sinners, and mix easily with the multitudes. He requires what has been called 'the genial obtuseness of the upright'. He is different with a difference, neither defensive, apprehensive, nor offensive, but comprehensive. His separation is from the spirit of the world and from the practice of wrong-doing, not a skirt-withdrawing refusal to face the facts of life and the actual clash and spatter of social intercourse. John Milton rightly refused to 'praise a fugitive and cloistered virtue' which withdraws from the arena of life's rough and tumble, 'where the immortal garland is to be run for, not without dust and heat'. The wrath of God is the obverse of His love; it shows that He cares enough to notice and punish. Even what appears the automatic recoil of impersonal nemesis is a manifestation of His personal will once the apparently automatic determinism of existence is seen as but the regular and measurable part of a personally directed universe. With the Hebrew heroes faced with the fiery furnace of Nebuchadnezzar we must say, 'Our God is able to deliver us, *but if not,* be it known unto you, O king, that we will not serve your gods or worship the golden image which you have set up' (Daniel 3:17f.).

Positive holiness

On the positive side there is no definable limit, though the minimum requirement is an attitude of encouragement rather than discouragement. There was a rule for naval officers which might be seared into the minds of every Christian: 'no officer shall speak discouragingly to his mate either on the watch or at mess, concerning the business on which he is or may be engaged.' Similarly with regard to people we do well to heed the sly dig of Sir Thomas Browne, 'he who discommendeth others obliquely commendeth himself.' Internally there is the the endless problem of personal grievance where we deem ourselves or someone dear to us damaged unfairly. Florence Nightingale wisely observed that 'in a difficult life it is always better clearly to decide for oneself what grievances one will bear, being inescapable, escape from, or try to remove.' Keep clear in mind the end-product, which is a certain type of character in community of family and kingdom, which reflects and imparts the glory of God. Home, work, leisure, and government are seen in the context of godlike qualities. In many ways our use of leisure reveals most clearly our standards when we are free to choose. In their leisure, said Reinhold Niebuhr, 'men either pray or get drunk'. This extreme form of statement is intended to be provocative. What he means is that freedom is used either to further some worthwhile end or to indulge the self. The difference is between what St Augustine called the major freedom, which is for responsibility, and the minor

N   183 freedom which merely desires to throw off restrictions, kick off its nappies, and kick its legs irrespective of other people's convenience.

Holiness highway code

The highway code of the Christian journey is most fully illustrated in the Sermon on the Mount. Turning the other cheek, going the second mile, giving more than requested, are creative responses to potentially destructive situations. Once they become an appendix of refined laws of conduct they lose their point which is surprise, originality, the outflanking of prepared positions. They are not handles for the unregenerate to twist to their own advantage. No one ought to be able to presume that we should not apparently fall from grace for a few minutes. The gracious attitude is not produced for the manufacture of spongers and exploiters. The Christian is not meant to be a doormat unless it serves a purpose for the feet of Christ. The aim is redemptive out-pouring of the self in saving service. The fruit of the Spirit is 'love, joy, peace, patience, kindness, goodness, faithfulness, gentleness, self-control: against such there is no law . . . If we live by the Spirit, let us also walk by the Spirit. Let us have no self-conceit, no provoking of one another, no envy of one another' (Galatians 5:22–26). Paul incidentally was talking within the Christian fellowship, and he would hardly waste space on non-existent problems. The Spirit he inculcates is the Spirit of the Father and the Son. The Trinity takes up residence within the believing self and the believing community, inducing obedient and trustful response to His blessed Self, and imparting the pattern, the purpose, the power, the promise, the purity, the passion, the process. Hence the Christian is governed not only by the law of gravity but by the spirit of hilarity. The believer is God-intoxicated, divinely inebriated. The law provides the skeleton, but the Spirit provides the supple sinews, muscles, shuddering together the scattered bones, as in Ezekiel's vision. There is a legal framework within the orbit of the Spirit. Christ's teaching in this form has been called His strange work, whereby He erects a fixed point for guidance, as sailors sail *by* rather than *to* the stars; He erects a standard which reveals deficiency; and, after man's introduction to the new life in the Spirit, He proffers a provoking challenge to man's attainment to prevent complacency and the misuse of grace to evade effort.

Summarized estimate of love

A simple pocket-edition of Christian love is Paul's lyrical effusion described by Henry Drummond as *The Greatest Thing in the World* (1 Corinthians 13). This love moves outward to help without consideration of reward or merit. The love of God is a fixed and dependable attitude towards mankind, working out the best for them in spite of their disobedience. Such love is spontaneous, creative, sacrificial, trustful, obedient, and reliable. It is holy love. Tongues, either as ecstasy or rhetoric without love are empty noise. Prophecy, inspired foresight, and capacity to communicate infectiously God's interpretation of events, can be applied harshly or offhandedly. Knowledge, either as initiation into hidden mysteries or as superior human wisdom, inflates a pompous balloon rather than constructs a community, without love. Even faith, one of the top three Christian virtues, can become self-display or reckless and feckless presumption. Compassion for the needy can be a corrupt exhibition, patronizing and pauperizing, salving the conscience. Martyrdom might seem immune, but the half-recognized aim may be spiritual glory or blackmail, doing 'the right deed for the wrong reason'. Each of these qualities can be refined by Christian love, or sullied without it. There is nothing in any of them apart from this distinctively Christian love.

Lasting power of love

This love is patient, long-tempered towards injurious and provoking people and circumstances. It overcomes the immediate reaction of annoyance or alarm, and seeks to assess the situation in calm perspective. Love acts like this because it seeks the best interest of the Kingdom of God rather than estimating everything in terms of the effect upon itself. The winner lasts out longest.

Kindly love

Kindness is another characteristic, the recognition of sharing kinship. To be kind is to deal with people as if they were one of the family. Life is full of inevitable inequalities, but the more favoured need not cruelly exploit their advantage, nor the less-favoured chip bits off the reputation of the more fortunate.

Humble love

Love does not swell itself up like the frog who boasted he could make himself as huge as an ox. 'Love saves a man from making a fool of himself by thrusting himself through consequential conduct into positions which betray his incompetence', said Marcus Dods. Littleness loves to assert itself with pompous self-importance. As the negro preacher once put it, 'Some people remind me of de bottom figger of a fraction. De bigger dey try to be, de smaller dey really is!' Humility means a proper and balanced estimate of our own powers and position in the plan of God. Self-depreciation is not humility, but an inverted form of drawing attention to oneself. Love is easy to work with, and never tries to make other people look small.

Courteous love

Love refines the rough, crude stuff of personality. Our Lord's presence demands courtesy. Strident tones and ugly gestures, are misplaced in the vicinity of the King of Kings. Love is not perverse. G. K. Chesterton's description of St Francis arouses a wholesome covetousness in a Christian: 'politeness flowed from him . . . like one of the public fountains in a sunny Italian market-place.'

Encouraging love

Love does not draw attention to itself, is not always jealously guarding its rights or making itself an unnecessary martyr. Love denies itself cosy devotional moments in order to serve the best interests of other people. It keeps no score of wrongs, as James Moffat put it. It is not quickly irritated because private plans are thwarted. Nothing withers the delicate bloom of good relationships like bad temper. Such love does not dig for nasty motives. It does not cackle with cynical laughter when some-body goes wrong, nor hold up pious hands in horror. It is not quick to expose a fault or mistake. Love does not think evil funny, but longs to see truth win. It is therefore always grateful, readier to thank than complain or dun.

Weather-proof love

Here is a limitless capacity for tolerance, hope, trust, patient endurance, when and where necessary. The various hindrances to love merely stimulate its endless capacity to be itself. Such love is weather-proof, with tough resilience, and a skin as thick as its heart is tender. A North American frontier proverb ran, 'There's nothing out today but crows and Methodist preachers.' The necessity for this tough love with resources beyond the ordinary is shown by a story told by Elliot Kendall from Communist China. A Christian doctor worked in a hospital where nurses, employees, and patients voted the salaries. This man's outstanding compassionate concern kept him near the top of the poll till it was accidentally discovered that he was a Christian. At the end of the month his salary slumped. The main drop was among the simple indoctrinated Communist soldiers, who explained, 'Formerly we thought you loved us as wounded soldiers of the People's Liberation Army. Now we know that we're mistaken; you do not love us only; you love us because you are a Christian, and love everyone; therefore we vote you a smaller number of points towards your salary.'

Learning the ropes

This love is complete, not partially or muzzily reflected as in one of the metal mirrors of Paul's day. In practice we are like apprentices learning a trade, each lesson opening up new possibilities, though with the perfection of heaven at each stage. We recognize God therein as He recognizes us first. There is nothing to add to love, except more and more love.

Love grows up

Here is maturity, growing up properly to the best of which one is capable. Though once, like a child, Paul babbled, chattered, and gesticulated violently without regard to other

187

people's position, he eventually abandoned such attitudes. Love looks outward from itself to the general good, and persists in patient endeavour after God's purposes.

Everlasting love

Such love lasts forever. Both faith and hope may be misplaced, but love never. Love has the secret of perennial youth; it never passes out of existence, and cannot be obliterated from the heavenly record; it is written in the indelible ink of the blood of Christ. Love's carbon-copy is in triplicate, in the heart of the eternal God, in the heart of history at Calvary, and in the human heart. Its transcript-image is everywhere and always a cross. Therefore we never finish with love, as the love of God never finishes with us. Love includes, transforms, fulfils, and perpetuates everything that is worthwhile in life. No flood can quench it, no fire consume it, no rust corrode it, no devil corrupt it.

Optimism of grace

The purpose of the top level talks now nears completion. The Christian Summit Meeting is expressed in actual process in the world. The nature of the Triune God is at work in human nature and the world at large. The general Biblical pattern of procedure has appeared, and some understanding has been gained of its significance and practicability. The optimism of grace has been sounded above the deep bass note of penitence and the pessimism of grace. The contradictions of human nature and history would fill the heart with despondency were it not for the plain promise of Scripture and the lives of the saints, famous and obscure. Jesus loved all-out folk. To the wealthy young overlord he said, 'One thing thou lackest' (Luke 18:22), but the lack was fatal. The unredeeming feature differs with individuals, but whatever substitute-worship dominates the heart must go, without qualification. 'All for Jesus. Christ for all. All for Christ.'

Christ must reign

At your heart this attitude and spirit of Christ must reign, however perverse the circumstances wherein your life is lived, and however little you are allowed to express it in action.

James Naylor, the Quaker who at one time was persuaded by misguided friends to believe that he was the returning Messiah, but made a marvellous recovery to sanity, wrote in the choice language of his religious persuasion of the inner change wrought by the work of Christ. 'There is a spirit which I feel, that delights to do no evil, nor to revenge any wrong, but delights to endure all things; its hope is to outlive all wrath and contention, and to weary out all exultation and cruelty . . . As it bears no evil in itself, so it conceives none in thought to any other . . . Its crown is meekness, its life is everlasting love unfeigned; it takes its kingdom with entreaty, and not with contention, and keeps it by lowliness of mind.'

Completing the process

Whatever else may be outside your control if you have any normal freedom at all, of the most residual kind, God's Spirit works thereon. 'A bruised reed he will not break, and a dimly burning wick he will not quench' (Isaiah 42:3). There is no limit which faith can set to the possibilities. 'It doth not yet appear what we shall be, but we know that when we see him we shall be like him, for we shall see him as he is. And every one who thus hopes in him purifies himself as he is pure' (1 John 3:2–3). The process is at work all the time under the surface, but cannot effectually work till it is brought to the surface in the acceptance by faith of new birth in Christ, when we become trustful and obedient children. As we proceed it becomes clear that a further section is required on completing the process, with reference to further elements in the shaping process, and with a dissertation on the meaning of glory, for we are to be changed from one glory to another.

Faith works by love

However far or deep or tortuous the road of thought on these profound matters may have been we end in prayer and praise. In verse form Charles Wesley's hymn with the opening lines, which mislead so many folk into supposing it is a morbid threnody, sums up the theme, including the note of mystic ecstasy which was so central to his brother's convictions about the blessing, and which in fact is a permanent rapture of ethical

love woven into the texture of time and space here and now
in human experience, but with a forward look to the fulness
yet to come. 'Come on, my partners in distress . . . to patient
faith the prize is sure, and they that to the end endure the
cross shall wear the crown . . . In hope of that ecstatic pause,
Jesus we now sustain the cross . . .' The whole hymn is a
model of Scriptural and experimental realism. The believer
marches, dances, fights, rejoices. Verbs abound as faith works
by love (Galatians 5:6). The very Greek verb *energoumene*
contains the quintessential word with which we began, and
which sums up the stuff of the universe through which everything, sanctification included, operates—energy. The participle
has complementary renderings which bring out different aspects
of the truth: faith is energized by love, and energizes through
love. The two attitudes are aspects of each other, and interact
upon each other, but love is the objective originator, with faith
as the response, whose subjective apprehension further releases
the power of love. 'There is no love, like the love of Jesus,
never to fade or fall . . .' As Cardinal Newman put it, 'The
concentrated energy of a look or a word is the instrument of
heaven.' The concentrated energy of the Spirit of God in Christ
fully at work in believers as saving persons *is* entire sanctification, which is both the promise of God and the natural response
to the promise.

As a tribute to my Father, George Meadley, through whom
I first learned to find my way around the Scriptures (through
whose life I saw the strong Son of God in the kind of unsenti-
mental love which battles on courageously and victoriously so
long as the physical base is available in fit form to use for
the purpose), I would close with a prayer he wrote for his
people at Claremont Street Methodist Church, Leicester:
'Thou Lamb of God, whose side wast cleft for love of sinners,
show me the secret of the love that drew me to Thee. Give
me the same gentle heart and constraining love that I may
draw others to Thee. As I pray Thou dost answer, for my
longing is begotten of Thy love. Thou art answering as I pray.
I believe that Thou wilt use me for the salvation of those
for whom Thou hast died. I rest upon the power of Thy love.'
Amen.

8   Concluding the process

'Then comes the end, when he delivers the kingdom to God the Father after destroying every rule and every authority and power. For he must reign until he has put all his enemies under his feet. The last enemy to be destroyed is death. "For God has put all things in subjection under his feet." But when it says, "All things are put in subjection under him," it is plain that he is excepted who put all things under him. When all things are subjected to him, then the Son himself will also be subjected to him who put all things under him, that God may be everything to every one.' (1 Corinthians 15 : 24–28.)

'And we all, with unveiled face, beholding the glory of the Lord, are being changed into his likeness from one degree of glory to another; for this comes from the Lord who is the Spirit . . . Though our outer nature is wasting away, our inner nature is being renewed every day. For this slight momentary affliction is preparing for us an eternal weight of glory beyond all comparison, because we look not to the things that are seen but to the things that are unseen; for the things that are seen are transient, but the things that are unseen are eternal. For we know that if the earthly tent we dwell in is destroyed, we have a building from God, a house not made with hands, eternal in the heavens.' (2 Corinthians 3 : 18; 4 : 16; 5 : 1.)

'And just as it is appointed for men to die once, and after that comes judgement, so Christ,

*having been offered once to bear the sins of
many, will appear a second time, not to deal
with sin but to save those who are eagerly
waiting for him.'* (Hebrews 9:27–28.)
*'Then I saw a new heaven and a new earth;
for the first heaven and the first earth had
passed away, and the sea was no more. And
I saw the holy city, new Jerusalem, coming
down out of heaven from God, prepared as a
bride adorned for her husband; and I heard a
great voice from the throne saying, "Behold,
the dwelling of God is with men. He will dwell
with them, and they shall be his people, and
God himself will be with them; he will wipe
away every tear from their eyes, and death shall
be no more, neither shall there be any mourning nor crying nor pain any more, for the
former things have passed away."'* (Revelation
21:1–4.)

WE have surveyed the scene, learned the language, compiled
the agenda, outlined the programme, watched the snags,
considered how the energy is generated and the operation
conducted. How does the whole affair culminate? What is the
conclusion of the process?

A final sifting

As the work began in the world of the spirit so presumably
it concludes there, and gathers up the earthly processes in
a final sifting of worthwhile and worthless, consigning the
latter either to oblivion or to some kind of perpetually
destructive incinerator, because it is self-destructive in essence.
The whole process requires the concept of a grand finale to
make sense; otherwise it is a largely pointless gyration of
energy to little purpose, temporarily significant but finally
meaningless. Wheat and tares grow together till the harvest,
and then the winnowing process sorts them out; the wheat
is gathered into the garner, and the chaff and tares are burned
with unquenchable fire.

All things in Christ

Apparently the purpose of God is to gather up all things in Christ (Ephesians 1 : 9–10), though this omnibus resolution is necessarily limited by obstinate refusal. The aim of God is to create a universe where personality in community may flourish, and the condition of the horizontal relationships between human beings is the commonly accepted vertical relationship to the One in control. 'Glory to God in the highest, and on earth peace among men of goodwill' (Luke 2 : 14).

Faith not sight

Once we begin to consider such a final state we are drawn far beyond any capacity of man for complete understanding or prediction. He is without qualification in the region of faith and hope, not of sight. Recall that the Biblical view of faith does not preclude evidence, reason, imagination, courage, experimentation. The contrast is with sight or measurability, not with reason or evidence. The immediate promise is that the exercise of such faith will have considerable, though not complete, verification in temporal experience. Through the Spirit, applying Christ and His reconciling work, we have a foretaste, a pledge, a first instalment, an engagement-ring (2 Corinthians 1 : 22; 5 : 5; Ephesians 1 : 14). This experience of pardon, holiness, and heaven is a sample offcut from the final constituent of the universe, but it is always imparted within the continuing and containing condition of time and change, space and limitation. At the beginning and end of things we shade off into the cloud of mystery, of unknowing, of the agnostic. 'Lord, wilt thou at this time restore the kingdom to Israel?' (Acts 1 : 6) was the main question asked by the apostles of the risen Jesus. 'It is not for you to know the times or the seasons which the Father hath put in his own power' (v. 7) was our Lord's reply, which cuts at the root of any suggestion of claims to special knowledge on the subject.

Incomplete and metaphorical

The most we can do is to study the clues in Scripture and

193

seek to fit them into the pattern already given. Inevitably the result of the investigation will be incomplete. We are neither wise nor good enough to possess such knowledge. It will not be surprising if the hints and pictures are not completely consistent. We do not necessarily conclude that they are mutually exclusive or incompatible. They are in the nature of the case parabolic, symbolic, with a limited purpose in each instance to bring out an aspect of the truth. The current use of the term *myth* is unhelpful because it is used in a highly specialized sense which does not convey to non-academic people what the academics mean. Myth in ordinary language implies totally imaginary situations in the category of fairy-tales. A far better term, less open to criticism, would be *parable,* or that which is laid alongside to convey meaning and indicate a framework of reference. It is obviously to our advantage to deal with this matter of language straightaway, (though reference has already been made in the chapter on 'Learning the Language'), for unless we are allowed to use metaphorical language we might as well go out of business, certainly in discussing final realities.

Two verbal ways of approach

There are roughly two verbal approaches to the Last Things, as theological jargon has it, and both are employed in Scripture. There is the agnostic way, saying what we don't know, and, on the other hand, the frank use of symbolic language, using images which evoke the appropriate ideas and sensations. To quote the seventeenth-century doctor with such a fund of recondite allusion and quaintly perspicacious turn of phrase, Sir Thomas Browne in *Religio Medici,* 'that elegant apostle who wrote of these things hath left us but a negative description thereof'. He refers to Paul's words, 'eye hath not seen, neither hath ear heard, neither hath it entered into the mind of man, what things God hath prepared for those who love him' (1 Corinthians 2:9). John Bunyan recognizes the difficulty when he comments in doggerel verse on the criticisms hurled at the simple visual imagery of *Pilgrim's Progress*. He was well aware of the perils of unimaginative interpretation.

Take heed . . . of playing with the outside of my dream;
Nor let my figure or similitude
Put thee into a laughter or a feud.
Leave this for boys and fools; but as for thee,
Do thou the inside of my matter see.
Put by the curtains, look within the veil,
Turn up my metaphors and do not fail.
There, if thou seekest them, such things thou'lt find
As will be helpful to an honest mind.

Bunyan knows that he is attempting to describe the indescrib-able, and to express the inexpressible, the reality of the spiritual world, the glory of accomplished purpose, the climax and triumph of the strivings of God and man. When he has given us a glimpse of the glories of the world beyond he falls back upon Sir Thomas Browne's approach. 'But, above all, the warm and joyful thoughts that they had about their own dwelling there, with such company and that for ever and ever— oh, by what tongue or pen can their glories be expressed!' Nevertheless he tried his best and pressed language to the uttermost. He properly used earthly pictures, as does the author of the Revelation, to symbolize and suggest unearthly glory, and to arouse the appropriate sensations here and now. Art must be harnessed to its noblest use, and language must be used to transcend language, which is the function of poetry. The measurable language of science and common sense is vital to our existence in this world, but cannot cope satisfac-torily even in this life with the values and relationships which make existence worthwhile. Francis Thompson speaks for us all when he exclaims,

Oh but the heavenly grammar did I hold
Of that high speech which angels' tongues turn gold.

The origin of the language
Language is a tool to cope with life. Great language is born of great experiences, which themselves involve the con-flict, misery and grandeur which are the stuff of human freedom. The Scriptural depiction of heaven borrows language from the raw history of the people of God before Christ came. 'The

city was pure gold, like unto clear glass. And the foundations of the wall of the city were garnished with all manner of precious stones' (Revelation 21:18b–19a). Here is an idealized picture whose roots were in the historical Jerusalem, the holy city, levelled to the dust of utter desolation, weeds its only decoration and wild beasts its only inhabitants. The inaccessibility of exile made the lost city inexpressibly precious. Those born in exile must perforce rely on glowing descriptions of the former glories, their imaginations unshackled by actuality. They pictured a restored perfection. After the brief Maccabean interlude of independence the Jews descended into the long trough of subjection. The more frustrated their experience, the more inflated became the city of their dreams, which they eventually attributed to God's workmanship, at last to descend from heaven. To meet the need a special class of literature arose called apocalyptic, unveiling the otherwise hidden power of God, couched in language full of meaning to the initiated but in cryptic cipher to mislead the tyrannical overlords. These Tracts for Bad Times originated in periods of hardship and persecution. Their audience was composed of the faithful, suffering for their faith. Their aim was to encourage continued loyalty in the face of brutal torture. Their method was to reveal in code the overthrow of the oppressor and to kindle the imagination with pictures of the ultimate state of victory, glory, and the blessedness to follow. Naturally the details of the picture were drawn from their own background, with an oriental flamboyance not always acceptable to the more restrained taste of those with the moderate Greek attitude based on the Golden Mean. The jewels and the gold represent the infinitely precious and valuable. Crowns speak of triumph and authority. Palms signify the flags and banners of a triumphal procession, like the torn-up ticker-tape of a New York reception for the famous. Harps were the national instrument, plucked for joy and gratitude. The silent harp bespoke grief, as when the exiles hung up their harps under the taunts of the Jew-baiters on Babylon's riverside.

The effect of the language
Anyone who dismisses such imagination as mere pipe-

dreaming fantasy should reflect that the images achieved their purpose. The precious proximity of the celestial world confirmed faith and maintained loyalty. No language is so vivid and powerful as that wrought in the fires of actual suffering. 'The trumpet sounds from the hid battlements of eternity' with martial vigour, sweet appeal and magical effect. Precious truths uttered in nerveless or abstract language lose force. It is easy to scoff but such vivid word-pictures produced the goods. Argument is inadequate when aggressive worldliness, with all the glittering panoply of successful secularism, flaunts its wares before men's gaze, especially when it reaches its logical climax in all the pressures of totalitarian government. Apostasy awaits the feeble in faith. Whether it is the pressures of persecution or the soul-destroying monotony and petty spitefulness of routine living which assaults the soul, there is nothing so effectual as 'the light that never was on land or sea' to reinforce and irradiate human life with dignity and destiny. 'You can only throw up your hat in this world when you believe in the next', exclaimed saintly Bishop King of Lincoln. Dean Inge may scorn 'the squalid sluttery of dissenting conventicles', but Dr Russell Maltby's implied rebuke to one who commiserated with his supposed distasteful memories of Methodist village Bethels in his childhood, is nearer to the truth. 'I only remember the shine on the faces of the people', and he was not referring to the effect of overheated chapels on the sweat-glands of the face. There was an inner glow which transfigured these social nobodies who were aristocrats of the faith, and incidentally contributed in no small measure to all that is best in social legislation and decent behaviour in this country.

> *The men of grace have found*
> *Glory begun below;*
> *Celestial fruit on earthly ground*
> *From faith and hope may grow:*
> *Then let our songs abound,*
> *And every tear be dry;*
> *We are marching through Immanuel's ground*
> *To fairer worlds on high.*

ISAAC WATTS

What is heaven?

The final hope of the Christian is that he will reach heaven, the dimension in which God is known without any hindrance or distortion caused by time, space, or sin. Heaven is another name for the direct presence of God. The English word means literally the sky, the overarching blue dome, the firmament apparently fixed above the earth, so far as man's unsophisticated observation goes, the expanse in which the sun, moon, stars and planets move. More technically it is interstellar space. In the first chapter of the Bible God is represented as responsible for the heavens as well as the earth, and the last book of the Bible visualizes a new heaven as well as a new earth. It is not hard to sense why the abode of God was considered as up above the bright blue sky. Primitive man has a sense of the nearness of spiritual powers in streams, trees, and localized objects, but once the idea of one God has been accepted the unity of His Being required something more adequate for His presence than diffusion through space. Even more when His power, majesty, and ethical holiness were understood it was natural to look up to the Being supremely superior in strength and character. The prepositions of spatial relationship are all that is available to symbolize a personal relationship, yet neither can be equated totally with the other without doing injustice to each. The prisoner of Patmos was both *in* the island concentration-camp and also *in* the Spirit. So also we both look *up* to a high mountain and to a person of superior authority and goodness. Patronizing references to simple believers of previous generations who thought that heaven was in fact above the literal skies are quite out of place. It is doubtful whether any instructed Christian ever reasoned so. Augustine summed the point up very early in the history of Christian thought: 'there is no distance from God except unlikeness to Him', and centuries previously the Psalmist knew that astromical ascent and geological descent did not exhaust the presence of God. Once more we are faced with the inevitable use of picture-language from crude human observation. The Hebrews used *galgal,* rolling clouds, and *shamayim,* the heaved-up things, and the Greeks *ouranos,* the sky and air, in each case employing the normal terms for supreme elevation.

The essence of the concept was the approach to the One in control from a status of eminence. To be approved and accepted in God's immediate presence is the supreme bliss, summarizing all other attendant benefits. Heaven therefore stands for the reward and final destiny of those who are properly adjusted to His will. Heaven above is the obvious material symbol of transcendence, which is the dimension of supreme spiritual worth, active within but not confined by the limited world of space/time. Our Lord discourages speculation about the topography of heaven. No celestial guidebooks are available, either for sale or free distribution. His main concern was that men should be living in line with the will and rule of God here and now. A curious question about the numbers qualifying for salvation was met by the practical exhortation, 'Strive to enter in at the strait gate' (Luke 13:24). Watch, pray, keep the loins girt and the lamps burning, endure to the end. The scenery and stage-setting is beyond our direct vision precisely because we are not yet living within the undiluted dimension where it is relevant. The inherited imagery is too precious to be jettisoned, though neither it nor any other conceivable form can achieve the precision which is reserved for direct vision.

The unclouded presence: eternal life

Heaven is the unclouded presence of God for those adjusted to Him. Thus it is in itself eternal life (John 3:15f; 6:47), that quality of existence which in its nature is incorruptible, the unquenchable, everflowing stream of right relationships with God which Amos longed to see in the land characterized by unreliably spasmodic water-supplies. The suitable ones 'drink of the water of life freely' (Revelations 22:17). This quality of relationship is available in principle now. Believers may sit now with Christ, through whom this possibility has reached its fulness, 'in the heavenly places' (Ephesians 2:6). They may 'abide now' (John 15:4) in Christ. They are citizens and colonists of heaven below (cf. Philippians 3:20; Luke 10:20). They may know not only the fellowship of His sufferings but also the power of His resurrection (Philippians 3:10). Nevertheless there is a simultaneity of pure perpetual vision reserved in the beyond, where adoration is

o

unencumbered by the inherent limitations of a contingent world. God is then and there seen 'face to face' (1 Corinthians 13:12) in the perfection of love. 'We shall see Him as He is' (1 John 3:2), and 'cry with a great voice' (Revelation 7:10) the praises of the Lamb who was slain. The heart of heaven is the adjusted relationship to the heart of the universe, the supra-personal matrix whence all existence emerges, and to which it returns, its destiny determined by its relationship. The Christian message relates to the nature of this matrix we call God, the concentrated creative repository of whatever is good, and the way of proper relationship thereto. In particular, the message deals with the way to re-enter that relationship when it has been lost, for whatever reason. The story of redeeming love through the life, work, death and resurrection of Jesus Christ is the central clue to everything, including heaven as the final state. 'In him we live and move and have our being, even as some of your (Greek) poets have said, for we are indeed his offspring . . . Now he commands all men everywhere to repent, because he had fixed a day on which he will judge the world in righteousness by a man whom he has appointed, and of this he has given assurance to all men by raising him from the dead' (Acts 17:28; 30–31). Charles Wesley's repeated phrase about 'pardon and holiness and heaven' summarizes the relationship of our theme to the celestial climax, except that it omits, more by assumption than neglect, the original context of the whole drama in the unspoiled creation, to that extent without the proven need of pardon. For Paul the life in Christ was essential heaven, the fulness of which drew desire towards its completion: 'for me to live is Christ, and to die is gain . . . I am hard pressed between the two. My desire is to depart and be with Christ, for that is far better . . .' (Philippians 1:21, 23.)

Unalloyed fellowship with others in Christ

All the way through we have to watch the tendency to see the process in primarily individualistic terms. Personality is a conjoint product, sanctification a social process, and heaven includes the communion of saints. The apocalyptic seer 'saw a great multitude which no man could number . . .' (Revelation

8 : 9–10). The grave may be 'a fine and private place', and 'je meurrai seul' (I shall die alone), but heaven is essentially corporate, and the beatific vision a congregational experience. Even now we have association with those who have completed the mortal race and fight. We are 'surrounded with an unseen cloud of witnesses' (Hebrews 12 : 1), who testify to the victorious power of God in Christ. As heroes of the faith, those faithful unto death who have received the crown of life (cf. Revelation 2 : 10), they see the accomplished purpose and final vindication more clearly than we can, but they are still concerned about their successors. Indeed, 'they without us shall not be made perfect' (Hebrews 11 : 40). United themselves with the great High Priest Himself they share His feeling for our infirmities. The joy of heaven, both for Christ and them, is compatible with suffering concern for those still enmeshed in the time-space-sin dimension. Our relationship to Jesus Christ includes within itself our total incorporation into the communion of those who are Christ's at his final coming, both past, present, and to come. A trans-temporal-eternal unity exists in worship, prayer, and faith with the glorious company of apostles, saints prophets, and martyrs. 'You have come to Mount Zion and to the city of the living God, the heavenly Jerusalem, and to innumerable angels in festal gathering, and to the assembly of the first-born who are enrolled in heaven, and to a judge who is God of all, and to the spirits of just men made perfect, and to Jesus the mediator of a new covenant, and to the sprinkled blood that speaks more graciously than the blood of Abel' (Hebrews 12 : 22–24). Heaven in its fulness includes our place in that company. We shall have joined the part of the host who have crossed the flood. Joseph Addison puts the point sombrely in *Reflections in Westminster Abbey*: 'when I read several dates of the tombs of some that died yesterday and some six hundred years ago, I consider the great day when we shall all of us be contemporaries.' C. H. Dodd truly remarked, 'for Christianity the true seat of eternal life is the communion of saints, and the individual is held to be immortal within that communion' (Ingersoll Lectures 1934–5, *The Communion of Saints*).

Blissful and obedient service

Fundamental to the Biblical conception of God is his continuous exercise of energetic purpose. 'My Father is working still, and I am working' (John 5:17). Service is the nub of this purposive energy, both serving the purpose and the participants therein. 'They serve him day and night in his temple' (Revelation 7:15). Angels are messengers able and willing to dart anywhere at the bidding of the Lord of all. Heaven is the dimension in which pure service continues without interruption or corruption. Worship and work are one indivisible ritual. There is nothing so delightful as permanent usefulness in a worthwhile cause. For this purpose Christ came; with this method He pursued his calling; and in this accomplished destiny He triumphs. No grit spoils the frictionless movement, and the oil of joy suffuses the whole activity. Hence the original and true unity is restored, and trustful obedience issues in blissful service, to which mankind can set no limit save his wilful refusal to cooperate.

Active rest

'There remains therefore a rest to the people of God' (Hebrews 4:9). Primarily this rest is the Sabbath, the periodic climax, the seventh day of the week, applied to the consummation of the trek from slavery to freedom in Canaan. The rest is not supine inactivity, but activity so natural and unfrustrated that labour is more restful than leisure; indeed labour and recreation are one and the same. One can appreciate the charwoman's epitaph without sharing its implications.

> *Don't pity me now;*
> *Don't pity me never.*
> *I'm going to do nothing*
> *For ever and ever.*

Nevertheless the essence of heaven is not such a permanently prone posture on an infinite chaise-longue. With relaxed strength our best self, together with those who share our faith, we pick up the threads, worn and sometimes broken, of human experience, and find them securely woven into the overall pattern of divinely purposive energy.

202

Accomplished purpose

The total purpose, which hitherto has been moving *to* fruition now operates *within* fruition. What appeared to close in twilight emerges into dawn. Victor Hugo, towards the end of his life as a novelist, commented, 'I have tried all, but I feel I have not said one thousandth part of what is in me. When I go down to the grave I cannot say I have finished my life. My day's work will begin again next morning. The tomb is not a blind alley, it is a thoroughfare.' The will of God includes accomplishment without loss of incentive to continued accomplishment. Grace reigns in perfect harmony and with a built-in simultaneity of experience. 'We all, with unveiled face, beholding the glory of the Lord, are being changed from one degree of glory to another . . .' (2 Corinthians 3:18). The inheritance 'is imperishable, undefiled and unfading, kept in heaven for you . . .' (1 Peter 1:4). The centre of everything is 'the throne of God and of the Lamb . . . and his servants shall worship him . . . and they shall reign for ever and ever' (Revelation 22:3, 5).

Freedom from evil distraction

The enemy of concentration is distraction, and concentration is the essence of purity of heart, which is the condition of the vision of God which is heaven. Sin, sorrow, successiveness all distract. Conquest *is* possible in the here and now, but the pressure of these three factors is relentless. God will 'wipe away every tear from their eyes and death shall be no more, neither shall there be mourning nor crying any more, for the former things have passed away' (Revelation 21:3-4). Also every symptom of diseased relationship is deleted; 'as for the cowardly, the faithless, the polluted, as for murderers, fornicators, sorcerers, idolaters, and all liars'. There is no place or opportunity to distract attention. The fate of this grisly crew is dealt with later. The main point is that 'nothing unclean shall enter it, nor anyone who practises abomination or falsehood . . .' (ibid. 21:27).

Harmonious home

Heaven is thus that state of being and relationship where man is at home with the source of his being. It is the consummation of the supreme quality of living, sometimes called eternal life, which is the Johannine equivalent of the Kingdom or Reign of God, central to the teaching of Jesus. Custom cannot stale its infinite variety. It is not so much interminable as simultaneous, 'forever beginning what never shall end.' No one need fear that he will ever be driven to utter the last word of spy Kim Philby's father, 'God, I'm bored!' The richer our relationship the less conscious we are of the passing of time. We are absorbed in whole-hearted commitment to love, service, compassionate service, beauty, worship. We are, in the profoundest sense of the phrase, at home, where all the best within us may flourish without impediment. Here is the finest friendship releasing the fullest potential of creative activity. 'I must have Coleridge with me,' exclaimed William Wordsworth, 'there is poetry in me only he can bring out.' Heaven is 'to know Thee, the only true God' (John 17:3), the One who said 'You are my friends . . . I go to prepare a place for you . . . In my Father's house are many rooms' (John 14:2), rather as an Eastern father added extensions to the family home to include his increasing family. Life is never dull with an incandescent friend. Here is solid reality and supreme dignity. In *The Great Divorce* C. S. Lewis describes the grass of heaven as sharp like spikes of glass, yet those properly adjusted walk easily thereon. One transparently beautiful and honoured lady is Sarah Smith of Golders Green. The narrative proceeds:

'And who are all these young men and women on each side?'
'They are her sons and daughters.'
'She must have had a very large family, Sir.'
'Every young man or boy that met her became her son— even if it was only the boy that brought the meat to her back door. Every girl that met her was her daughter.'
'Isn't that a bit hard on their own parents?'
'No. There *are* those who steal other people's children. But her motherhood was of a different kind. Those on whom it fell went back to their natural parents loving them more. Few men looked on her without becoming, in a certain fashion, her lovers. But it was the kind of love that made them not less true, but truer, to their own wives' (pp. 98–9).

For those who accept the adjustment to the Divine Will this harmonious home is the centre and climax of all when the Son shall deliver up all things to the Father, including those whom the Father has given Him (1 Corinthians 15:24 ff. and John 17:6).

Unmitigated glory

Possibly the supreme word for the heavenly state is glory. Each facet of heaven so far discussed implies glory. Like all comprehensively supreme words it eludes exact definition, precisely because definition, by derivation, sets categorical limits. Yet we cannot be satisfied with Humpty Dumpty's scornful dogmatism in *Alice Through The Looking-Glass,* 'There's glory for you . . . a nice knockdown argument . . . When I use a word it means just what I choose it to mean— neither more nor less.' Two elements appear in the Biblical occasions of glory—shining brightness and weight. I recall a midnight swim at Cuxhaven at the mouth of the River Elbe in Schleswig, Germany. The water had a phosphorescent quality. Against the purple velvet darkness of the sky each stroke of the arms brought a flash of light, clear and splendid, an unforgettable experience. Glory speaks of a public occasion, a cavalcade of triumph, with brilliant colours in pennants and accoutrements, purple and scarlet, glittering armour reflecting the shining of the sun, shimmering irridescence of flower and foliage, fountains and effulgent panoply. Every voice joins in the swelling chorus of joyous praise. All the wealth of the community is on display, heavy with the weight of jewels and the flourishing economy of the country. The robes for the occasion are massive and copious; medals, decorations, coronets are in full display. Glory covers all as the waters cover the sea. When the monarch of Great Britain is crowned the poor soul seems almost smothered and borne down by the weight of symbolism, but nothing else does justice to the event. We live in a dusty, gritty age, flattening and levelling to the point of meanness. Man yearns for exultation, and is not satisfied with utility alone. Shining songs of glory reverberate throughout the Scriptures such as humanism never knew. Noble ethics exist apart from the full revelation in Christ.

Stoicism towers in history, but it does not overflow in choral glory. 'Epictetus announces a hymn to Zeus', said T. R. Glover, 'but he never starts the tune.'

A distinctive note of the early nineteenth-century Ranters was precisely this glory. 'A glimpse of bright glory overpowers my soul . . . My soul's full of glory which inspires my tongue; Could I meet with angels I'd sing them a song . . . O brethren, keep believing . . . we're going home to glory (repeated three times) . . . Come and taste along with me, glory, glory, glory; wherefore should I feast alone, glory, glory, glory . . . Blow ye the trumpet, blow . . .'

Often they would meet in a cowshed with the farmyard odours of Edom still fresh upon their corduroy trousers (the nether garments of royalty, the arty-crafty, and the yokel), and their song would be 'On all the kings of earth in pity we look down', on ten shillings a week with a family to keep. Nevertheless glory crowned the mercy-seat, and they were dignified, bright, weighty men, who, though social, financial, and educational nobodies, helped to transform the crude and callous indignities of the new industrial working class, and eventually won the popular vote. One aim of the Gospel is 'to bring many sons into glory'. To impart this glimpse of heaven Christ came with its miraculous expression in Suffering Servant form to open the doors and windows. The imagery of the Apocalypse conveys the glorious triumph of the Lamb slain from the foundation of the world, who is the Lion of Judah, breaking every chain.

Silence in heaven

The climax in Revelation of the greatest choral festival of glory ever presented was—silence (cf. Revelation 8:1). The scene centres on the sealed book containing the secrets of the divine purpose. The innumerable company of Christian believers is gathered round the throne of final government. The Lord Jesus, having completed His stint of active communication in space and time, breaks each seal in turn, and each new insight releases the pent-up feelings of the immense gathering in a swirling tempest of exultant joy. When the seventh and final seal is ripped and the deepest mysteries unveiled, the tumult and the shouting subsides into the sound of a gentle stillness. This strange sequel displays the touch of the artist. The theatrical technician would have brought every instrument and voice to a crescendo of crescendos, an earsplitting fortissimo. The disciplined craftsman knows that supreme emotions are silent, transcending sound. When we visit the bereaved we have nothing to say; hand grips hand, and deep calls to deep. The sound waves of the spirit exceed the speed of speech. 'Set the important in silence' advised a drama teacher. The effective pause is part of the communication. Such silence speaks. In the countryside the absence of the city hum can keep the townsman awake. 'Don't forget to play your rests', said Sir Walter Parratt. The most hair-raising part of the Hallelujah Chorus is the uncanny pause prior to 'the kingdoms of this world'.

Sound is a sea, and melody it makes,
But silence is the shore on which it breaks.

Half an hour is a curious time-detail to insert into eternity, but presumably it is meant to emphasize the profundity of the impression created. Two minutes is a long silence on Remembrance Day. Half an hour would be an unforgettable interval at the theatre. This celestial silence has a threefold quality. Everyone is amazed, like 'stout Cortez . . . silent upon a peak in Darien', at the new world displayed. Jesus stressed the element of surprise at the judgement. First and last may well be reversed. The nature and extent of holy love over-whelms the spirit with wonder. Everyone is also ashamed. 'Kings shall shut their mouths because of him' (Isaiah 52:15). All the self-confident human interpretations of history fade away. Luther, imagining the Judgement Day, remarked, 'I can bear anything but the silence of God.' The faithless fears, the querulous self-pity, the petulant complaints, all melt into penitential tears. Above all, everyone adores. Many strands weave the garment of adoration. Gratitude is often tongue-tied. 'We mean the thanks we cannot speak.' Awe hushes the voice, and praise sits silent on our tongues. The intimate communion of friends needs not the wearisome labour of manufacturing conversation. 'We do not know each other yet. We have not dared to be silent together', said Maurice Maeterlinck in *The Treasure of the Humble*. Supremely, adoration culminates in ecstasy, rapture, bliss. A peasant said in church, 'I just looks at Him, and He looks at me.' John Donne expresses the human equivalent in 'The Extasie',

> *All day the same our postures were,*
> *And we said nothing all the day.*

The fullness of rapture is one of the distinctive marks of the Methodist movement. Charles Wesley often returns to this theme. He catches up this particular Scriptural moment as he exhorts the Christian pilgrim to press towards the celestial hill. The various evidences of the costly reconciling work of Christ:

> *. . . conspire our rapture to complete;*
> *And lo! we fall before His feet,*
> *And silence heightens heaven.*
> *In hope of that ecstatic pause*
> *Jesus, we now sustain the Cross . . .*

Here the inner meaning of mysticism, which so often loses its way in unhistorical deserts and a morass of internal sensation, in spite of ascetic disciplines of concentration, is brought to its true centre and climax. Entire sanctification is a permanently-shared rapture of holy love, which is nothing less than the divine nature imparted. In heaven this already mundanely experienced relationship is relieved from the undulating nature of all temporal existence. Here is the fullness of what had been already tasted, 'the silence of eternity, interpreted by love.' The engine runs smoothly and silently because every part is perfectly adjusted. Father, Son, and Holy Spirit, together with the whole family of trustful and obedient love are within each other, not absorbed but reconciled.

Immortality

Against this background the concept of immortality is to be understood. In itself it is more Greek, aesthetic and metaphysical than the Biblical approach. So far as it goes the notion is legitimate. The existence of a desire implies *possible*, though *not inevitable*, satisfaction. The sheer mortality of man assaults his dignity, and the premature thwarting of his unfinished purposes offends him. He thinks he was not made to die. He has a pathetic revulsion from extinction the higher he rises in the scale of values. A certain greyness afflicts his culture eventually when the brightest attractions of his earthly environment display symptoms of corruption, physical or moral. We should not know thirst if drink did not exist, and likewise with hunger and food, sight and light. There is no guarantee that the fulfilment is available when required, but the existence somewhere of fulfilment is inherent in the existence of the experience and capacity. Life initiates purposes unfulfilled in time, therefore it is not irrational to continue the dotted line into eternity. The advantage of the Christian assertion is that this human outreach is met by a presence from the eternal world, not merely of ideas but of personal and communal purposes, namely the first and the last and the living One (Revelation 1 : 17f.). Thereby the human concept of immortality, valid within its limits, is filled with profounder meaning. He has abolished (i.e. taken the power out of) death, and 'has brought life and immortality *to light* through the Gospel' (2 Timothy 1 : 10). Thereby the otherwise alternative views of eternal life and immortality are reconciled. There remains to relate this reconciled understanding to the particularly Biblical view of resurrection.

Appropriate embodiment

Implied in the whole Christian drama of revelation is continuing identity of the individual within the continuing fabric of the believing community. We are not destined to be no more than drops in an infinite ocean of being. The form of heavenly existence is therefore up for question. We are to be distinguishable selves in society. Being raised from the dead implies both that death is an empirical reality, with its associated spiritual experience, and that a new dimension of existence is available. We are familiar with the fact of organic adaptation to environment in this world, and the reciprocal relation of environment to organism. Henry Drummond introduced us to natural law in the spiritual world, but he was only applying a thoroughly Biblical procedure. 'Speak to the earth and it shall teach you', taught Job (12:8). Paul follows the same idea in the most extended treatment of the theme in the New Testament. He draws a distinction between the flesh and the body, and until this is clearly seen we are likely to have grisly nightmares of gravestones flying, skeletons reassembling, and attendant queries about cremated remains. The flesh, as particles of measurable matter, shares the fate of the rest of creation. 'Dust you are, and to dust you return . . . All flesh is grass, and the goodliness thereof as the flower of the field. The grass withers, the flower fades. Surely the people is grass.' Genesis and Isaiah concur. Paul agrees that 'flesh and blood cannot inherit the kingdom of God' (1 Corinthians 15:50). 'The first man was from the earth, a man of dust' (v. 47). Not that the apostle despises the physical framework. There is no oriental abhorrence of man's physical nature. The carnal spirit, which idolizes and exploits its flesh for its own use or pleasure, irrespective of the will of God, is to be rejected, but the psychosomatic unit which is our present habitation is sacred because it is the temple of the Holy Spirit. By using the term *body* Paul intends us to understand the whole person in whatever form is suitable to a given dimension of existence. Thus he insists that a suitable body is provided (vv. 35–38). He draws his analogy from any back garden, the mystery of the seed, which might be no more than a handful of sand, till sown. The first, rather uninteresting shape decays, the old body is shed, and a new shape of use and beauty appears which would be quite inconceivable until produced and observed. Such death was necessary for the new life to appear. 'Except a corn of wheat fall into the ground and die it abides alone' (John 12:24), as Jesus commented. Where the old tissues and cells refuse to die, a cancerous state ensues.

The power of this new life was ironically illustrated in Hanover cemetery, where a woman disbeliever in the resurrection left instructions for her tomb to be so piled up with massive slabs of marble and granite, secured with steel clasps, that if such a misfortune occurred the resurrection would not reach her. The epitaph read, 'This grave must never be opened.'

A tiny seed fell among the slabs and began to feel for the light. By its own internal nature it reached for light and air, and finally grew into a tree which burst the bonds asunder.

Paul proceeds to assert that the necessary new shape of embodiment is provided, adapted to the new surroundings, with the appropriate qualities to exist therein. The personality will not be diminished, but rather enhanced, since it is free of the cramping limitations previously necessary to clamp it into disciplined shape. The new body is in a sense preparing now as the inner glory of the butterfly awaits the shedding of the chrysalis. The spiritual body does not depend on the state of the earthly body at death. Beneath many a crippled, distorted, and even paralysed form a beautiful spirit, temporarily concealed, awaits deliverance. Whether psychic phenomena provide a clue to the transitional area between the one and the other is a matter for speculation. Some are persuaded, others not, but the significant point either way is the quality of the life in relation to the opportunity in Christ. The incorruptible one is Jesus Christ, in whom the spirit of holiness dwelt in completion. The Bible does not have much truck with the merely psychic. Though Paul claimed such gifts of nature he kept them strictly in their subordinate place. What matters is the whole-hearted relationship of trust, obedience, and love in the Father's family of acceptance, as made available in the costly work of His Son, experienced in the fellowship of the Holy Spirit. Heaven below and heaven above are both known in and through Jesus Christ, and linked through Him. We are raised with Him in a form appropriate to the heavenly dimension; hence our faith includes the resurrection of the body, as well as immortality and eternal life.

Hell

Since the proper climax of entire sanctification is heaven, and since a partial freedom is assumed in men, it follows that some may miss the way. No normal person contemplates such a fate for himself or any other with equanimity. Our Lord's approach in this as in all other matters was practical. Make sure you are on the right road! He did not come to condemn, but to rescue, but loss is a possibility. How shall we interpret

211

this sad fate? The English word hell originally means a covered place, hence the underworld, the mysterious abode of the buried. The reference in the Apostles' Creed to our Lord's descending into hell has no original suggestion of a place of torment or punishment. It was inserted from the Sirmian Creed at the Council of Ariminum in A.D. 359 to combat any idea that our Lord was not truly human and shared to the full the experience of death. The original form of words ran, 'and went down into the lower world'. Only later was the English term used for the place of the damned rather than the dead. For the most part the term disappears in modern translations, not because of any dislike of the doctrine but because it conveys an inaccurate idea. The Hebrew Sheol and the Greek Hades mean only what the English Hell first meant—a rather grey, amorphous underworld of departed shades.

Our Lord's picture

The picture which our Lord uses, implying some kind of painful destruction, is Gehenna, the valley of Hinnom, where such abominations had been practised at one time immediately outside the Holy City that it had been destroyed under a ban, and retained only as a refuse tip (2 Kings 23:10; Jeremiah 7:31). It was a fitting symbol of abominable curse and perpetual incineration, the refuse-heap of the universe. Since our Lord drew the parallel we cannot ignore the warning. John Milton expresses the point:

> *The pleasant valley of Hinnom, Tophet thence*
> *And black Gehenna called, the type of Hell.*

Dante's *Inferno* has elaborated the labyrinths of punishment, but his concern was more with his own day, and particular individuals he thought needed the treatment, though he includes types of people as well. As powerful parabolic preaching this is great stuff, but it does harm if it is assumed to indicate some special knowledge of the topography of judgement. Presumably the most refined interpretation would be of endless conscious suffering, realized as punishment, and separation from God even in His extremest mercy. The possibility of such a state would appear to be present in Scripture, but it is

212

doubtful whether we are able to dogmatize about the actual nature of such a state. It is certainly not our function to usurp the prerogatives of God and assign individuals or groups to the everlasting bonfire. When our Lord comments forcibly on the subject the conditions relate to ordinary compassion neglected. 'The eternal fire prepared for the devil and all his angels' (Matthew 25:41) is the destination of those who are uncompassionate to the humblest folk. It is hard to see the compassion of Christ in the furrowed brows and pursed lips of those who insist on emphasizing the penal element, with a kind of repressed ferocity.

Wesley and hell

It is instructive to note that John Wesley makes little reference to the subject; 'fewer than twenty references in almost 8,000 printed pages!' (D. Dunn Wilson, *Proceedings of the Wesley Historical Society,* Vol. XXXIV, p. 12). Wesley accepts the Scriptural references at their face value, but uses them not so much to threaten as to plead. He notes that frequent insistence on such punishment 'generally hardens them that believe not and discourages them that do' (Minutes 1746). Three different states are mentioned in *Notes on the New Testament.* Tartarus (2 Peter 2:4) is a place where fallen angels are like condemned criminals for 'safe custody as if bound with the strongest chains in a dungeon of darkness, to be reserved unto the judgement of the great day'. Hades is 'the invisible world. In the intermediate state, the body abides in death, the soul in Hades.' This condition has two apartments, one for those like Dives and another, Paradise or Abraham's bosom, for the Lazarus type. Gehenna he acknowledges as 'a fit emblem of hell'. The condemned 'gnaw their tongues for anguish and pain; they will curse God and look upward. There the dogs of hell—pride, malice, revenge, rage, horror, despair—continually devour them' (Sermons: 'The Great Assize').

The essence of hell

The essence of hell is separation from God the ground of our confidence, of exclusion from His family, condemned to be a permanent outsider, compelled to exist in a perpetual state of maladjustment. For practical purposes the function of such a state is sanitary, the elimination of disease and fumigation to prevent infection. In so far as hell is the state of nothingness, the abolition of values and purposive control for good ends, it is the abyss from which the Beast, Abaddon, emerges (Revelation 9:11). This Beast is energy in organized destruction, because impersonal energy is accepted as the ultimate, resulting in the worship of force, the idolatry of power, with its inevitable explosion into violence. The wages of such a rule is death. 'War is sin's apocalypse' (P. T. Forsyth, *Theodicy*). Since personal beings exist, such impersonal force is always mixed with personal aims of some kind on the corporate scale, and it issues in demonic forces of destruction, the more efficient and damnable the more merely human civilization advances. Thus hell is the ingurgitating vacuum of the spirit, the Maelstrom sucking its victims into its central emptiness. Here is a state of endless dissatisfaction. 'He'd like well to scratch; but even when he can scratch no more he'd rather itch than not' (C. S. Lewis, *The Great Divorce*). When Lewis's traveller seeks to locate the return journey to hell from heaven he is directed to an almost invisible slit in the ground. 'Do you mean that hell—all that infinitely empty town—is down some little crack like this?' The guide replies 'Yes. All hell is smaller than one pebble of your earthly world: but it is smaller than one atom of this world, the Real World . . .' 'It seems big enough when you're in it, Sir.' 'And yet all loneliness, angers, hatreds, envies and itchings that it contains, if rolled into one single experience and put into the scale against the least moment of joy that is felt by the least in Heaven, would have no weight that could be registered at all. Bad cannot succeed even in being bad as truly as good is good . . . A damned soul is nearly nothing; it is shrunk, shut up in itself.'

Hell the opposite of heaven

Hell is maladjustment to the final environment of the personality, to the world of the Holy Spirit as incarnated in Jesus Christ. Hell is the state of a compulsively unreconciled relationship. For a person whose idea of bliss was Saturday night at the local, to be confined to a perpetual prayer-meeting would be damnation. If heaven is the unclouded presence of God then hell would be the clouded presence, a shadowed relationship. If heaven is unalloyed fellowship with others in Christ than Jean Paul Sartre's definition would be precise: 'hell is other people'. If heaven includes blissful and obedient service, then hell is the wilful refusal to cooperate. In so far as heaven is active rest, hell is restless inaction. In so far as heaven is accomplished purpose, hell is purposelessness, motion without meaning. In so far as heaven is freedom from evil distraction, hell is the very concentration of this sorry state, never able to concentrate on anything worthwhile. In so far as heaven is harmonious home, hell is alienation and disharmony. In so far as heaven is unmitigated glory, hell is a state of dull meanness. In so far as the climax of heaven is the silence of the integrated mystic ecstasy, the rapture of holy love, the climax of hell is the deafening clamour of disintegrating hate, 'weeping and wailing and gnashing of teeth' (Luke 13:28), 'where their worm dieth not, and the fire is not quenched' (Mark 9:48). Self-centred isolation in enforced propinquity is the built-in essence of damnation, with an ever-increasing thirst for an ever-decreasing satisfaction. Ingurgitation of artifical stimuli expands to a dropsy of the spirit. Whether such a state ever culminates in oblivion who can say? Whether there is still an escape-hatch, and how such a state relates to the sovereign love of God and the joys of the blessed would appear to be speculations beyond the wit of man. The emphasis of our Lord was always on the practical distinction and the absolute importance of making the right response while opportunity remained.

Points of transition

In their concentrated essence these states exist beyond time, to be reached via a transitional junction. The terminus of time for the individual is death, and for society the end of the world as habitable for man. The teaching about the return of our Lord, and the association thereof with the final judgement, guarantees that these terminal points are not merely inevitable events without further control or significance. However, for

P

ourselves death is the more immediate transitional point of departure for final destiny.

The fact of death

The one most certain fact of life is death, which we have only observed and not personally experienced. 'In Adam all (everyman as human) die . . .' (1 Corinthians 15:22). Heart transplant operations pose with particular difficulty the question of the exact moment of death. Nevertheless, for all practical purposes, in its completeness it is the time when the mechanism of the heart, the circulation of the blood in the body, the act of breathing, the control of the nervous system by the brain, all cease. Death is 'thermodynamical equilibrium' (Schrödinger, *What is Life?*). 'Dust you are, and to dust you shall return' (Genesis 3:20) is the laconic comment of Holy Scripture at the very commencement of the human drama. The undertaker is one tradesman never likely to be unemployed.

Apparent finality of death

Death is not unique to human beings. Dying is a zoological fact; having to die is a human experience. The sense of anticipation, foreboding, frustration constitutes the peculiarly human dilemma. If personality is merely a more complex form of animal existence, a neuro-chemical phenomenon, then death is the end-product. The last word is with death, whose coronation procession we daily observe. The corpse needs only hygienic disposal by the local sanitation department. Human life is to that extent devalued, and there remains no spiritual authority to limit permissible maltreatment of human beings. Man cannot suppress for ever the question baldly asked in the old Ranter hymn, 'And am I only born to die?' Death as final reduces life to nonsense, denies overriding purpose, and saps the dynamic for civilized behaviour.

Attempts at mitigation

George Eliot sought substitute motivation in the longing to join the Choir Invisible of folk who had contributed to the betterment of future generations, a laudable attempt which merely postpones the question to the final death of the human

race. She evades the real issue, the corporate worthwhileness
of existence. The void eventually returns. George Meredith
counselled resigned acceptance, sensible but hardly invigorating.

> *Into the breast that gave the rose*
> *Should I with shuddering fall?*

More common is the recommendation of Ecclesiastes and
Omar Khayyam: 'Let us eat, drink, and be merry for tomorrow
we die.' Accumulated experience soon teaches people prudential
ethics, the avoidance of too drastic squeezing of the nervous
system for anodyne sensation. Mutual self-interest erects social
rituals to mitigate the worst effects on the community of too
logical an expression of this attitude. But the upshot is the
same: how to fill in time satisfactorily until the undertaker
calls.

The contribution of the Burial Service

The Burial Service poignantly focuses the great Biblical
themes as they affect mankind faced with the ultimate query.
The liturgy representatively summarizes the doctrines of
creation, providence, judgement, redemption, the end of the
world, the return of the Lord, heaven and hell. The dimensions
of time and eternity are concentrated in one moment in relation to a specific individual. Where, if anywhere, do we go
from here? If somewhere, what is its nature, and how do
we qualify? Eternal life is the very nature of God, and in the
Gospel that life we are invited to share, which offer brings us
back to our main theme, entire sanctification, or the complete
impartation of the divine nature. The Burial Service, therefore,
is in its very essence holiness evangelism, quite apart from
its therapeutic overtones.

The end of the world

In days of deceptive calm the end of the world is a thought
men seek to evade, or consign to Jehovah's Witnesses and
Armageddon News. It is the scientists who repeatedly bring us
back to facts. As President of the British Association, Sir
Richard Gregory gave an eye-witness account of the first experimental nuclear explosion in the Mexican desert prior to the

traumatic event of Hiroshima. He could find no more accurate description than the Scriptural prophecy that 'the heavens will vanish with a crackling roar, the stars will set ablaze and melt' (2 Peter 3:10). The Greek words indicate the sound of a rapid motion through the air, with a searing flash of fierce flame at fever heat. Under the headline 'How the World Could End' Tom Margerison, Science Correspondent of the *Sunday Telegraph* (20 June, 1966), reviewed Professor Barry Commoner's *Science and Survival*. From four to five years after a major nuclear attack atomic dust could blot out ten per cent of the sun's light, thus introducing a new Ice Age which could last about ten thousand years. Hot or cold, the closure is a possibility. The film of Nevil Shute's novel *On the Beach* in its final shots shows the empty streets of Melbourne, a flapping Salvation Army banner, and the last relics of human faith and energy pathetically fighting their doomed rearguard action. The 'one far-off divine event to which the whole creation moves' seems neither far-off nor divine.

Standard human reactions

If such be the last word, sanctification is anchorless. None of of the five alternative human reactions will suffice. Some ignore Cassandra's wolf-crying, and fall back on the stability of a paralysed imagination or a cynical resistance to what seems the all too familiar salesroom talk. 'Positively the last day' ceases to impress when indefinitely extended. Flesh-creeping secretes its own immunization. Some resort to the irrepressible optimism of Mr Micawber, genial but bankrupt. A prospective euphoria, a spiritual *spes phthisica,* bubbles up from the inner depths of fantasy. Despair is the most rational reaction. The prophet of evolutionary optimism, H. G. Wells, concluded *The Fate of Homo Sapiens* in this frame of mind. Realistic Bertrand Russell reached the same conclusion much earlier in *A Free Man's Worship.* As Luther commented on Ecclesiastes, 'He rides in his socks, without boot or spur.' Intoxication is a popular escape. 'As in the days of Noah' men guzzle the artificially stimulated sensation of expansion. Its logic is the momentary ecstasy of the methylated-spirit drinker as his throat gasps at the sharp intake of air. Psychedelic drugs are the latest short-cut to rapturous evasion. There remain the trigger-happy button-pressers whose bravado attracts the very destruction which fascinates them. For a moment they enjoy the sense of being arbiters of final destiny, even though like Samson they pull the temple down around them. Such destructive conclusions are the very nadir of entire sanctification.

Standard Christian reactions (a) Solemn urgency

Contrariwise the standard Christian reactions, which see the end of the habitable world in the context of God, further sanctification. 'Are there not twelve hours in the day? Work therefore, for the night cometh when no man can work' (John 11:9). The dilatory are stirred to action by the approaching examination or audit. Alertness is stimulated by the unpredictable imminence of the last opportunity. The householder who understands the proximity of the burglar is not caught asleep. In Richard Baxter's phrase we can preach as 'a dying man to dying men'. Fear may be an inadequate total motive, but it provides a negative impetus to escape from the City of Destruction. Men are not scorched into penitence over the nether flames, but they may be prodded to flee from the wrath to come. Even the gentle John Keble could sing, 'Save, Lord, by love or fear.' Nevertheless the panic of the end cannot finally sustain the required motive power. 'De Lawd' notes that even the flood did not achieve its end, never mind the thunderbolts desired by the Angel Gabriel, to stab the spirit broad awake. 'The dog returns to its vomit' (2 Peter 2.22).

Standard Christian reactions (b) Serene assurance

The apostolically-commended attitude is serene assurance. The best results are not achieved by a frantic last minute rush. Steady preparation is the best method. If the end comes early the watchers are ready; if late, there is all the more opportunity for amendment of life and long-suffering patience. Continuous struggle to the end is realistically recognized. Wars and rumours of wars constitute the interim state, building up to a final showdown, an Armageddon at the decisive battlefield. The interaction of good and evil is too complex for a final assessment in this world. Every technical and sophisticated advance may fertilize both wheat and tares, which grow together until the harvest. Sin and holiness alike are related to the end of all things. Holiness alone fosters a soundly serene assurance. The end takes meaning only from the divine purpose, directly related to sanctification.

The return of the Lord

Neither death for the individual nor the end of the world for corporate humanity constitute the meaning of human life, though both raise the question. Only the concepts of judgement and the return of the Lord Jesus can extrapolate the meaning otherwise hidden under the clutter of existence or sunk in the morass of aimlessness. A proper conclusion includes the expectation of a final advent to wind up the process. This teaching is not added as a complication but because the Christian revelation demands and offers it. What God began in Jesus Christ must be consummated. 'We see not yet all things put under his feet. . .' (Hebrews 2:8), but 'then comes the end when he shall deliver up the kingdom to God the Father' (1 Corinthians 15:24). The climax is not return to chaos but to manifestation of control. The personal conquest of the Lord Jesus must be irreversibly obvious, so that at the name of Jesus every knee shall bow, and every tongue confess that Jesus is Lord to the glory of God the Father (cf. Philippians 2:11). Then and then only, the thin barrier between time and eternity, the finite and the infinite, merges into unity. Meanwhile we wait for His appearing as those who long to say to an awaited friend of final competence, 'Thank God you've come.'

Understanding the Lord's return

The early Christians were puzzled by the delay; contemporary Christians are more often perplexed by the expectation. In either case the believer is subject to the apparent mockery that the same old world is still here. 'Where is the promise of His coming?' (2 Peter 3:4). Two thousand years of Christianity seems to have made so little difference, and the New Testament question still echoes. The sheer inertia of existence wears the hope threadbare, and consequently for many the purpose-built fabric of sanctification sags and snaps. For others the need to maintain the hope creates miasmas of millenarian fantasy which cloud the vision and suffocate the reason, however much they temporarily satisfy the heart. The whole subject is surrounded with pitfalls and will-o'-the-wisps which affront the common sense of mankind, yet without an intelligible doctrine of final return the whole theme of sanctification tails off into the sand. It is therefore necessary to signpost the blind alleys as well as the through road

Apocalyptic jigsaw

Any attempt to fit the bits and pieces of apocalyptic imagery into a neat jigsaw picture is doomed to failure. The upshot is confusion and discord. An elderly couple nearly ended their hitherto happy marriage when the wife saw the Lord's return as a thief in the night, with silent stealth, while the husband selected the sound of a great trumpet. The symbols of the final triumph of the Lord should be treated as brilliant flashes of light and glimpses of significant elements imparting sufficient knowledge for practical action. The beginning and the end of all things are inevitably shrouded in mystery and beyond the reach of neat abstract systems of thought. Parables and dramatic pictures alone are adequate to convey the meaning, and then only in part. The reconciling factor is the person and work of the Lord Himself. In Him alone all things fit together and every joint is compacted together.

Time-table

Equally it is impossible to construct a time-table. The Church's waste-paper basket overflows with discarded time-charts for the final showdown. Man is not granted a confidential peep into God's diary with D-Day ringed in red. Pooh's dictum can hardly be bettered, 'Nobody knows, tiddly-pom!' Claims to foreknowledge here are clairvoyance, not responsible prophecy. Disenchantment awaits such plum-stone eschatology. Marx, Lenin, Stalin, each increasingly elongated the time-schedule for the millenial end of the dictatorship of the proletariat. 'This year, next year, sometime . . .' is the formula of postponement. The final phrase abandons the hope. An ironical advertisement was published in *The British Journal of Astrology* for October 1939: 'owing to the uncertainty of the immediate future this Quarterly will not be published till further notice'! The significant point about the return of the Lord is neither gradualness nor suddenness, immediacy nor incalculability, but certainty. 'It shall come to pass . . .' is the undergirding conviction of the Christian believer.

Contemporary application

One great temptation is to apply the teaching exclusively to one's own day. There are always wars, rumours thereof, and disasters enough to fit the Lord's words about the Last Days. Each generation's delusion of grandeur is to see itself as the centre of history, with an egotistic tendency to foreshorten the future. The *Nuremburg Chronicle* (12 July, 1493) contained a summary of 'events most worthy of notice from the beginning of the world to the calamity of our times', and added six blank pages at the end to record significant events from then till judgement-day. At that very moment a young sailor left the Tagus astern at Lisbon *en route* to discover a new world and open up a whole new era of history. The application of this message to our own times in principle is always relevant. The Lord is always coming in judgement and victory. The underlying patterns of large-scale, long-term human behaviour in relation to the creative processes remain the same, sometimes hidden, sometimes manifest. In a sense the less obvious the connexion the greater the relevance, and the necessity for exposing the patterns.

Interpretation (a) The end supplies the clue

In all walks of life men have to begin at the end. Last things must come first, otherwise no one knows what he is aiming at. The site foreman needs the architect's plans and the artist's impression of the finished product. It is hard to resist the temptation, when selecting a novel or a play, to sneak a glance at the last page to see how it all ends. 'How does it end?' is a natural question to ask. There the mystery is supposed to be resolved and all else made plain. The end is not merely a conclusion but also the climax, and to that extent contains the clue to the whole series of events. The Lord's return is just such a climactic event, linking and personalizing the other climactic events of death, the end of the world, and final judgement.

Interpretation (b) **The end has appeared**

The crucial element in Christian understanding of this theme is that in fact a preview of the last page has been vouchsafed. In one sense the final scene has already been displayed, because the One to come has already come. He who died as an apparent failure in violent disgrace, even Jesus Christ, is 'the first, and the last and the living One' (Revelation 1:8) who has the keys of death and the grave, and is also the 'Lion of Judah . . .' (Revelation 5:5) who breaks every chain. His basic work of dealing with the arch-betrayers of man's confidence, death and sin, has been completed at the central point of struggle for power, namely the Cross, seen always in the light of the Resurrection. The plan of the drama was there revealed in obedient sacrifice and reconciling love, The Holy Spirit, operative therein and now also, applies continuously the completed work and imparts understanding of its purport. Man has seen the One who rules and the way he rules. The principle of selection, differentiation, assessment, are all based on man's present attitude to Jesus. The judgement is based on the mutual identification of Christ and the believing community in doing His compassionate works, sharing the Cross and public commitment.

The end game

In chess after a given move is made the end becomes inevitable. A long delaying action may well be feasible but mopping-up operations are the order of the day. The chessplayer in the advantageous position may not force the closure prematurely, but the end is still inevitable. God presumably does not force the closure yet because he respects the free choice of his children. Nevertheless the last move will vindicate the *fait accompli* on the Cross. God's love dominates at last.

> *They that set at nought and mocked him*
> *Shall the true Messiah see!*

Interpretation (c) **Living in the interval**

The Christian sees himself and his fellow-believers as living in the interval between the first coming of the Lord and His final arrival. In so far as the same contingency necessary to his existence as a being with the dignity of freedom still is a main factor in existence, he operates with uncertainty about immediate decisions. A brilliant whist-player, also a devout Christian, once likened his position *vis-à-vis* the Lord as playing opposite the Perfect Partner. He did not know what cards were in the Partner's hand at the beginning of the game, but he trusts for a proper lead, responding thoughtfully and learning to deduce the proper responsive move as the game proceeds. He believes his Partner has the Ace of Trumps, and that at the last trump we shall know whether impersonal nature or personal Godhead is the final reality. The ultimate conviction is the clue and the foundation of the whole situation.

Interpretation (d) **Critical reaction**

The criterion for assessing the final return of the Lord relates to His first arrival. In so far as men are convinced that the clue and the criterion are in Jesus Christ as portrayed already in the Gospels and in personal, and corporate, encounter, just so far can they have confidence in the Lord's return at the last. Nothing will finally convince men about the final coming unless they are fully persuaded by personal knowledge of the first coming. Sheer truth must compel conviction, or else mankind is clueless and lost. Herein is the basis of triumphant survival for the most precious values in life; the victory of creative, holy love, already established amidst the destructive forces of sin, ignorance, and death, is visible at Calvary. Here is the divine nature, destined to outlast all the hostile forces, and impartable to mankind.

Improper response to teaching

Where the proper balance of understanding is deficient at least two possible unsatisfactory attitudes emerge, both reflected within the New Testament. Some responded to the supposed nearness of the end with a lazy irresponsibility. Downing tools they became parasites, bomb-happy bums (in the American sense of the term). The sense of the overwhelming inevitability of the end of the present order through nuclear explosion has been known to make even city councils refuse any kind of preparations for protection. It was in this context that Paul laid down the principle often attributed to Karl Marx, 'If any will not work, neither let him eat' (2 Thessalonians 3:10). The opposite reaction is equally destructive. Unstable folk lost equilibrium, became jumpy, tautly listening in the dark for the footsteps of the intruder, their nerves frayed with unnatural tension. Whatever else may be supposed to flow from the expectation of the end of the world and the return of our Lord such reactions are plainly alien to the hope of entire sanctification.

Proper response

A fourfold attitude is recommended in this context. Believers should be *expectant*, 'looking for and hasting to the coming of the day of God . . . We, according to his promise, look for new heavens and a new earth, wherein dwelleth righteousness' (2 Peter 3:12f). Life degenerates without purpose and a possible achievement. As the Fifeshire farm-labourer remarked to Robert Louis Stevenson, 'Him that has aye something ayont need never be weary.' Believers should also be *ready*, loins girt, lamps burning, on prayerful watch. Since the hour is unpredictable, 'as a thief in the night, what manner of person ought ye to be, in all holy conversation and godliness? . . . Wherefore, beloved, seeing that ye look for such things, be diligent that ye may be found of him in peace, without spot and blameless' (2 Peter 3; 10, 11, 14). Saint Augustine remarked that 'the Last Day is hidden that all days may be observed.' In the early nineteenth century the Connecticut Legislature was sitting when a great darkness enveloped the land. Some thought it was the last day and moved the adjournment. An old Puritan arose and said, 'If the Lord was coming I would desire to be found at my post.' He moved that candles be brought and the business proceed. The third strand in the believer's response is *gratitude*. An assurance of vindication and present survival is infinitely precious. God is 'not willing that any should perish . . .'. Therefore we should 'account that the longsuffering

225

of the Lord is salvation' (2 Peter 3, 9–15; cf. 18). Delay implies further opportunity for repentance and further growth in grace. Expectant, ready, grateful, the believer is finally *patient*. 'Beware lest you fall away from your own steadfastness . . . The Lord is not slack concerning his promise, as some men count slackness . . . One day is with the Lord as a thousand years, and a thousand years as one day' (2 Peter 3:17–19). God works on a large canvas, and the end is not yet. It is hardly accidental that the passage in Habakkuk which provides Paul with his Scriptural base for the doctrine of justification also provides the word for our relationship to the day of the Lord. 'If it tarry, wait for it; it will surely come. In the end it will speak and not lie; for the just shall live by his faith' (Habakkuk 2:3). Habakkuk has the broad Abrahamic type of faith in mind. Paul narrows the focus to justifying faith in relation to the forgiveness of sins. We may coalesce the two in our doctrine of sanctification, whereby the precise personal trust in a personal Saviour and the work of the Holy Spirit catches up again the wider context of conviction about the ultimate triumph of righteousness and the necessity to stake all on the adventurous trek of the human spirit for a city out of sight and a Promised Land. Patient endurance, grateful readiness, prayerful watchfulness, all founded on the constant *nisus* towards the final consummation of all things in Christ, are essential elements in the work of sanctification. Each separately and all together are manifested as the response of faith in its fullest sense to the proffered grace of God as directed towards the culmination of the creative and sanctifying process in Christ.

Making ends meet

A number of closure-points have been mentioned—death, the world's end, the return of the Lord. Two terminal-points have been elaborated—heaven and hell. The question, so practical on the mundane level of economics, remains on this exalted level of final destiny: how do we make ends meet? The evidence set forth demands some assessment, which involves judgement. 'It is appointed to men once to die, and after that the judgement' (Hebrews 9:27). The principles are

226

known and the procedures available. When curious questions about the statistics of salvation were asked our Lord's reply was realistic and practical: 'Strait is the gate and narrow is the way, and few there be that find it' (Matthew 7:14). In essence Jesus concentrates on the practical issue of the conditions for qualification. There is no exit in case of emergency. 'We must all be made manifest before the judgement seat of Christ; that each may receive the things done in the body, according to what he has done, whether it be good or bad' (2 Corinthians 5:11). The standards applied are ethical and universal. 'Be not afraid of them that kill the body, but are not able to kill the soul; but rather fear him which is able to destroy both body and soul in hell' (Matthew 10:28). 'I was hungry, and you gave me meat . . . inasmuch as you did it to the least of these my brethren, you did it to me . . . Inasmuch as you did it not . . .' (Matthew 25:35 ff.). The inward attitude to the person and work of Jesus, reflected in its outward compassionate expression, is the inbuilt test.

The inescapability of judgement

The moment of truth always comes. Life is built for testing. Days of judgement are not arbitrary but structural. Codes, principles, moral legislation are only divine and valid when they are extrapolations from the substructural patterns of energy which go to make up total existence. 'With what judgement you judge you will be judged' (Matthew 7:1 ff.). The tape-recorder illustrates the point. One imaginery scene of judgement is to be set in the centre of the heavenly crowd while a recording of all we have said and thought, never mind done, is played back to us. Our own mouths and memories condemn us. To silence by throwing the culprit's words back at him is an ancient technique. Hecklers and children know the art of confusing by innocent repetition—'but you said . . .'. The parable is a form of lure to self-judgement as David discovered after Nathan's story of the poor man's one ewe-lamb. When Peter denied association with Christ, Jesus said nothing. The words re-echoed in the miserable disciple's ear with their own condemnation. Before His judges the Lord said nothing until compelled in some form, and even then His replies implied the same principle of judgement. Jesus does not recommend evasion of judgement, but the acknowledgement that every judgement is a self-judgement because it reveals our standards of judgement. He himself blistered the Scribes and Pharisees, and in the next verse (Matthew 7:6) describes some types as swine who would trample pearls under foot. Jesus has no truck with easy-going tolerance which seeks to spike the guns of adverse criticism of oneself. Our expressed judgements give ourselves away, whether right or wrong. The continued refusal to accept the challenge of the holy love of God induces spiritual stupefaction which decreases and distorts the capacity to assess life properly. 'They were hardened; as it is written, God gave them a spirit of stupor, eyes that they should not see, and ears that they should not hear, until this very day' (Romans 11:8). So critical is this inbuilt assessing process that love demands severity to warn and rescue. 'If your hand or foot offend, cut it off and cast it away from you: it is better for you to enter into life lame or maimed, rather than possessing both hands and two feet to be cast into eternal fire' (Matthew 18:8). This process applies even more to corporate bodies than to individuals. Injustice and disobedience eventually come home to roost. The concept of final judgement is simply the focusing in one final occasion, a crescendo of crescendos, when the continuous process is manifest without ambiguity and with irresistible vindication. Its purpose is not primarily, but only incidentally, condemnation. Jesus comes not chiefly to condemn, but to save, and impart the incorruptible life of God which alone survives all pressures to break. Entire sanctification includes the acceptance of the necessity, validity, and finality of this eternal moment of truth in the total context of the kind of saving God we see and meet in Jesus Christ. He alone is the standard and the agent of saving judgement.

The integration of judgement

The concept of a Judgement Day, related to the return of our Lord, integrates the closure-points of individual death and the corporate end of the world with each other and with the cosmic vindication of Christ, at the same time serving as the transitional procedure to the terminal-points of heaven and hell, rewards and punishments, and the conclusion of the process, either negatively or positively. Equally the parable of the Great Assize integrates the otherwise disparate patterns of historic judgement, interim and partial, which otherwise eventually dissolve into the formless void of oblivion. These interim patterns provoke assessments, temporary recognitions of genuine testing. They tease man's odd taste for comment, praise, and blame, while at the same time arousing a sense of the absurd arrogance involved. C. Day Lewis catches this mood in his poem 'A Relativist'.

> *He raged at critic, moralist—all*
> *That gang who with almightiest gall*
> *Lay claim to the decisive vote*
> *In separating sheep from goat.*
>
> *So on the last day when he's got*
> *His breath back again, it will not*
> *Be goats or sheep that rouse his dudgeon*
> *But the absurdity of judging.*

The necessity and the absurdity of such final judgement is prevented from destructive dichotomy by accepting the Scriptural promise of divine sovereignty and responsibility for the occasion. The irony of judgement is a theme which threads its way throughout the Scriptures. 'He that sitteth in the heavens shall laugh . . . Yet have I set my King upon the holy hill of Zion . . . Thou art my Son; this day have I begotten thee . . . Be wise therefore, O ye kings: be instructed, ye judges of the earth. Serve the Lord with fear, and rejoice with trembling. Kiss the Son, lest he be angry, and ye perish from the way, when his wrath is kindled but a little. Blessed are all they that put their trust in him' (Psalm 2:4, 6-7, 10-12). The paradox of supreme absurdity and supreme solemnity is reconciled in the Cross of Christ, which is the supreme surd, the irremovable factor which stands, however irrational, and must be incorporated into any total system of interpretation of life. The principle of self-judgement against a background of given sovereignty, already outlined, provides the reconciling clue. At Calvary man judges himself by his judgement of Christ, and is condemned by the same instrument which provides the way of escape and renewal. The Crucifixion, as man's judgement upon God, boomerangs back upon himself. Man's guilt and God's holiness here wrestle for the fall. The victory remains with holy love, which is always and invariably itself woven through without seam or fault, and too compact of incorruptible creative personal energy to be denied resurrection. The victory which overcomes the world is the combination of this gracious deed of saving power with corporate trust in its historic effect and eternal significance. The testing energy is always at work, but lacks purposeful finality unless related to the Cross-cum-Resurrection event in the setting of the Holiness of God.

Summary

The parable of the Top Level Talks and the Christian Summit Meeting has now been worked through, though not exhausted. We began in the immeasurable world of the Spirit and we end there. After completing the survey for the first scene-setting to continuous conduct of operation, we have presumed to peer into the conclusion of the process, so far as acceptable evidence has been vouchsafed to us. We have sought to demonstrate some kind of reasonable coherence in profound themes which in the nature of the case are never fully within human grasp, either theoretically or practically. Man can only recognize his true master, in whose control is perfect freedom. Accepting Jesus Christ in His Scriptural background provides the necessary clue. The energy of holy love He incarnated and projected into the total situation of man is at once the sample and the source of entire sanctification. Nothing less than perfection will suffice. Once the passion for perfection flags, the rot sets in for a nation, a civilization, a business, a person. The scientist cannot be satisfied with less. Let the artist Michael Angelo speak for all: 'Nothing makes the soul so pure, so religious, as the endeavour to create something perfect; for God is perfection, and whoever strives for perfection strives for something that is God.' All sub-personal activities of man share in this necessary craving, but the reconciling factor is the total personality engaged in the service of the divine. This reconciling total person is Jesus Christ, Son of Man and of God, Lord and Saviour. The function of the Church is to serve and manifest His sovereignty, whose diverse gifts of the Spirit are to be perfectly joined together, through the faith that energizes by love. The intention is that we should 'all come . . . unto a perfect man, unto the measure of the stature of the fulness of Christ' (Ephesians 4:13). Such a total climax cannot be treated in isolation from the whole range of Christian thought from Creation to the Last Things. The doctrine of Entire Sanctification has to be understood in terms of the Christian revelation of God as personal saving energy of the type embodied in Jesus Christ, and especially the concentrated essence of his saving work in the atoning deed of Calvary. The Christian is called to embody personally and corporately this same nature and work so far as the limits of his situation permit, and to pioneer creatively and surprisingly the extension of those limits. Christians are those who accept the challenge-offer of freely disciplined movement towards such total social coherence as accords with the will of God for His earthly family. The precise form of this life is never fully codifiable. It is a spirit, an attitude, a relationship, which constantly seeks to unearth the inbuilt principles of the divine order and to earth the application thereof in the constantly changing and developing circumstances, material and cultural, of the mundane scene. Variety and originality as well as coherence and obedience are indigenous to this saving work of Christ for us, in us, and through us. Its final expression is the overflow of praise. Gratitude is its motive, theme, and note.

> *Above the rest this note shall swell:*
> *My Jesus has done all things well.*

Conclusion

The conclusion of the process must transcend the temporal and finite world which is our familiar setting, although that limited and dependent dimension is an essential part of the plan of God, and by its interim actuality enriches the Godhead. Thus the precarnate Son 'takes to heaven a human brow', and incorporates the actual interior experience of created man into the Creator God's experience. After the processes and events summed up in death, the world's end, the return of the Lord, and the Last Judgement there remains the possibility of the Millenium, the thousand-year reign of the Lord with His saints in a regenerated universe, 'where the wolf also shall dwell with the lamb, and the leopard shall lie down with the kid; and the calf and the young lion and the fatling together; and a little child shall lead them . . . They shall not hurt nor destroy in all my holy mountain: for the earth shall be full of the knowledge of the Lord as the waters cover the sea' (Isaiah 11:6-9). Also 'the streets of the city shall be full of boys and girls playing in the streets thereof' (Zechariah 8:5). Marxism shares this Biblical view, though in a secularized version, of the winding up the experienced processes of creation and history, and the inauguration of a qualitatively different dimension of existence within the space-time universe. To what real state this vision can be attached, who can say? Presumably its intention is to safeguard faith in some real transformation within the familiar dimensions accepted as a going concern, and to prevent a mere deferment of all genuine consummation to the eternal world of the spirit. To this extent we must hold on to this conviction, however little we can focus its fulfilment. At the same time, the simple fact that a time period, however long and however conventionally generalized, is mentioned (Revelation 20:2-8) suggests that even this restored Paradise has its end. The climax is in the heavenly places, a vast corporate relationship of adoring love and an experience of glory and bliss. The reward of trustful and obedient reception of the gracious gift of this blessing is to share the fullness of the divine nature imparted in the saving energy. 'His servants shall serve him; and they shall see his face . . . and they shall reign for ever and ever' (Revelation 22:3-5).

The sovereign energy of the universe, from which all specific forms of energy derive, is holiness. The nature of that holy energy includes the production of personality in society as its loftiest phenomenon. Death and sin are the resistant factors, and both need radical treatment and mastery if the energy is to have full sway. Jesus is the supreme person, the radical master of death and sin, by reason of his tackling both in their complex lair at Calvary and the garden-tomb. Here the saving energy is concentrated in its maximum effectiveness. Trust the Proper Man and his energetic victory at the Cross, and the new nature and the same divine energy flows through you as you are grappled to God in Christ in a united relationship. Faith energizes by love to join men perfectly together, to create, salvage, recreate and renew fair dealing, loyalty and mutual helpfulness over the whole range of human values and relationships. Negatively this implies destruction of everything which hinders this development. 'I hate them with a perfect hatred' (Psalm 139:22). Positively it requires the commitment of the total self within the confidently urgent powers and purposes of God in Christ and a constant reaching towards the continual coming of the Lord Jesus in the mode of His Spirit. A great world requires a great destiny, and great times call for great men. Neither can be produced without the habitual vision of greatness, transcending all experiences of disillusionment and degradation. At every point for this transcendent vision of God we need the Lord Jesus. Let this theme resume its rightful place on the agenda of the Church. 'Even so, come, Lord Jesus. The grace of our Lord Jesus Christ be with you all' (Revelation 22:21).

Select Bibliography

Aldis, W. H., *The Message of Keswick and its Meaning*
Arminian Magazine (1778)
Aumann, J. R., and Greenstock D. L., *The Meaning of Christian Perfection,* Bloomsbury
Baker, E. W., *The Faith of a Christian,* Epworth, 1958
Barker, J. H. J., *This Is the Will of God,* Epworth, 1956
Carré, A. M., *Holiness,* Aquin
Chadwick, S., *A Call to Christian Perfection,* Epworth, 1966
Chambers, O., *My Utmost For His Highest,* Marshall, Morgan and Scott
Champness, T., *Plain Talks on Perfection,* Joyful News Bookroom, 1897
Cleall, C., *Music and Holiness,* Epworth, 1965
Cook, T., *New Testament Holiness,* Epworth, 1902
Cooper, D., ed., *The Dialectics of Liberation,* Pelican, 1968
Cresswell, A. S., *The Second Blessing, Advance Magazine,* 26 December, 1963
Fison, J. E., *The Blessing of the Holy Spirit,* Longmans
Fletcher, J., *Morals and Medicine,* Gollancz, 1955
Flew, R. N., *The Idea of Perfection in Christian Theology,* O.U.P., 1934
Ford, J., *What the Holiness People Believe,* Church of the Nazarenes
Forsyth, P. T., *Christ on Parnassus,* Hodder and Stoughton, 1911
Forsyth, P. T., *Christian Perfection,* Hodder and Stoughton, 1899
Forsyth, P. T., *The Church, the Gospel, and Society,* Epworth, 1962
Forsyth, P. T., *The Taste of Death and the Life of Grace,* James Clarke, 1901
Forsyth, P. T., *This Life and the Next,* Independent Press, 1918

234

Galloway, J. B., *Holiness from the Early Church Fathers*, West Publishing Company, Apollo, Pa., U.S.A.

Gardeil, A., *The Holy Spirit in Christian Life*

Glover, T. R., *The Disciple*, C.U.P., 1942

Goodwin, J., *A Being Filled with the Spirit*

Hadfield, J., *Psychology and Morals*, Methuen, 1923

Henschen, W. G., *Christian Perfection Before Wesley*, Beacon Press, Kansas City, Missouri, U.S.A.

Hunt, J., *Letters on Entire Sanctification*

Jessop, T. E., *The Christian Morality*, Epworth, 1960

Joly, H., *The Psychology of the Saints*, Burnes, Oates and Washburn, 1919

Jones, O. R., *The Concept of Holiness*, Allen and Unwin

Law, W., *A Serious Call to a Devout and Holy Life*, Dent, Everyman Series

Lindström, H., *Wesley and Sanctification*, Epworth, 1946

Lloyd-Jones, D. M., *Studies in the Sermon on the Mount*, 2 vols. I.V.F., 1959

Montefiore, Hugh, *Awkward Questions on Christian Love*, Fontana, 1964

Moulton, W. J., *John Wesley's Doctrine of Perfect Love*, The *London Quarterly*, 1925

Neill, S. C., *Christian Holiness*, Lutterworth, 1960

Niebuhr, R., *An Interpretation of Christian Ethics*, S.C.M., 1936, (especially chapter 4)

Otto, R., *The Idea of the Holy*, O.U.P., 1923

Perkins H. W., *The Doctrine of Christian Perfection*

Pierce, C. A., *Conscience in the New Testament*, S.C.M., 1955

Proceedings of the 10th World Methodist Conference (Oslo), Epworth/Abingdon

Roberts, T. D., ed., *Contraception and Holiness*, Fontana, 1965

Rogers, E., *God's Business*, Epworth, 1955

Sangster, W. E., *The Path to Perfection*, Hodder and Stoughton, 1943

Sangster, W. E., *The Pure in Heart*, Epworth, 1954

Smith, C. Ryder, *What Do Ye?*, Epworth, 1944

Sugden, E. H., ed., *Wesley's Standard Sermons*, Epworth (especially vol. ii, 147–77; 442–60)

Telford, J., ed., *Wesley's Veterans,* Epworth
Theobald, H. W., *The Concept of Energy,* Spon, 1966 (especially pp. 160–65, 176–78)
Thompson, F., *Health and Holiness,* Burnes and Oates, 1905
Wesley, J., *A Plain Account of Christian Perfection,* Epworth
Wilson, M., *The Church is Healing,* S.C.M., 1966
Woolman, J., *Journal,* Dent, Everyman Series

Subject Index

abstract thought, 44
adoption, 22
altar, 23
Apocalyptic, 75, 221
Assurance, 23
Atonement, 22, 51

backsliding, 164 ff.
beauty, 103 f.
Bible, 6, 59–89, 75 f., 121, 178 ff.
blessing, 32 f., 98, 115

Church, 55, 80 f., 107 f., 109, 122, 166 ff.
conscience, 95
conversion, 22
Covenant, 20, 46 f.
Creation, 40 f., 56, 120
Cross, 86, 120 ff., 125 ff.

death, 215
Devil, 13
doctrine, 100

ecstasy, 180, 206 ff.
energy, 41 f., 52, 117 ff., 123 ff., 190
English words, 30 ff.
Entire Sanctification, 2 ff., 30, 87, 135, 180, 190, 230 f.
eschatology, 162 f., 217 ff, 226
Eternal Life, 199, 209
evangelism, 174 ff.
evolution, 60
expiation, 22

faith, 23 f., 67 f., 147 f., 193
Fall, 63 ff.
freedom, 64
fullness, 29 f.

glory, 204 ff.
Grace, 101 ff., 188
Greek words, 26
guidance, 181
guilt, 21, 48, 148 f.

health, 45, 55
heaven, 15 f., 81, 198 ff.
Hebrew words, 24 ff.
history, 61, 76 ff.
holiness, 10, 18, 26, 55, 58, 91 ff., 119, 182 ff., 232
Holy Spirit, 79, 136
humility, 111

immortality, 208
intercession, 53

Jesus Christ, 10, 77 ff., 87, 124
judgement, 227 ff.
Justification, 21, 48

Kingdom, 120

language, 10 f., 19 f., 35, 194 ff.
Law, 21, 62, 66
linguistic analysis, 35 ff.
Lord's Supper, 170 ff.
love, 85, 176 ff., 184 ff.

man, 41, 63 ff.
maturity, 115 f.
Mediator, 56
Millenium, 231
ministry, 177 f.
moral codes, 82 ff., 184 f.
myth, 62, 194

omnipotence, 7

pain, 137 f.
Paradise, 9, 63
patience, 145
penalty, 49, 136
Pentecost, 131
perfection, 27 f.
prayer, 24, 140, 153, 155ff.
preaching, 172 f.
priesthood, 23, 53, 168
process, 144 f.
propitiation, 22

Providence, 74
psychology, 135
purity of heart, 161

reason, 103 f.
reconciliation, 22
Redemption, 20, 48
Regeneration, 22, 50
Remnant, 72
Resurrection, 130 f., 209
Revelation, 60 f., 66
root (of sin), 101

sacrifice, 23
saints, 95, 180 f.
salvation, 20, 56, 141
sanctification, 12, 22, 51, 87
scholarship, 75 f.
Second Blessing, 32 ff., 88 f.
Second Coming, 220 ff.
self, 110 f.

self-denial, 113 f.
self-righteousness, 114
separatism, 71
sex, 105 f.
sin, 21
social reform, 106 f., 151
Spirit, 8
substitution, 73
suffering, 73, 128

temptation, 63 f.
'tongues', 79, 133
transference, 73 f., 135
Trinity, 13 ff., 38, 53 f.

verbs, 34 f.
vicariousness, 49

Wesley, 2 f., 34, 180 f., 213 f.
world, 43, 45
worship, 173 f.

Index of Scripture Passages

GENESIS 69	**2 SAMUEL** 69	**PROVERBS** 69
1:1–31 43	6:3 25	1:7 8
1:1–3 ....6 f., 60	22:20 104	3 84
1:26 ....14, 41, 60		9:10 157
1:26–30 ....16, 43	**1 KINGS** 69	14:31 41
2–3 ....62 ff.	7:51 25	23:23 181
2:15 16		24:16 164
2:26 ff. 41	**2 KINGS** 69	
3:4–6, 20 64	15:13 25	**ECCLESIASTES** ...69
4:10 65	23:10 212	7:16 90
17:7 14		
17:11 7	**1 CHRONICLES**...69	**SONG OF**
18:25 ff. 68	28:9 26	**SOLOMON** 69
22:8 68	29:9, 19 26	
37 114		**ISAIAH**
49:6 114	**EZRA** 74	6:1 ff. 25, 72
		11:6 ff. 75, 232
EXODUS 69	**NEHEMIAH** 74	38:3 25
1:8 68	1:3 ff. 115	42:3 189
3:14 39		52:15 207
20:3 62	**ESTHER** 69	53 136
22:31 25	4:8 ff. 115	53:3 f. 138
	5:1–13 115	53:11 142
LEVITICUS 69		53:12 53
15:3 25	**JOB** 69	60:9 62
19:2 10	1 13	65:5 93
22:4–6 25	12:8 ....43, 210	65:8 25
NUMBERS 69	**PSALMS** 69	**JEREMIAH**
	2:4 ff. 229	7:31 212
DEUTERONOMY 69	18:19 104	8:7 43
	18:33 90	17:9 ....95 f.
JOSHUA 69	22 142	27:5 40
7:18–26 25	29 25	31:31 ff. 67
	34 84	
JUDGES 69	77:10 163	**LAMENTATIONS** 69
7:8 ff. 115	99:24 25	1:12 ....137 f.
16:20 86	103:7 60	
	106:2, 8 60	**EZEKIEL**
RUTH 69	111:10 157	24:18 139
	121:4 39	36:23 58
1 SAMUEL 69	137:3 72	44:9 25
16:7 163	139:22 233	
	145:4–12 60	

DANIEL
3:17 f. 183
6:10 72
7:13 72

HOSEA
7:4 116
11:1 f. 67

AMOS
4:13 ....41, 76

OBADIAH 17 107

HABAKKUK
3:19 90

HAGGAI
1:6 117

ZECHARIAH
8:5 232

MALACHI
3:2 28

MATTHEW 70
5:8 ....31 f.
5:16 58
5:48 ....10, 83
6:9 f., 13 7
7:1–14 227–8
7:16 85
10:28 227
12:34 f. 83
15:19 83
16:26 66
18:8 ....228 f.
23:23 96
24:28 97
25:35 227
25:41 213
26:8 55
27:42 127
28:19 55

MARK 70
4:1 ff. 43
4:26 ff. 42
8:34 113

9:48 215
12:1 ff. 120

LUKE 70
2:14 193
2:35 126
2:49 125
10:20 199
11:13 136
12:48 84
12:49 119
13:24 198
17:32 115
18:22 188
23:34, 43 141
23:44 119
23:46 143
24:21 119

JOHN 70
1:1 ff. ...10, 15, 42, 60
1:12 f. 50
1:30 15
3:3–8 50
3:15 119
4:23 173
5:17 ....125, 201
6 ....133, 152
6:47 199
8:58 15
9 104
12:24 ....114, 210
13:36 ff. 113
14:2 204
14:30 86
15:4 199
17 ....18, 55
17:3 204
17:6 205
17:20–25 38
19:26 f. ....141 f.
19:30 142
21:15–19 113

ACTS 70
1:6 193
2:4 117
2:11 19
2:23 38
2:24 49
2:38 169
4:23 164

7 70
9:2 85
10:46 134
19:2 85
19:6 134
20:35 115
24:14 ff. 85

ROMANS 70
1:4 ....18, 87
1:16 117
5:8 169
6:4 ff. 169
7:12 67
8:18–23 52
8:37 ....149 f.
11:8 227
12:1 f. 84, 144

1 CORINTHIANS 70
1:10 28
2:4 172
2:9 194
8:1 131
10:4 78
10:12 182
13 ....185 ff.
13:12 200
14 133
15 ....209 ff.
15:20–28 ....38, 91
15:22 216
15:24 ff. ...191, 205, 220
15:46 106
15:47 210
15:50 210
15:56 65
15:58 131
16:1 131

2 CORINTHIANS
1:22 193
3:18 ....191, 203
4:7 124
4:16 191
5:1 191
5:5 193
5:11 227
5:17 29
11:14 96
12:16 f. 175
13:14 55

240

GALATIANS 70
2:20 113
3:22 64
4:4 ff. 77
4:6 54
5:6 ....85, 143, 190
5:22 ff. 184

EPHESIANS 70
1:9–10 ....39, 193
1:14 193
2:6 199
3:9–11 13
3:19 30
4:2 85
4:13 ......83, 175, 231
6:10–20 13

PHILIPPIANS 70
1:21 ff. 200
2:10 78
2:11 220
2:12 f. 59
2:15 84
3:10, 20 199

COLOSSIANS 70
1:15 f. 42
1:17 f. 42, 77
1:24 139
1:28 10
2:9, 15 78
3:1 ....55, 118

1 THESSALONIANS
...................70
4:1 ff. 83, 144
4:22 181
5:16–22 144
5:22 84
5:23 30

2 THESSALONIANS
3:10 225

1 TIMOTHY 70
3:16 39
4:7 98
6:15 7
6:17 43

2 TIMOTHY
1:10 ....130, 209
1:12 150
3:2 114

TITUS 70
1:7 114

HEBREWS 70
1:1 ff. 78
2:8 220
2:8 ff. 132
2:9 78
2:10 ff. 10, 37, 76
4:9 202
8:5 6
9:27 f. 191, 226
10:36 145
11 .... 147 f.
11:6 157
11:39 108
12:1 201
12:2 112
12:22 ff. 201
12:29 8
13:21 10

JAMES 70
2:10 21

1 PETER 70
1:3 ....50, 117
1:4 203
1:8 150
1:10 ff. 59, 88
1:12 ....5, 13
1:23 50

1:25 59
2:4–9 144
2:19–25 136
3:18 117
3:19 130

2 PETER
1:4 10
2:4 213
2:10 10
2:22 219
3:4 220
3:10 ....218, 225
3:9–18 ....225 f.

1 JOHN 70
1:5 7
1:7 ....52. 122
3:2 ....86, 200
4:18 85
5:4 148

JUDE 70

REVELATION 70
1:8 223
1:17 209
2:10 201
7:10 200
7:15 202
8:1 ....39, 140, 206
8:9 f. ....200 f.
9:11 214
13:8 ....17, 44
17:14 7
19:6 7
20:2–8 232
21:1–4 ......192 f., 203
21:18 f. 196
21:27 203
22:1–3 17
22:3 ff. 203, 232
22:21 233

Pine Heart 31/32 .